Shakespeare in the Theatre: The King's Men

SERIES EDITORS

Peter Holland, Farah Karim-Cooper and Stephen Purcell

Published titles
Patrice Chéreau, Dominique Goy-Blanquet
The American Shakespeare Center, Paul Menzer
Mark Rylance at the Globe, Stephen Purcell
The National Theatre, 1963–1975: Olivier and Hall,
Robert Shaughnessy
Nicholas Hytner, Abigail Rokison-Woodall
Peter Sellars, Ayanna Thompson
Trevor Nunn, Russell Jackson
Cheek by Jowl, Peter Kirwan
Peter Hall, Stuart Hampton-Reeves
Yukio Ninagawa, Conor Hanratty

Forthcoming
Sir William Davenant and the Duke's Company,
Richard Schoch and Amanda Eubanks Winkler
Sarah Siddons and John Philip Kemble, Fiona Ritchie
Phyllida Lloyd, Elizabeth Schafer

Shakespeare in the Theatre: The King's Men

Lucy Munro

THE ARDEN SHAKESPEARE
LONDON • NEW YORK • OXFORD • NEW DELHI • SYDNEY

THE ARDEN SHAKESPEARE
Bloomsbury Publishing Plc
50 Bedford Square, London, WC1B 3DP, UK
1385 Broadway, New York, NY 10018, USA
29 Earlsfort Terrace, Dublin 2, Ireland

BLOOMSBURY, THE ARDEN SHAKESPEARE and the
Arden Shakespeare logo are trademarks of Bloomsbury Publishing Plc

First published in Great Britain 2020
This paperback edition published in 2021

Copyright © Lucy Munro, 2020

Lucy Munro has asserted her right under the Copyright, Designs and
Patents Act, 1988, to be identified as the author of this work.

For legal purposes the Acknowledgements on pp. ix–x constitute an
extension of this copyright page.

Series design by Dani Leigh
Cover image: Sketch of the Globe Playhouse
(© Cyril Walter Hodges / Folger Shakespeare Library)

All rights reserved. No part of this publication may be reproduced or
transmitted in any form or by any means, electronic or mechanical,
including photocopying, recording, or any information storage or retrieval
system, without prior permission in writing from the publishers.

Bloomsbury Publishing Plc does not have any control over, or
responsibility for, any third-party websites referred to or in this book.
All internet addresses given in this book were correct at the time of
going to press. The author and publisher regret any inconvenience
caused if addresses have changed or sites have ceased to exist, but can
accept no responsibility for any such changes.

A catalogue record for this book is available from the British Library.

Library of Congress Control Number: 2020934534

ISBN:	HB:	978-1-4742-6261-3
	PB:	978-1-4742-6259-0
	ePDF:	978-1-4742-6263-7
	eBook:	978-1-4742-6262-0

Series: Shakespeare in the Theatre

Typeset by Integra Software Services Pvt. Ltd.

To find out more about our authors and books visit www.bloomsbury.com
and sign up for our newsletters.

CONTENTS

List of Illustrations vii
Abbreviations and Note on the Text viii
Acknowledgements ix
Series Preface xi
Preface: 1603 xiii

Prologue: Playing the Court, 1604–5 1

1 The Art and Faculty of Playing: The King's Men and Their Roles 9

   Interlude: Playing the Court, 1612–13 45

2 Collaboration, Competition and Candlelight: *Othello* and *The Alchemist* 51

   Interlude: Playing the Court, 1619–20 83

3 Painful Adventures: *Pericles* and the 'Traffic' of the Stage 87

   Interlude: Playing the Court, 1633–4 117

4 Men, Women and Magic: Shakespeare, the Merry Devil and the Prophetess 123

   Interlude: Playing the Court, 1636–7 145

5 Summer Days at the Globe: *Richard II*, *Henry VIII* and the Politics of Playing 151

Epilogue: *Hamlet* without the Prince, 1642–60 177

Appendix 185
Notes 195
References 207
Index 222

LIST OF ILLUSTRATIONS

1 and 2   Account of Edmund Tilney, Master of the Revels, 1604–5, AO 3/908/13, The National Archives, Kew   2–3

3   'The Actors Names', in *The Tragedy of the Dutchesse of Malfy* (London, 1623), General Collection, Beinecke Rare Book and Manuscript Library, Yale University   13

4   'The persons presented', with manuscript annotations, in *Philaster* (London, 1634), Art Inv. 271 no. 10e (2). Used by permission of the Folger Shakespeare Library   14

5   'The Persons of the Play', in *The Alchemist*, with manuscript annotations, in *The Workes of Benjamin Jonson* (London, 1616), 49968, The Huntington Library, San Marino, California   58

6   'The principall Comœdians', in *The Alchemist*, with manuscript annotations, in *The Workes of Benjamin Jonson* (London, 1616), 49968, The Huntington Library, San Marino, California   59

ABBREVIATIONS AND NOTE ON THE TEXT

Abbreviations

BL	British Library, London
LMA	London Metropolitan Archives
Shakespeare Documented	Folger Shakespeare Library et al. (2016–), *Shakespeare Documented*, Washington, DC: Folger Shakespeare Library, https://shakespearedocumented.folger.edu
TNA	The National Archives, Kew

Unless otherwise noted, all quotations from the works of the central dramatists of the King's Men are from the following editions: the Arden Shakespeare Third Series; Fredson Bowers, gen. ed., *The Dramatic Works in the Beaumont and Fletcher Canon*, 10 vols, Cambridge: Cambridge University Press, 1966–97; David Bevington, Martin Butler and Ian Donaldson, gen. eds, *The Cambridge Edition of the Works of Ben Jonson*, 7 vols, Cambridge: Cambridge University Press, 2012; Philip Edwards and Colin Gibson, eds, *The Plays and Poems of Philip Massinger*, 4 vols, Oxford: Clarendon Press, 1976; Gary Taylor and John Lavagnino, gen. eds, *Thomas Middleton: The Collected Works*, Oxford: Oxford University Press, 2007. Dates of plays, unless otherwise noted, are from Martin Wiggins, in association with Catherine Richardson, *British Drama 1533–1642: A Catalogue*, 9 vols, Oxford: Oxford University Press, 2011–18, and information about the biographies of individual actors is from Gerald Eades Bentley, *The Jacobean and Caroline Stage*, 7 vols, Oxford: Clarendon Press, 1941–68, volume 2, unless another source is cited.

ACKNOWLEDGEMENTS

My greatest debt is to Farah Karim-Cooper, my general editor, who invited me to write this book at an ungodly hour in Stratford-upon-Avon in 2014. It wouldn't exist without her intellectual and practical stimulus, and I hope she likes it. I'm also very grateful to Clare McManus and Tanya Pollard for reading and commenting on the draft text at ridiculously short notice, and I'm sorry that there isn't (even) more on (a) boy actors in *Othello* and (b) Richard Burbage in what follows. I also want to thank Jane Hwang Degenhardt, Edmund King, Jeremy Lopez, Clare McManus, Cyrus Mulready, Marion O'Connor and Neil Vickers for invitations to present work-in-progress; Tamara Atkin, Hannah Leah Crummé, Laura Estill, Kristen Poole, Lauren Shohet and Andrew McConnell Stott for inviting me to write essays involving various aspects of the King's Men; and Deb Callan and James Wallace for helping me to run a 'Winter Playing' workshop on casting at Shakespeare's Globe. Students on the Shakespeare Studies MA at King's College London and Shakespeare's Globe have helped me to sort out some of the ideas presented here through their enthusiastic contribution to seminars on the King's Men. John Astington, Julie Sanders and Tanya Pollard wrote me references for fellowships at the Huntington Library (2016) and the Folger Shakespeare Library (2018), which supported some of the research; I'm indebted to the staff at both of these libraries for all of their help, and to staff at the Beinecke Library, Yale University, for help with images. Holger Schott Syme shared unpublished work with me, for which I'm very grateful. I'd also like to thank Margaret Bartley, Lara Bateman, Mark Dudgeon and Linda Fisher at the Arden Shakespeare for their encouragement and patience during the writing and production process. Colleagues at King's and Shakespeare's Globe have been characteristically generous and supportive, as have Andy Kesson and Callan Davies, my colleagues on Before Shakespeare. For comments, suggestions and provocations I'm especially indebted to Roberta Barker, Sarah Dustagheer, Roslyn Knutson, Sarah Lewis, Jemima Matthews, Gordon McMullan and Will Tosh. As always, I couldn't have written this without Matt Haynes.

SERIES PREFACE

Each volume in the *Shakespeare in the Theatre* series focuses on a director or theatre company who has made a significant contribution to Shakespeare production, identifying the artistic and political/social contexts of their work.

The series introduces readers to the work of significant theatre directors and companies whose Shakespeare productions have been transformative in our understanding of his plays in performance. Each volume examines a single figure or company, considering their key productions, rehearsal approaches and their work with other artists (actors, designers, composers). A particular feature of each book is its exploration of the contexts within which these theatre artists have made their Shakespeare productions work. Thus, the series not only considers the ways in which directors and companies produce Shakespeare, but also reflects upon their other theatre activities and the broader artistic, cultural and socio-political milieu within which their Shakespeare performances and productions have been created. The key to the series' originality, then, is its consideration of Shakespeare production in a range of artistic and broader contexts; in this sense, it de-centres Shakespeare from within Shakespeare studies, pointing to the range of people, artistic practices and cultural phenomena that combine to make meaning in the theatre.

Series editors:
Peter Holland, Farah Karim-Cooper
and Stephen Purcell

PREFACE: 1603

In May 1603, a document was issued that transformed the status of the playing company that had hitherto been known as the Lord Chamberlain's Men. In the name of the new king, James I, it addressed 'all Justices Maiors Sheriffes Constables hedborow*es* [parish officers] and other our Officers and louinge Subiect*es*', informing them that

> Wee of our speciall grace certeine knowledge & mere motion haue licenced and aucthorized and by theise p*r*esentes doe licence and aucthorize theise our servaunt*es* lawrence ffletcher Willi*a*m Shakespeare Richard Burbage Augustyne Phillippes John Heninges Henrie Condell Willi*a*m Sly Robe*r*t Armyn Richard Cowly and the rest of theire Assosiates freely to vse and exercise the Arte and faculty of playinge Com*m*edies Tragedies Histories Enterludes Moralls pastorall*es* Stageplaies and suche others like as theie haue alreadie studied or hereafter shall vse or studie aswell for the recreation of our loving Subjects as for our Solace and pleasure when wee shall thincke good to see them duringe our pleasure And the said Com*m*edies […] and suche like to shewe and exercise publiquely to theire best Com*m*oditie when the infection of the plague shall decrease aswell within theire nowe vsuall howse called the Globe within our County of Surrey, as alsoe within anie towne halls or moute halls or other conveniente places within the liberties and freedome of anie other Cittie vniversitie towne or Boroughe.[1]

In issuing such 'letters patent', James reinstated the idea that the monarch should exercise direct patronage over a leading company of players, which had lapsed somewhat in the 1590s, when troupes such as the Chamberlain's Men and the Admiral's Men began to eclipse Queen Elizabeth's own company. The king would also extend the idea of royal patronage to other companies: the Admiral's Men became Prince Henry's Men and another leading company, Worcester's Men, became Queen Anna's Men; the queen also took on the patronage of one of the all-boy playing companies hitherto associated with the choir schools and grammar schools, the Children of the Chapel becoming the Children of the Queen's Revels (Gurr 1996: 168–9).

The relationship between the company that James took under his patronage in 1603 and the second man named in the list of 'our servauntes', William Shakespeare, is the subject of this book. *Shakespeare in the Theatre: The King's Men* explores points of connection between theatre history and literary criticism and interpretation: the moments at which the 'Arte and faculty of playinge' – as the letters patent term it – has a direct impact on the character and composition of the theatrical repertoire. It argues that the King's Men, as theatre-makers in their own right, exercised a generative and transformative influence on Shakespeare's plays, and that their practices over four decades shaped traditions that would define Shakespearean performance. The King's Men, it suggests, shaped what we now know as 'Shakespeare', in terms not only of our understanding of the player-dramatist's career but also of the uses of his plays as theatrical commodities.

An intertwined set of concerns – authority, service, commodity and collaboration – are central to both the letters patent and this book. When the King's Men showed their copy of this document to the local authorities in Surrey, the City of London or the country at large, they re-inscribed their position as dependent upon royal favour. In the text itself, James licenses and authorizes the performances of the King's Men 'of our speciall grace certeine knowledge & mere motion [individual inclination]', and the letters refer twice to the company as 'our servauntes'. The 'recreation of our loving Subjectes' appears to be subordinated to the king's 'Solace and pleasure'. Yet the very reference to 'public' performance and the use of the resonant term 'Commoditie' – which carried a range of meanings including income, revenue, benefit and convenience – admit that commercial performance is crucial to the company's activities. As David Schalkwyk notes in the context of Shakespeare's own representations of service, the actor 'embodies his enabling relationship to the master by whose grace his personations are permitted; as a member of a commercial theatre dependent on a paying audience, he enacts service in a more modern, market sense' (2008: 10). As I will explore further in the chapters that follow, this double sense of 'service' was crucial to the operations of the King's Men, and it inflected their repertory in a variety of ways.

The list of the actors' names registers the importance of their collaborative 'art' – their combined creative and practical skills – in the work of the King's Men. These were the company's 'sharers', the men who had invested their money into it and drew a regular share of its profits, and some of them also held shares in the company's playhouse. Collectively, they controlled the company and were crucial to its success as performers, playwrights (in the case of Shakespeare and, possibly, Armin), investors and administrators. The reference to 'the rest of theire Assosiates' also points to the other theatrical labour that underpinned the company's activities – for instance, that of the hired men, who were paid by the week to take smaller roles and did not share in the company's profits, or the apprentices who played female and juvenile roles.[2] In what follows I will explore the contribution of these men and boys to the theatrical enterprise. I will also attend to the regular shifts in the membership of the company, which were an issue even at the moment at which the letters patent were drawn up. The company was shortly to lose a leading performer, Thomas Pope, who died in July 1603 and does not figure in the letters patent, but in the same year it recruited John Lowin, who was to be central to its activities in the coming decades.

In their reference to 'theire nowe vsuall howse called the Globe', the letters patent also signal the importance of this outdoor playhouse near the south bank of the Thames, which the company had occupied since 1599. In 1608 the King's Men also gained access to an indoor playhouse, the Blackfriars, which was situated on the western edge of the City of London, north of the Thames. This book will explore in detail impact of the company's playhouses on their theatrical output. At the same time, it will also look at a striking example of a moment at which they exercised their right to play in 'other conveniente places': the performances of Shakespeare's *Othello* and Ben Jonson's *The Alchemist* in Oxford in September 1610, another time at which the 'infection of the plague' placed limits on the company.

The stipulation that the company are licensed to perform 'Commedies Tragedies Histories Enterludes Moralls pastoralles Stageplaies' and the reference to pieces 'theie haue alreadie studied or hereafter shall vse or studie', also point to the importance of repertory construction and design to the King's Men. A successful roster of plays necessitated a combination of different modes of drama, plays produced by different writers, new plays and old plays. Between 1603 and 1642 the King's Men commissioned plays from most of the leading dramatists of the period: Shakespeare, Jonson, Middleton, Beaumont, Fletcher, Webster, Ford, Massinger, Brome, Davenant and Shirley. They also employed intriguing figures such as George Wilkins, Shakespeare's collaborator on *Pericles*, whose playwrighting career appears to be confined to a brief period around 1606–8, John Clavell, a reformed highwayman turned dramatist, who wrote *The Soddered Citizen* for them around 1630, and courtier-dramatists such as Lodowick Carlell and Thomas Killigrew. The combined output of these playwrights represents one of the richest bodies of drama produced in the period.

Shakespeare was at the heart of the company's activities for nearly four decades, as player, playwright and theatrical commodity, and this book explores in detail these three interconnecting versions of 'Shakespeare'. The first is the actor who held shares in his playing company and its playhouses and was 'fellow' to a tight-knit group of actors, one of whom, Phillips, named him in his will and others of whom – Burbage,

Heminges and Condell – are named in his own will (Honigmann and Brock 1993: 73, 107). Shakespeare may not have been as central to company's business dealings as Burbage or Heminges, but he features prominently in the 1603 patent and had earlier been named alongside Burbage and an actor who had since left the company, William Kemp, as a payee for the performances of the Chamberlain's Men at court during the Christmas season of 1594–5.[3]

The second 'Shakespeare' is the writer retained by the company as its leading dramatist, whose plays emerged from a dialogue with other writers and were shaped by the skills of the actors who performed them. The third is the theatrical commodity, a set of plays that would continue through their regular revival to fuel actors' ambitions and playwrights' imaginations for decades to come. These two aspects of 'Shakespeare' are not always easy to untangle. Between 1603 and 1613, the plays that Shakespeare newly composed, often in collaboration with dramatists such as Wilkins, Middleton and Fletcher, were essential to the aesthetic and financial health of the King's Men. These plays sat in the repertory alongside other newly commissioned works and older plays by Shakespeare and others. Evidence of this interplay between old and new Shakespearean plays can be seen in two of the most complete sets of records of court performance that have survived, for 1604–5 and 1612–13.[4] *Othello* and *Measure for Measure* were performed at court in the Christmas season of 1604–5 alongside *The Merry Wives of Windsor*, *The Comedy of Errors*, *Love's Labour's Lost*, *Henry V* and *The Merchant of Venice*, while *The Tempest*, *Cardenio* and *The Winter's Tale* were performed there in 1612–13 alongside *Julius Caesar*, *Much Ado About Nothing*, *Othello*, 'The Hotspur' (*1 Henry IV*) and 'Sir Iohn Falstafe' (either *2 Henry IV* or *The Merry Wives of Windsor*). It is likely that the court seasons of other years, which are not nearly so well documented, saw similar line-ups of old and new Shakespearean works.[5]

After Shakespeare's retirement, his plays continued to be central to the court and commercial repertoire, and to the ongoing identity and practices of the King's Men. The period between 1613 and 1660 is often glossed over by scholars, but it was crucial to the development of traditions that would shape Shakespearean performance in the Restoration and beyond. This book is interested not only in performance 'firsts' – Burbage's appearance as Othello around 1604, for example – but in what happened when a play was revived and new actors took on its roles. This is the first period in English theatre history at which we possess sufficiently detailed information to be able to track in detail the movement of roles between actors; the successive performance contexts of individual plays, and the 'Shakespeare' that they produced, would leave a long shadow.

In exploring these various versions of 'Shakespeare', this book seeks to bring together questions relating to repertory design and performance practice, and to forge connections between theatre history and other currents within Shakespearean and early modern studies. In his important recent work on the 'textile black body' in *Othello* and *The Merchant of Venice*, Ian Smith has demonstrated the ways in which 'an initial inquiry largely identified with the theatre historian's research' can have wider ramifications for the ways in which we interpret early modern plays (2016: 170; see also Smith 2013). This book responds to Smith's challenge, pursuing a set of inquiries that start with theatre historians' questions – Who performed this role? Where was this play performed? What does this eyewitness response mean? – then drawing on a wider range of interpretative techniques in order to address them.

In addition, this book repeatedly asks questions of the documentary materials on which it draws, questions that should also be asked of the letters patent that I have explored here. For example, it is noticeable that the list of the actors' names is headed not by a longstanding member of the company such as Shakespeare or Burbage, but by Lawrence Fletcher, a favourite actor of King James who appears to have newly arrived in London. It has often been thought that Fletcher's presence was merely nominal, a mark of respect to the new king that had little impact on the company itself, but he also appears in a 1607 list of the men to whom payments were due as James's 'Players of Interludes', and his membership of the company may have been more significant than we have so far realized.[6] Fletcher's presence in these documents is a reminder, therefore, that the paper trail on which theatre history depends is both fractured and complex.

The documentary record is also central to this book because it provides us with material not only for its five main chapters but also a series of mini-chapters – a Prologue and four Interludes – that give it a chronological spine. Each of these mini-chapters explores the shifting relationship between Shakespeare's plays and those of his colleagues and successors through a single resonant document: a record of the plays performed at court in a specific season. Richard Dutton (2016) has recently made a powerful case for the impact of court patronage on Shakespeare's plays. My interest in the court seasons here lies in what they tell us about the company's repertory. Plays selected for performance at court indicate what the King's Men thought would please the monarch and his family, but they also offer evidence about what the King's Men offered their broader public because court plays appear generally to have been selected from the current commercial repertory.[7] I therefore use these records to chart the impact of individual actors' careers and life-events, the arrival of new dramatists, shifts in theatrical patronage as the children of James I reached political maturity and changes in the tastes of playgoers. For readers who would like an even broader overview, an Appendix presents a summary of the evidence for the performance of Shakespeare's plays by the King's Men between 1603 and 1642.

The Prologue and first Interlude focus on the court seasons of 1604–5 and 1612–13, in which Shakespeare could himself have actively participated as playwright and, possibly, player. The first of these seasons is documented by an extensive manuscript account drawn up for the Master of the Revels, Sir Edmund Tilney, which details the various expenses for which the Revels Office sought repayment. Now catalogued as AO 3/908/13 in the National Archives, Kew, it has a colourful history of its own. In the 1840s it was taken from the official archive by a theatre historian, Peter Cunningham, and not returned until the 1860s; in the decades that followed it was routinely accused of being a forgery (see Streitberger 1986: xxx–xxxi; Freeman and Freeman 2004: 403–10).[8] Information about the 1612–13 season comes from a document deriving from a later stage in the official paperwork, having been drawn up for the Treasurer of the Chamber, Sir John Stanhope, Baron Stanhope of Harrington, whose office was responsible for issuing payments to Tilney's successor Sir George Buc (Taylor 2012: 22). It would have drawn its information from a document similar to the 1604–5 account. This document has also had a chequered history. The manuscript of which it is part, now housed in the Bodleian Library, Oxford, and catalogued as MS Rawl. A. 239, ended up in the papers of Samuel Pepys. Along with a number of Pepys's official papers, it was rescued from waste-paper dealers by the antiquarian Richard Rawlinson (Lupić 2012: 102–4). Rawlinson then bequeathed his collection to the Bodleian on his death in 1755.

The second Interlude, which focuses on the court season of 1619–20, takes us to a very early stage of the process of court performance. It explores the contents of a set of fragmentary notes made by Buc, in which he appears to have listed the plays that he thought would be appropriate for court performance. He then reused the paper for making notes on corrections to his history of the career of King Richard III, and the notes are preserved with the manuscript of his draft in the British Library, where it is catalogued as Cotton MS Tiberius E.X (Marcham 1925; Chambers 1925). The third Interlude takes us to the moment of performance itself, albeit in a heavily mediated form. It draws on a set of notes on the plays performed in 1633–4 by Buc's successor, Sir Henry Herbert, that were transcribed by the eighteenth-century theatre history Edmond Malone and published by him in 1821 (Shakespeare 1821, 3: 233–4; see Bawcutt 1996: 184–8, Collins 2013: 30–41). The fourth and final interlude explores the court season of 1636–7, which is documented by a list of plays drawn up by the King's Men themselves and then attached by a court official to the warrant for payment.[9] Now catalogued in the National Archives as AO 3/908/22, it was also among the documents taken by Cunningham in the 1840s, but its authenticity has been less frequently called into question. The fragmentary nature of the documentary record is demonstrated by the fact that, while all or most of these documents would have been produced for each court season, they only survive sporadically.

The Interludes are interspersed between five full-length chapters, each of which deals in a different way with the questions of authority, service, commodity and collaboration outlined above. Chapter 1, 'The Art and Faculty of Playing: The King's Men and Their Roles' summarizes the information that has come down to us about the roles played by individual actors and explores the skills on which they were able to draw in performance. It focuses in turn on three key groups of performers: leading actors, specialist performers of comic roles and apprentice players who took female and juvenile roles. In doing so, it starts to trace the relationship between the company's plays and the 'repertory' of roles performed by individual actors, a relationship that will be crucial to the chapters that follow.

Like scholars such as Joseph R. Roach and Marvin Carlson, I am interested in relationships between the different roles played by the same actors, and between the same roles as they are played by different actors, relationships that they characterize in various terms as ghosting, surrogation and replacement. Carlson writes of the 'recycled body of an actor' whose performances 'will almost inevitably in a new role evoke the ghost or ghosts of previous roles' (2001: 8), while Roach notes that '[e]ven in death actors' roles tend to stay with them. They gather in the memory of audiences, like ghosts, as each new interpretation of a role sustains or upsets expectations derived from the previous ones' (1996: 78). Early modern audiences may not have expected the same level of interpretative novelty from actors as their twenty-first-century counterparts, but they were nonetheless acutely aware of the process of transition that occurred when a role moved from one actor to another, or an actor took on a new role.

The remaining chapters build on Chapter 1 to explore in more detail a set of interactions between Shakespeare's plays and the broader performance practices of the King's Men. Drawing on documentary materials such as actor-lists and eyewitness accounts or reports of performances, they look at casting, revivals, repertory design and the ways in which specific plays exploit the capabilities of the company's two playhouses, the Globe and Blackfriars. Each of them focuses on a Shakespeare play or a pair of Shakespeare plays: *Othello*; *Pericles*; *The Tempest* and *The Winter's Tale*; and *Richard II* and *Henry VIII, or All is True*. This miniature canon, consisting of some of the most successful plays of the period in terms of their recorded performances and influence, confirms what we think we know about the value of plays such as *Othello* and *The Tempest*, which still dominate the stage and school syllabi today. However, it also disrupts such expectations given the current relative lack of interest in *Pericles* and *Henry VIII*, and the fact that these two hugely popular plays were co-written with other dramatists – Wilkins and Fletcher – also unsettles some persistent myths about Shakespeare's artistic autonomy.

The chapters offer case-studies of the stage-lives of these plays and their successive interactions with other plays of the repertory, telling a set of interrelated stories about Shakespearean performance between 1603 and 1642. Chapter 2, 'Collaboration, Competition and Candlelight: *Othello* and *The Alchemist*', argues that these plays were popular because they offered outstanding showcases for the talents of successive actors, who must collaborate intensively in order to do justice to their representations of conflict and competition. Tracing in detail the evidence that survives of successive performances of the plays at the Globe and Blackfriars, it discovers that the casting of both plays was more complex than has often been recognized. Although Joseph

Taylor succeeded Richard Burbage as the leading actor of the King's Men, he did not take, or in some cases retain, all of the roles taken by his predecessor. The chapter explores the reasons why Taylor apparently preferred to play Iago and Face over Othello and Subtle, deploying his authority as the company's leading actor in ways that were different from those of his predecessor. In doing so, it argues that the technical demands posed by performance at the Blackfriars, and their impact on the plays' structures of collaboration and competition, have been underestimated.

Chapter 3, 'Painful Adventures: *Pericles* and the "Traffic" of the Stage', looks in detail at the stage-life of Shakespeare and Wilkins's hugely popular *Pericles, Prince of Tyre* over three decades, reading it through a set of later plays that respond to its narrative structures and theatrical conventions: Fletcher and Massinger's *The Custom of the Country* (c. 1619), Massinger's *Believe as You List* (1631) and Killigrew's *The Princess* (c. 1635–6). Looking at this group of plays together offers a fresh perspective on both the popularity and the textual problems of *Pericles* – the forms in which the play was itself 'trafficked'. More than this, however, the chapter also takes a broader view of workings of stage traffic, looking at the relationship between narratives of bondage and subjection within the plays and the trafficking structures of the company itself. The relationships of actors to their companies were regulated by financial bonds that restricted their freedom to operate independently; apprentices were 'bound' to their masters until their terms expired; and in 1633 the King's Men was awarded the right to take actors from other companies, a practice that may have existed also in earlier times. *Pericles* and its dramatic successors thus both embody and critique the King's Men's commercial 'trafficking' of plays, plots and players.

Chapter 4, 'Men, Women and Magic: Shakespeare, the Merry Devil and the Prophetess' follows the figure of the magic-worker from Peter Fabell in *The Merry Devil of Edmonton* (1603), through Shakespeare's Prospero and Paulina, to

Delphia, the title character in Fletcher and Massinger's *The Prophetess* (1622). Exploring the uses to which these plays put theatrical space and the actors available to them, it deconstructs familiar narratives about the relative prominence of the King's Men's two playhouses and returns to questions of authority, collaboration and service, exploring in detail the interplay between leading actors and apprentice players. Where plays such as *The Merry Devil of Edmonton* and *The Tempest* place the leading actor at the centre of attention, *The Winter's Tale* and *The Prophetess* instead demonstrate how boy actors and female characters might inhabit and control theatrical space.

Chapter 5, 'Summer Days at the Globe: *Richard II*, *Henry VIII* and the Politics of Playing', explores in detail the ability of the King's Men to negotiate not only the opportunities offered by the king's patronage but also its dangers. It analyses a remarkable but largely neglected aspect of the King's Men's repertory design: the performance of political and topical drama at the Globe over a span of forty years. Scholars have overlooked this tradition, and the role of Shakespeare's plays within it, because they have followed accepted wisdom that the Globe became a secondary, downmarket venue when the King's Men acquired the Blackfriars. Drawing on eyewitness accounts and reports of performances of *Richard II* and other plays on the same topic (1601, 1611 and 1631), *Henry VIII* (1613 and 1628), Fletcher and Massinger's *Sir John Van Olden Barnavelt* (1619) and Middleton's *A Game at Chess* (1624), the chapter argues that the success of these plays was due not only to their controversial subject-material but also to the ways in which the King's Men used verbal and visual effects, and the casting of particular actors, to render politics and politicians 'familiar' to spectators.

The final chapter thus points to some of the political tensions that existed within the structures of the theatre industry, tensions that are visible in the attempt of the letters patent to balance the competing demands of 'the recreation of our loving Subjectes' and the king's own 'Solace and pleasure'.

The Epilogue pushes these questions further into the period of the Civil War, Commonwealth and Protectorate, tracing what happened to the Shakespeare and the King's Men when the structures of royal authority were removed. In doing so, it acknowledges that playing did not disappear in 1642, when Parliament ordered that the playhouses be closed as a way of maintaining public order in the early days of the Civil War, but it also registers the extent to which commercial playing was disrupted.

As a whole, then, this book argues that the King's Men's part in shaping the earliest Shakespearean performance traditions has been underestimated. Its explorations of patterns within the company's repertory and casting practices bring theatre history into dialogue with other areas of Shakespearean and early modern studies, providing a richer and more suggestive perspective on the plays and their performance. We cannot understand the place of Shakespeare's plays on the early seventeenth-century stage without understanding the uses to which the company put his plays, or their creative input into the ways in which they were staged. Shakespeare could not have known in 1603 that his plays would still be holding the stage many decades later. *Shakespeare in the Theatre: The King's Men* tells the story – or, rather, the multiple stories – of how they got there, and how they changed along the way.

Prologue: Playing the Court, 1604–5

A striking picture of the relationship between Shakespeare and the King's Men is offered by the set of accounts drawn up by the Master of the Revels, Sir Edmund Tilney, when he sought repayment for the expenses laid out on the court season of 1604–5 (Figures 1 and 2). Alongside lists of the charges for candles, benches, rushes for the floor, canvas for the tiring house, wages for the Revels office staff and other expenses is a list of the plays performed by three companies – the King's Men, the Queen's Men and the Children of the Chapel – between Hallowmas Day, 1 November 1604, and Shrove Tuesday, 12 February 1605.[1]

The King's Men performed seven plays by Shakespeare: 'The moor of venis', now better known as *Othello*; 'the Merry wiues of winsor'; 'Mesur for Mesur'; 'The plaie of Errors', better known as *The Comedy of Errors*; 'Loues Labours Lost'; 'Henry the fift'; and 'the Martchant of venis'. The last was performed twice, the second time 'Againe Commanded By the Kings Majestie'. They also performed two plays by Ben Jonson, his hugely popular 'humours' comedies *Every Man out of his Humour* and *Every Man in his Humour*, and a lost play by an unknown author, 'A Tragidye of The Spanishe Maz', or 'Maze'. In addition to providing the names of the plays, the list offers

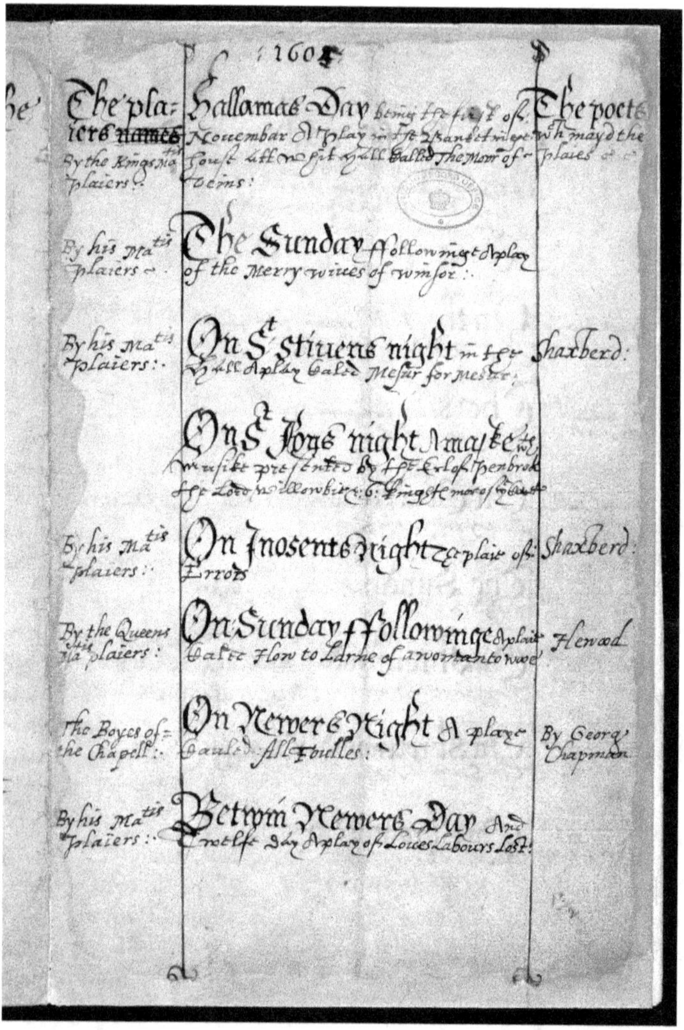

1604

The plaiers names		The poets wh mayd the plaies
By the Kings Matis plaiers:	Hallamas Day being the first of Nouembar A play in the Banketinge house att Whithall Called The Moor of Venis:	
By his Matis plaiers:	The Sunday ffollowinge A play of the Merry wiues of Winsor:	
By his Matis plaiers:	On St Stiuens night in the Hall A play Caled Mesur for Mesur:	Shaxberd:
	On St Iohns night A maske with musike presented by the Erl of Penbrok the Lord Willowbie & 6 Knightes more of the Court	
By his Matis plaiers:	On Inosents night The plaie of Errors	Shaxberd:
By the Queens Matis plaiers:	On Sunday ffollowinge A plaie Called How to Larne of a woman to wooe	Heywood
The Boyes of the Chapell:	On Newers Night A playe Cauled All Foulles:	By George Chapman
By his Matis plaiers:	Betwin Newers Day And Twelfe day A play of Loues Labours Lost:	

FIGURES 1 and 2 *Account of Edmund Tilney, Master of the Revels, 1604–5, AO 3/908/13, The National Archives, Kew.*

The plaiers		The poets
	On Twelfe Night...	
By his Ma^{tis} plaiers:	On the 7: of January was played the play of Henry the fift:	
By his ma^{tis} plaiers:	The: 8: of January: A play Cauled Every on out of his Umor	
By his Ma^{tis} plaiers:	On Candelmas night A play: Every one In his Umor	
	The Sunday ffollowing A play...	
By his Ma^{tis} plaiers:	On Shroufunday A play of the Marthant of Venis	Shaxberd
By his Ma^{tis} plaiers:	On Shroumonday A Tragidye of the Spanishe Maz:	
By his Ma^{tis} plaiers:	On Shroutusday A play Cauled The Marchant of Venis Againe Comanded By the Kings Matie:	Shaxberd

FIGURES 1 and 2 *(Continued)*

an intriguing perspective on relationships within the company. The left-hand column, headed 'The plaiers', lists the names of the playing companies; the central column lists the dates of the performances with the titles of the plays; and the right-hand column lists the names of 'The poets w^{c}h mayd the plaies'. The 'poets' are in fact named only sporadically, perhaps as they were not essential to the process of ensuring that the companies were paid for their labour. The name of Shakespeare – or 'Shaxberd', as it is rendered here – features only four times, and Jonson goes entirely unnamed, as does the author of *The Spanish Maze*. In contrast, the 'plaiers' are named against almost every performance, the exception being a 'play provided And discharged' on 3 February. The list thus presents the poet's labour alongside that of the players, but it also subordinates playwrighting to playing in a way that may feel odd or transgressive to twenty-first-century readers. Important as poets were to dramatic creation, authority lay with the players.

Three of the plays were probably new to the repertory. *Measure for Measure* and *Othello* both appear to have been written during the plague-disrupted months between James's accession in March 1603 and the beginning of the court season in November 1604, while *The Spanish Maze* is likely to have exploited the topicality of Spanish material in the wake of the peace treaty that the new king signed with Spain on 18 August 1604. Twelve members of the King's Men and eleven members of Queen Anna's Men were recruited to swell the numbers of Grooms of the Chamber for this event, and even if they were simply there 'to impress the Spaniards with the good looks and bearing of the king's servants', as Lois Potter suggests (2012: 308), it would not have hurt the King's Men to advertise the connection within their repertory. Moreover, the company appear to have been intrigued by the possibilities of political drama in 1603–4, performing Jonson's drama of conspiracy and empire in ancient Rome, *Sejanus*, in 1603, and a lost play, *The Tragedy of Gowrie*, which probably dramatized a conspiracy against King James earlier in his Scottish reign, around 18 December 1604

(Wiggins 2011–18: 5.168–9).[2] Both of these plays aroused controversy on their initial performances; in contrast, *The Spanish Maze* may have negotiated more successfully the demanding balance between topicality and decorum. The other plays were older. *The Comedy of Errors* was first performed between 1589 and 1593, *Love's Labours Lost* between 1594 and 1597, *The Merchant of Venice* between 1596 and 1598, *The Merry Wives of Windsor* between 1597 and 1602, Jonson's *Every Man in his Humour* in 1598 and *Every Man out of his Humour* and *Henry V* in 1599.

Given that he was an actor and company sharer as well as a poet, Shakespeare was probably involved in some measure in the choice of the plays that the King's Men performed before James and his family. It is also possible that he acted in some or all of them, given that he appears in the list of the principal actors in *Sejanus* (1616: 2O3v), performed only a couple of years earlier. Shakespeare appears never to have been thought of as a great actor; by the end of the seventeenth century he was remembered as 'a much better Poet, than Player' (Wright 1699: 4). However, Jonson – not generally a man moved by sentiment – placed his fellow playwright second in the list of actors in *Sejanus*, behind Richard Burbage and ahead of John Heminges and Augustine Phillips. He was thus considered by at least one contemporary to be a significant player as well as playwright.

We do not know how much consideration Shakespeare gave to the relationship between his old plays and new compositions, but the plays of the 1604–5 court season speak to each other in intriguing ways. Plays such as *Othello* and *The Comedy of Errors* dramatize pan-Mediterranean cultures, and both *Othello* and *The Merchant of Venice* deal with questions of racial and religious identity and alterity. Given Spain's fraught history of religious and ethnic conflict, these connections also prompt us to consider how such questions may also have been explicitly or implicitly handled in *The Spanish Maze*. Furthermore, *Othello* has itself been linked specifically with the racial and religious politics of Spain via the figure of Iago (see Hall 2007: 204–5; Griffin 2009: 168–206). Performing *Othello* alongside *The Spanish Maze* may have made such connections especially pointed, highlighting a complex set of racial, religious and geographical issues that are not as readily visible to twenty-first-century readers and spectators.

Elsewhere in the repertory, the comic structures that pervade *Henry V* are brought to the fore if we consider it alongside Jonson's humours comedies. This is, after all, a play first printed in 1600 as 'THE CRONICLE History of Henry the fift, With his battell fought at *Agin Court* in *France*. Togither with *Auntient Pistoll*', a description that gestures not only to the historical narrative but the disreputable Pistol, who is mentioned in the advertisement of 'the humours of sir Iohn Fal-*staffe, and swaggering* Pistoll' on the title-page of the second part of *Henry IV*, which was also published in 1600. Jonson's representation of the extremes of human emotion in *Every Man in his Humour*, especially his portrayal of Thorello's possessively jealous treatment of his wife, Bianca, clearly resonated with Shakespeare when he was writing *Othello*, but Jonson also probably had an eye to *The Merchant of Venice* and, especially, *The Merry Wives of Windsor* when he was composing his own play.

These connections would have been heightened when the plays were performed by the same group of actors, and the 1604–5 repertory demonstrates the complexity of casting patterns deployed by the King's Men. Line counts are a relatively crude way of gauging the importance of characters within a play, given that characters with few lines can nonetheless make significant interventions within individual scenes, and characters' silent presence or gestures can be as important as their dialogue. Nonetheless, the distribution of lines alerts us to some of the structural conventions that the company deployed: outsize roles designed for leading players (such as the King in *Henry V*, Berowne in *Love's Labour's Lost* and Duke Vincentio in *Measure for Measure*); challengingly large roles for boy actors (such as Portia in *The Merchant of Venice*, the longest role in that play); leading duos (such as Othello and Iago in *Othello*); and more balanced ensemble playing (for instance, in *The Merry Wives of Windsor*, *The Comedy of Errors* or *Every Man Out of his Humour*).

Richard Burbage appears to have taken many of the plays' leading roles: there is evidence that he played Othello and he is also likely to have played Henry V, Berowne, Duke Vincentio and Thorello in *Every Man in his Humour*. He did not, however, dominate every play. As I will explore in greater detail in Chapter 2, Othello is not the largest role in the play that takes his name; Iago, played by a new recruit to the King's Men, John Lowin, has around 200 lines more in both the quarto and folio texts (King 1992: 220–2). The largest role in *The Merry Wives of Windsor*, Falstaff, was probably also played by Lowin in 1604–5, and the largest role in *Every Man out of his Humour*, Carlo Buffone, has been plausibly attributed to neither Burbage nor Lowin but a comic specialist like Thomas Pope or Robert Armin.[3] Rotating plays with different structures allowed the King's Men to offer opportunities to its sharers and leading boy actors, and it also allowed them to preserve the overall strength of the company. As I will explore in more detail in Chapter 1, the leading actors were crucial to the company's success, but they never dominated and – as Holger Schott Syme argues in a recent essay – the structure of the repertory may have been designed to protect individual players from exhaustion or overload (2019b).

The preceding discussion has opened up many of the central concerns of this book: the place of Shakespeare's plays within a changing theatrical repertory; the role of multiple audiences in helping to shape and sustain that repertory; the performance of plays across multiple venues; and the impact of both individual players and the broader structures of the playing company on the performance and reception of plays. The list of plays in Tilney's accounts offers the three versions of 'Shakespeare' outlined in the Preface: the actor/sharer; the playwright; and the theatrical commodity, whose plays are selected and repackaged for the court. It presents 'Shaxberd' as a product of the King's Men, produced and reproduced through the company's collective endeavour.

1

The Art and Faculty of Playing: The King's Men and Their Roles

One of the earliest histories of the English stage, James Wright's 1699 book *Historia Histrionica*, is also a history of the King's Men, the actors that made up the company in successive decades, and the roles that they took. The book takes the shape of a dialogue, in which a Restoration playgoer, Lovewit, questions an older man, Truman, about the actors of the period before the Civil War. Early in their conversation, Lovewit laments the fact that earlier printed plays do not carry 'the Actors Names over against the Parts they Acted', because if they had 'one might have guest at the Action of the Men, by the Parts which we now Read in the Old Plays' (Wright 1699: 3). Truman comments that some early plays indeed carry such information, listing among them five plays of the King's Men, and under Lovewit's questioning he also describes in some detail the leading actors of the 1630s and early 1640s:

> in my time, before the Wars, *Lowin* used to Act, with mighty Applause, *Falstaffe, Morose, Vulpone,* and *Mammon* in the *Alchymist; Melancius* in the *Maid's* Tragedy, and at the same time *Amyntor* was Play'd by *Stephen Hammerton,*

(who was at first a most noted and beautiful Woman Actor, but afterwards he acted with equal Grace and Applause, a Young Lover's Part) *Tayler* Acted *Hamlet* incomparably well, *Jago, Truewit* in the *Silent Woman,* and *Face* in the *Alchymist; Swanston* used to Play *Othello: Pollard,* and *Robinson* were Comedians, so was *Shank* who used to Act Sir *Roger,* in the *Scornful Lady.* These were of the *Blackfriers.* Those of principal Note at the *Cockpit,* were, *Perkins, Michael Bowyer, Sumner, William Allen,* and *Bird,* eminent Actors. and *Robins* a Comedian. Of the other Companies I took little notice.

(4)

Truman offers tantalizing glimpses of these players in action. He recalls the physically imposing John Lowin, who not only inherited roles such as Falstaff, the manipulative, malingering Volpone in Ben Jonson's play of that title – a role originally played by Richard Burbage – and the grotesquely noise-intolerant Morose in Jonson's *Epicoene,* but also created Sir Epicure Mammon in *The Alchemist* and the regicidal war hero Melantius in Francis Beaumont and John Fletcher's *The Maid's Tragedy*.[1] Lowin's closest colleague, Joseph Taylor, is brought to mind in a series of roles that he inherited from other actors: Hamlet, Iago, the mouthy gallant Truewit in *Epicoene* and the servant-turned-conman Face in *The Alchemist.* The glamorous Stephen Hammerton is remembered as the wavering Amintor in *The Maid's Tragedy,* and another leading performer, Elliard Swanston, is recalled as Othello. Truman also recollects comic actors such as Thomas Pollard, William Robins (also known as Robinson) and John Shank, who played the parson Sir Roger in Beaumont and Fletcher's *The Scornful Lady.*

Some of the actors that Wright associates with the Cockpit also performed with the King's Men. Richard Perkins was with them around 1622–5, before leaving for a new company under the patronage of Queen Henrietta Maria, with which he spent the rest of his career. The others became King's Men at the high point of their acting lives: Michael Bowyer and William Allen appear to have joined the company around 1637, followed by Theophilus Bird at some point between May 1638 and August 1639; William Robins was with them by 1641, and most likely a few years earlier. In addition to his account of Hammerton's career, Truman provides further information about the actors who played female and juvenile roles, such as the famous Restoration actors Charles Hart and Walter Clun, who 'were bred up Boys at the *Blackfriers;* and Acted Womens Parts, *Hart* was *Robinson*'s Boy or Apprentice: He Acted the Dutchess in the Tragedy of *the Cardinal,* which was the first Part that gave him Reputation' (3).

Wright's book offers an account of the King's Men that is incomplete and fragmented – giving us only partial insights into long careers – but it also provides a long view of the company's internal structures, its personnel, parts and performances. His narrative brings to the fore such issues as the existence of different ranks and specialisms within the company, the variety of interactions that existed between actors, the styles of performance and techniques that they employed and the range of roles that an individual performer might present. It also underscores the crucial function of spectators, who experience and remember individual actors and performances, and it creates in the process a submerged history of a family of playgoers. Wright, who was born in 1643, apparently draws on the memories of his father, Abraham, born in 1611, whose manuscript transcriptions of extracts from plays that he saw or read around 1640, and his notes on them, were preserved by his son.[2]

Truman's recollections of the actors and their roles offers a good deal of Shakespearean material, but the same cannot be said of other forms of evidence. The central performers and casting practices of the King's Men are uniquely well documented in comparison with their contemporaries, but one thing is notable for its absence. Although tiny fragments of casting information survive in printed texts of plays such as *Romeo and Juliet, Much Ado About Nothing* and *The Two Noble Kinsmen* (Shakespeare 1599: K3v; 1600: G3v–G4v; Shakespeare and

Fletcher 1634: I4v, L4v), we have yet to discover any manuscript or printed source that provides comprehensive information about the casting of a Shakespeare play. Instead, we have to look at the rich materials that do survive for the plays of his contemporaries and successors. A series of plays include detailed cast-lists that attribute roles to individual actors. Five of them are mentioned by Truman in *Historia Histrionica*: John Webster's *The Duchess of Malfi* (Figure 3), which presents the casts of an early performance around 1613 and a revival around 1620–3; Philip Massinger's *The Roman Actor*, performed in 1626, and *The Picture*, performed in 1629; Lodowick Carlell's *The Deserving Favourite*, performed around 1629; and Fletcher's *The Wild Goose Chase*, which presents the cast of a revival around 1632.[3] We now also know, as Truman did not, that similar cast-lists appear in manuscript copies of John Clavell's *The Soddered Citizen* (*c.* 1630) and Arthur Wilson's *The Swisser* (1631), and that actors' names appear in the stage directions and other parts of the playhouse manuscripts of Middleton's *The Second Maiden's Tragedy* (1611), Fletcher and Massinger's *Sir John Van Olden Barnavelt* (1619) and Massinger's *Believe As You List* (1631).[4] Moreover, the 'plot' of the second part of *The Seven Deadly Sins*, a playhouse document that tracks the entrances, exits and stage business for the purposes of managing a performance, includes the names of most of the members of the Chamberlain's Men – the predecessors of the King's Men – around 1597–8.[5]

In contrast with the 1623 folio edition of Shakespeare's plays, which presents a single list of 'The Names of the Principall Actors in all these Playes' – a list headed by Shakespeare himself – the 1616 folio of Jonson's *Works* and the 1679 second folio of the *Comedies and Tragedies* of Fletcher and his collaborators include lists of the names of the principal actors in individual plays. A more detailed actor-list was also printed with the quarto edition of John Ford's *The Lover's Melancholy*, performed by the King's Men in 1628 and printed in 1629 (A1v). Although these texts do not assign roles to individual actors, seventeenth-century readers sometimes

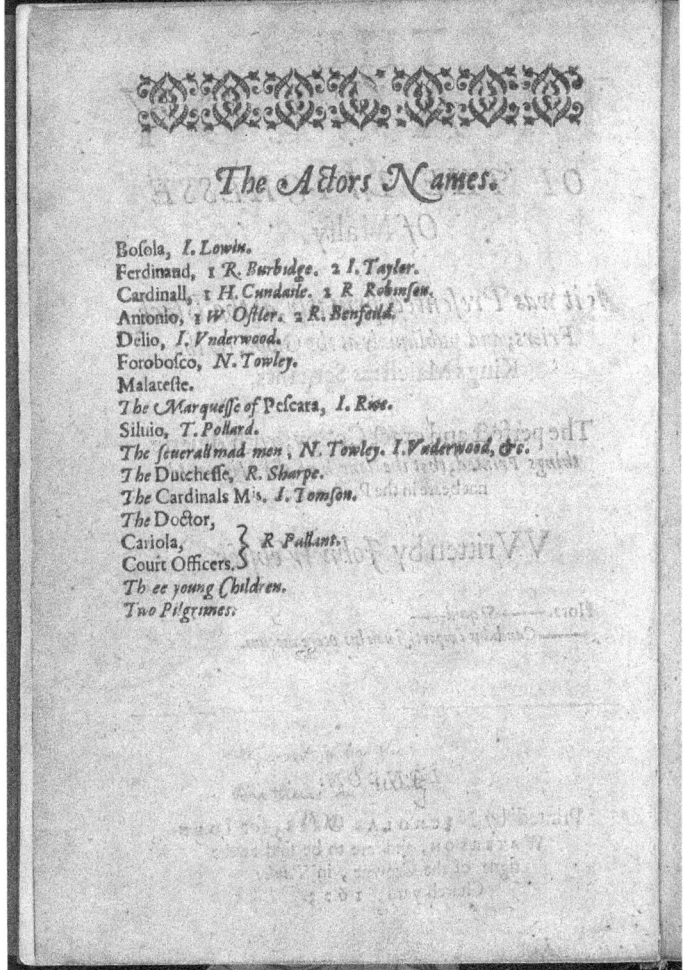

FIGURE 3 *'The Actors Names', in* The Tragedy of the Dutchesse of Malfy *(London, 1623), General Collection, Beinecke Rare Book and Manuscript Library, Yale University.*

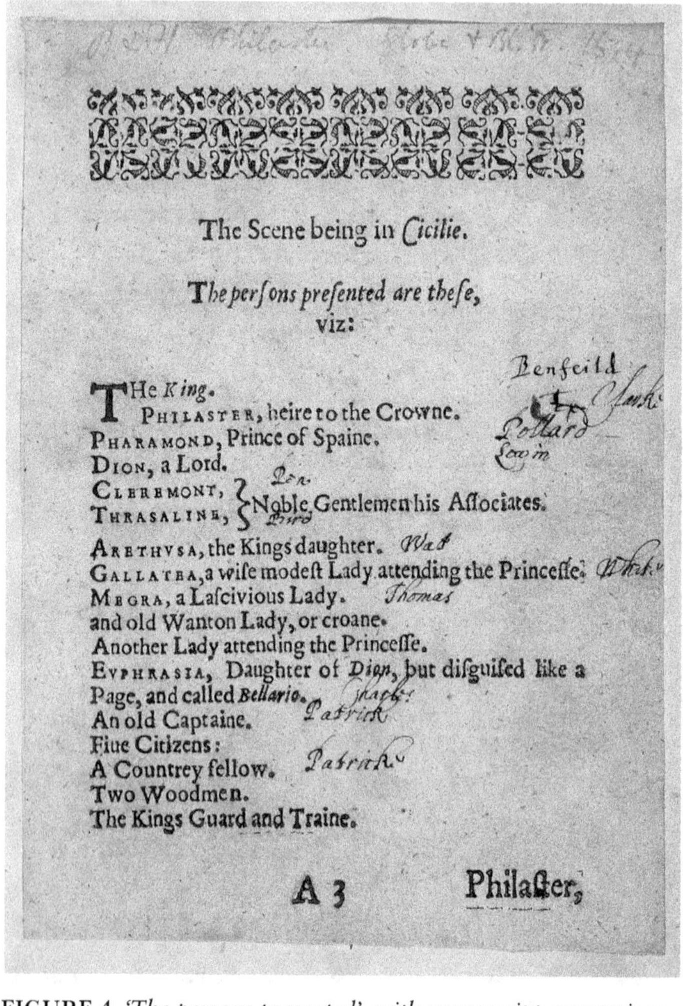

The Scene being in *Cicilie*.

The persons presented are these, viz:

THe *King*.
PHILASTER, heire to the Crowne.
PHARAMOND, Prince of Spaine.
DION, a Lord.
CLEREMONT, } Noble Gentlemen his Associates.
THRASALINE,

ARETHVSA, the Kings daughter.
GALLATEA, a wise modest Lady attending the Princesse.
MEGRA, a Lascivious Lady.
and old Wanton Lady, or croane.
Another Lady attending the Princesse.
EVPHRASIA, Daughter of *Dion*, but disguised like a Page, and called *Bellario*.
An old Captaine.
Fiue Citizens:
A Countrey fellow.
Two Woodmen.
The Kings Guard and Traine.

A 3 Philaster,

FIGURE 4 *'The persons presented', with manuscript annotations, in* Philaster *(London, 1634), Art Inv. 271 no. 10e (2). Used by permission of the Folger Shakespeare Library.*

added this information. For example, the owner of a copy of the Jonson folio wrote actors' names against some of its character-lists and character names against some of its actor-lists, providing detailed information about the casts of revivals of *Volpone* and *The Alchemist* around 1616–18.[6] Similarly, the owner or owners of a copy of the 1634 quarto of Beaumont and Fletcher's *Philaster* wrote the names of the actors against those of the characters (see Figure 4).[7]

These sources shed a good deal of light on the casting practices and performances of the King's Men. They help us to track arrivals and departures; the roles and perceived characteristics of different groups of actors, such as leading men, comic specialists and the trainee players who performed female and juvenile roles; and the structures through which the company ran and maintained itself. All of these events, processes and conventions factored into the practices of the King's Men, and they shed light on the ways in which the company shaped the stage-lives of Shakespeare's plays, from the way that the company's composition shaped their patterns of new commissions and revivals, to the ghostly interactions between actors and roles that helped to structure spectators' responses.

Leading men

The surviving sources document successive generations of the leading performers in the King's Men. A constant presence throughout is John Lowin, who seems to have joined the company from Worcester's Men in 1603 or early 1604 (Syme 2019a: 239–40), perhaps as a replacement for Thomas Pope. Lowin was in his mid-twenties at this time, eight years younger than Richard Burbage, who was firmly established as the company's leading actor. One of the earliest actor-lists for a King's Men play, printed with Jonson's *Sejanus* (1616: 203v), is headed by Burbage, who probably played the title role. Lowin, who is the seventh of the eight actors named, appears to have taken a supporting role in Jonson's tragedy – perhaps playing Silius, as Thomas Whitfield Baldwin thought (1927: casting chart between pages 434 and 435), or Macro, as Shoichiro Kawai has more recently argued (1992: 26). However, he quickly rose to prominence within the company, perhaps in part as a result of the death of Augustine Phillips in May 1605, and he appears in a list of the sharers compiled in late 1607.[8] He played the demanding part of the disturbed and manipulative serving-man Bosola in *The Duchess of Malfi*, and his roles of Eubulus in *The Picture* and Dion in *Philaster* – both of which are variations on the early modern stock character of the loyal but outspoken courtier – are among the largest in these plays. His known Shakespearean roles include Iago, Falstaff (a role that he may have picked up from William Kemp or Pope), and King Henry in Shakespeare and Fletcher's *Henry VIII, or All is True*. Alongside these more serious roles, the fact that he was renowned for playing Falstaff, Epicure Mammon, Sir Politic Would-Be and the bashful would-be lover Belleur in *The Wild Goose Chase* suggests his ability to play comedy effectively. It is, therefore, perhaps unsurprising to find a prologue apparently written for Lowin to speak before William Davenant's 1635 play *The Platonic Lovers*, in which the actor describes himself to the audience as '*I (your Servant) who have labour'd here / In Buskins, and in Socks, this thirty year*' (1636: A3r). The prologue's references to the buskins conventionally worn by tragedians in classical theatre and the socks worn by comedians pay tribute to Lowin's versatility.

A similar versatility was required of Burbage, who heads the actor-lists in all of the plays of Jonson in which he appeared and features prominently in all of the surviving Fletcherian actor-lists for plays performed by the King's Men during his lifetime. He probably continued acting until not long before his death on 13 March 1619, as he features in the list of the leading actors in Fletcher's *The Loyal Subject* (Beaumont and Fletcher 1679: 2K4r), licensed by the Master of the Revels on 16 November 1618 (Bawcutt 1996: 185). His known roles include King Gorboduc and the rapist Tereus in the second part of *The Seven Deadly Sins* (c. 1597–8), Shakespeare's Richard III, Volpone, Subtle in *The Alchemist* and Ferdinand in *The Duchess of Malfi*. Other roles are listed in an elegy that commemorated his death:

> hees gon, & wth him what a world is dead?
> by him reuiu'd, now to obliuion goe,
> no more young Hamlett, old Hieronimo
> Kinge Leer, the greeu'd Moore; & more besid*es*
> (that liued in him) are now for euer dead.[9]

This elegy is attributed in one manuscript – the one from which I quote here – to John Fletcher, a former collaborator of Shakespeare who by 1619 had taken his older colleague's place as the most regular playwright for the King's Men. It thus marks a series of interactions within the company: between Shakespeare and Burbage, who gave life to his roles, between Shakespeare and Fletcher, and between Burbage and Fletcher. Moreover, it also points to the ways in which Shakespeare's roles existed in dynamic tension with those of other playwrights, here captured in the juxtaposition of 'young Hamlett' and 'old Hieronimo', the revenging father of Thomas Kyd's *The Spanish Tragedy*.

Despite the prominence of Burbage and Lowin, other actors challenged their hold over the company's plays. William Ostler, who joined the King's Men around 1609 after beginning his career with the Children of the Chapel, later the Children of the Queen's Revels, is listed second after Burbage in three of the five actor-lists that survive from the early to mid-1610s (Beaumont and Fletcher's *The Captain* and Fletcher's *Bonduca* and *Valentinian*) and fourth in the other two (*The Alchemist* and *The Duchess of Malfi*). Another graduate from the Chapel/ Queen's Revels company, Nathan Field, played Face opposite Burbage's Subtle in *The Alchemist* around 1616–18. Both of these actors died young, Ostler in 1614 and Field – who may have been recruited to replace him – in 1619 or 1620.

The deaths of Burbage and Field led to changes in the company's casting patterns. Burbage was quickly replaced by Joseph Taylor, who picked up some of his predecessor's roles, such as Hamlet and Ferdinand. This process of transition is demonstrated vividly in the actor-list printed with *The Duchess of Malfi* in 1623, in which both appear (Figure 3). However, Taylor did not simply take over Burbage's repertoire. Lowin appears to have played Volpone in Burbage's place; Taylor was instead renowned as Mosca (Flecknoe 1665: E2v–E3r), inheriting the role from Henry Condell, who appears to have retired from performing around this time.[10] Taylor did not take Burbage's role of Subtle in *The Alchemist* either, instead acquiring Field's role of Face (Wright 1699: 3). Other roles that Taylor inherited at various dates include Iago – a problem to which I will return in Chapter 2 – and leading parts in Beaumont and Fletcher plays such as Arbaces in *A King and No King* and Amintor in *The Maid's Tragedy*. Fletcher and Massinger wrote a string of important roles for him in the 1620s and 1630s, such as the comic anti-hero, Mirabel, in Fletcher's *The Wild Goose Chase*, the title role in Fletcher and Massinger's *Rollo, Duke of Normandy, or The Bloody Brother*, the beleaguered actor, Paris, in Massinger's *The Roman Actor*, the wavering husband, Mathias, in *The Picture* and the persecuted former king, Antiochus, in *Believe as You List*.[11]

Lowin and Taylor, who was around a decade younger than his colleague, nearly always head the actor-lists that survive for Fletcher's 1620s plays, and they often take the largest roles in plays of the late 1620s and early 1630s, such as *The Picture* or *Believe as You List*. As I will explore in Chapter 3, dramatists such as Massinger exploit their on-stage chemistry and spectators' desire to see them in scenes of comradeship or conflict. Yet even these performers did not appear in every play: Taylor, for instance, is assigned no role in *The Soddered Citizen*, in what may be a rare surviving example of the broader strategy for preserving actors' energies that is also suggested by the structures of plays for which no cast-lists survive.[12]

As the 1630s wore on, younger performers began to challenge Lowin and Taylor's dominance. Richard Sharpe, born in 1601, was apprenticed to Heminges on 21 February 1616 and played the Duchess in *The Duchess of Malfi* around 1620–3 (Kathman 2004a: 9–10). Having graduated from female and juvenile parts by the mid-1620s, he had started to play leading male roles shortly before his early death in 1632. In Carlell's fervid tragicomedy *The Deserving Favourite*, for example, in Sharpe's role, Lysander, is the largest, with 635 lines; Taylor, playing the Duke, has 552 lines (King 1992: 119). The play also perhaps encourages long-time spectators to recall Sharpe's earlier excellence in female roles, as it has two substantial roles for John Honeyman, playing Clarinda (499 lines), and John Thompson, playing Cleonarda (448 lines).

In the following years, Elliard Swanston – who had been a sharer in the company since around 1624 and was probably in his early thirties at the time of Sharpe's death – also rose to prominence. In *The Picture*, Massinger creates two eye-catching comic roles for Swanston and Thomas Pollard, the sleazy courtiers Ricardo and Ubaldo, discussed in detail below. Within a few years Swanston was taking leading roles such as the protagonist of George Chapman's *Bussy D'Ambois*. A 1630s playgoer, Edmund Gayton, remembered Swanston and Taylor in his book *Pleasant Notes Upon Don Quixot*, which features a sporadic embedded commentary on the theatres in the years before the Civil War. Gayton describes a man who imagines himself an Emperor as 'instantly Metamorphoz'd into the stateliest, gravest and commanding soule, that ever eye beheld. *Taylor* acting *Arbaces*, or *Swanston D'Amboys*, were shadowes to him; his pace, his look, his voice, and all his garb was alter'd' (1654: E1r). Later in the seventeenth century Swanston was to be described in another evocation of the pre-Civil War stage as 'a brave roaring Fellow' (Shadwell 1676: 14).

Swanston's performance as Bussy is the subject of a prologue printed with the play in 1641, which probably dates to a 1630s revival. It lists three actors who have played the fiery central role:

> Field is gone,
> Whose action first did give it name, and one
> Who came the nearest to him, is denied
> By his grey beard to show the height and pride
> Of D'Ambois' youth and bravery; yet to hold
> Our title still a-foot, and not grow cold
> By giving it o'er, a third man with his best
> Of care and pains defends our interest;
> As Richard he was liked, nor do we fear
> In personating D'Ambois he'll appear
> To faint, or go less, so your free consent,
> As heretofore, give him encouragement.
> (Chapman 1965: Prologue, 17–19)

The prologue offers a commentary on the movement of roles between actors as they died, aged or became infirm. Field, who originated the role of Bussy when the play was performed by the Children of the Queen's Revels around 1604 (see Munro 2005: 170), probably brought the play to the King's Men. It has been plausibly suggested that the second man is Taylor, picking up the role after Field's death (Chapman 1910: 547), and the third is Swanston. In its statement that the third actor was 'liked' as 'Richard', the prologue also suggests that Swanston played the title role in Shakespeare's *Richard III*, which was performed at court on 17 November 1633, a few months before *Bussy* was performed there on 7 April 1634 (Bawcutt 1996: 184, 188). If Taylor originally inherited Burbage's role of Richard III, as seems likely, by the early 1630s it had been taken up by a younger man.

This process did not stop with Swanston. In the cast-list for *Philaster* (Figure 4), it looks to me as if one hand has written in the name 'Benfield' as the King and has started to write the name 'Eyliard [Swanston]' against Philaster, leaving only 'Ey', but another hand has deleted 'Ey' and written 'Clarke', before going on to add other names against other roles. 'Clarke' is Hugh Clarke, who began his career playing female and juvenile roles with Queen Henrietta Maria's Men at the Cockpit in the mid-1620s before graduating to adult male roles. He joined the company around 1636, when he was probably in his mid-twenties.[13] A prologue written for a later revival of *Philaster* pays tribute to Taylor and Clarke in terms that suggest that both played the title role:

> Could we as well revive those Actors too,
> who in those days, to th' life, those parts did doe,
> faire spoken Taylor, fame'd Roscius of his time,
> or handsome Clarke, when he was in his prime;
> who with their well tune'd Accents charm'd the Eare
> of Each Spectator, in the Theatre;
> we then might hope that something might appeare,
> worthy your coming, or your staying here[14]

It is possible, therefore, that Swanston replaced Taylor as Philaster at some point in the mid-1630s before being succeeded in turn by Clarke in the late 1630s, or that the first annotator of the cast-list was mistaken in thinking that Swanston played Philaster.

As the prologue to *Philaster* and Gayton's remarks suggest, a good deal of commentary survives on the performances of individual 'star' actors and what the 1603 letters patent term 'the Arte and faculty of playinge'.[15] 'Faculty' had a variety of meanings in the early seventeenth century, encompassing qualities such as: ability and aptitude; physical and mental capability and power; will, reason and memory; branches or departments of knowledge; art, trade and occupation; and the liberty or licence to do something (*OED*, faculty, *n.*). These shades of meaning inform early seventeenth-century commentaries. Thomas Gainsford, for instance, presents a summary of the skills required for good acting:

Player hath many times, many excellent qualities: as dancing, actiuitie, musicke, song, elloqution, abilitie of body, memory, vigilancy, skill of weapon, pregnancy of wit, and such like: […] Player must take heede of wrested and enforced action: for if there be not a facility in his deliuerance, and as it were a naturall dexteritie, it must needes sound harsh to the auditour, and procure his distast and displeasure.

(1616: Q1v)

Gainsford intriguingly blends together the physical and cognitive abilities that good acting requires, and he emphasizes both the player's innate talents – such as memory and wit – and the need for him to train and hone his skills. As Evelyn Tribble notes, the skilled performance described here also depends on the actor's interaction with a range of technologies, conventions and practices: 'the playhouse itself, governed by shared conventions of movement across the stage; cognitive artefacts such as the part and the plot; the strong social bonds fostered by the system of sharers […] and the regimes of training and education that undergirded their practice' (2017: 4). While Gainsford stresses, like many other commentators, a need for the actor's performance to appear unforced if it is to please spectators, the phrase 'as it were a naturall dexteritie' also suggests the artifice, skill and training that lay behind 'natural' performance.

Assessments of an actor's ability to appear 'natural' in their roles are not, therefore, especially helpful in themselves because they appear in so many different periods and contexts. It is practically a cliché, repeated across different eras and cultures, that good acting is 'natural', that the best actors of the present moment are 'natural' and that the acting of the past – even the very recent past – was artificial or 'unnatural'. Indeed, it is almost inevitable that different theatrical cultures will perceive naturalness in different styles and techniques – acting styles change over time, shaped by developments in performance spaces and modes, the requirements of individual plays and broader social shifts in attitudes towards voice, gesture and deportment. As Paul Menzer observes, '[t]o talk about acting in terms of "artificial" versus "natural" is to pursue an infinite regression' (2006: 84). Instead, we can look to the specifics of early modern commentaries on what Gayton terms the actor's 'pace', 'look' and 'voice'.

Gainsford sets out the physical and cognitive assets required by any actor, but other early modern writers describe specific types of performer, or even individuals. One of the most detailed accounts of a leading man is 'An Excellent Actor' (1615), which appears to have been written by John Webster (2007: 441–3, 454–6). It draws heavily on other modes of expression in order to convey the actor's impact in performance:

> Whatsoever is commendable in the grave Orator, is most exquisitly perfect in him; for by a full and significant action of body, he charmes our attention: sit in a full Theater, and you will thinke you see so many lines drawne from the circumference of so many eares, whiles the *Actor* is the *Center*. [...] By his action he fortifies morall precepts with example; for what we see him personate, we thinke truely done before us [...] Hee is much affected to painting, and tis a question whether that make him an excellent Plaier, or his playing an exquisite painter. Hee addes grace to the Poets labours: for what in the Poet is but ditty, in him is both ditty and musicke.
>
> (Webster 2007: 483)

The references to painting suggest that 'An Excellent Actor' describes Richard Burbage, who appears to have been skilled at painting as well as acting; in 1613 he collaborated with Shakespeare in devising an impresa used by the Earl of Rutland in the birthday tilting at court (Chambers 1923: 2.309, 4.257). A pun on the word 'painting' itself, which also referred to the cosmetics used by the actor onstage, also captures something of the actor's attention to detail and his broad interest in representation.

Less specific to Burbage is the comparison between actors and orators, who needed similar skills of voice and gesture.

This comparison is often used to the detriment of the actor, as in Abraham Fraunce's claim that the orator's gestures 'must followe the change and varietie of the voyce [...] yet not parasiticallie as stage plaiers vse, but grauelie and decentlie as becommeth men of greater calling' (1588: O7v). However, in 'An Excellent Actor' the actor's 'full and significant action of body' is said to outdo the orator's techniques in its power and persuasiveness. It is telling that the image Webster uses to reinforce this claim is that of the full outdoor playhouse and its 'circumference of so many eares' with the actor at its centre. We are often encouraged to believe that the outdoor playhouses went into decline after the King's Men took over the Blackfriars playhouse in 1608, and that the swift reconstruction of the Globe after the 1613 fire was a nostalgic or sentimental gesture (Gurr 1996: 117–18). However, the fact that the image of the actor capturing and holding the attention of a packed outdoor playhouse could be used in 1615 to epitomize the charismatic presence of the leading man that is evoked by Gayton and the author of the *Philaster* prologue suggests the lasting appeal of these large-scale spaces to both spectators and performers.

More precise details of Burbage's performance are offered in the Fletcher elegy, which describes the actor's 'action of body', his vocal technique and the interplay between body and voice:

> oft haue I seene him leape into a graue
> suitinge the person wch he seemd to haue
> of a sad lover, wth soe true an eye
> that there (I would haue sworne) he ment to die.
> [...]
> how did his speech becom him? & his pace
> suite wth his speech? & euery acc*i*on grace
> them both alike? Whilst nare a word did fall
> without iust weight to ballast it wth all.[16]

Fletcher offers glimpses of Burbage at work: the exuberance of his swift leap into the playhouse's trap during the altercation with Laertes in Act 5 of *Hamlet*; the pathos of death scenes that threatened to convince not only spectators but his fellow actors; and the precision of his movement, gesture and vocal delivery.

Fletcher, like Webster, would have been familiar with Burbage's acting through his work for the King's Men, and comments also survive by men who could have seen Burbage act in their youth. Richard Flecknoe, who was born in 1600, writes that there was

> as much difference betwixt him and one of our common Actors, as between a Ballad singer who onely mouths it, and an excellent singer, who knows all his Graces, and can artfully vary and modulate his Voice, even to know how much breath he is to give to every syllable. He had all the parts of an excellent Orator, (animating his words with speaking, and Speech with Action) his Auditors being never more delighted then when he spake, nor more sorry then when he held his peace; yet even thên, he was an excellent Actor still, never falling in his Part when he had done speaking; but with his looks and gesture, maintaining it still unto the heighth, he imagining *Age quod agis* ['do what you are doing'], onely spoke to him[.]
>
> (1664: G5v–6r)

Like Webster, Flecknoe draws comparisons between acting, oratory and music, and he does so in ways that draw attention to both the crucial process of interpretation that the actor brings to his role, and the strong technique that supports this process. His description is intriguing because he is able to talk in some depth about the performance tactics that made Burbage appear natural onstage: controlling his vocal delivery, working gesture and speech in tandem and maintaining his performance when he was not speaking.

Webster emphasizes the restraint shown by his 'Excellent Actor' in performance, writing that he 'doth not strive to make nature monstrous, she is often seen in the same Scæne with him, but neither on Stilts nor Crutches; and for his voice tis not lower then the prompter, nor lowder then the Foile and Target' (2007: 483). In contrast, some younger playgoers remembered Burbage as a more overtly histrionic performer. Thomas Bancroft, born around 1596, invokes Burbage's ability to move between different emotional states when portraying the heightened passion of the lover or revenger:

> Such, like our *Burbage* are, who when his part
> He acted, sent each passion to his heart;
> Would languish in a scene of love; then look
> Pallid for fear; but when revenge he took,
> Recall his bloud; when enemies were nigh,
> Grow big with wrath, and make his buttons fly.
>
> (1658: D6v)

In contrast with the measured emotional restraint, or 'signifying inhibition', that Menzer identifies in early seventeenth-century commentaries on acting (2006: 104), Bancroft describes a performance in which emotion is thrillingly legible. In doing so, he brings to the fore some of the problems in assuming that an earlier period's 'natural' acting is like our own – the Burbage described here displays a full-blooded, enjoyably excessive charisma that Gayton, quoted above, associates with Taylor and Swanston.

A similar impression is given in the comments of a near contemporary of Flecknoe and Bancroft, the courtier and playwright William Cavendish, Duke of Newcastle, born in 1592. Cavendish's 1635 play *Wit's Triumvirate* includes a character called Phantsy who constantly lapses into lovelorn, quasi-philosophical verse, a tendency that the physician, Clyster, tries to correct. In Act 4, Phantsy takes to verse, only to be interrupted by Clyster:

> Take nothing from no place and add it here,
> Or take something that's here, put it nowhere?
> Impossible! In understanding's spite,

Enter CLYSTER.

All must confess our love's world's infinite.

CLYSTER
How now, at verse again?
PHANTSY
No, faith, sir, I was at my prayers.
CLYSTER
What, so loud, and acting, as if Burbage's soul had newly revived Hamlet and Jeronimo again, or Alleyn, Tamburlaine?
PHANTSY
Nay, sir, rather Field in *Love Lies a Bleeding*.
(Cavendish 1975: 4.4.586–600)

Scholars are accustomed to setting the performance styles of Edward Alleyn and Burbage against each other – for instance, when Hamlet's comments on acting, or the player's speech in the same play, are interpreted as satire against Alleyn's supposedly outmoded style.[17] However, for Cavendish, who is likely to have been familiar with Burbage and Field's performances of the late 1610s, when he was in his twenties, the opposition is between the older generation of Burbage and Alleyn, and his own contemporary, Field.

Gathered together, these commentaries on the performances of the leading actors in the King's Men suggest both that there were normative ideas about what constituted 'good' acting and that the performances of individual actors might at times challenge or transgress those norms. Most importantly for my purposes in this book, they argue that spectators were aware of the different impressions that actors might make in the same role, and the connections that might be drawn between roles. In his elegy on Burbage, Fletcher fantasizes that his roles 'are now for euer dead'. Yet theatrical commodities such as *Hamlet*, *The Spanish Tragedy*, *King Lear* and *Othello* would not be allowed to disappear; instead, actors such as

Taylor, Swanston and Clarke would take Burbage's place at the centre of what Webster calls 'the circumference of so many eares'.

Comedians

In addition to his commentary on Burbage, Flecknoe offers some insights into comic performance in his character of '*one who imitates the good companion*', written in 1654: 'HE is one, who now the Stage is down, acts the Parasites part at Table, and since *Taylors* death none can play *Mosca* so well as he. [...] His mimick Gesture, together with his Buffoon faces, is all his mirth, excepting an old story or two, which you grow weary of presently, and then he must change his bank, or change his style' (1665: E2v–E3r). The man described here is a hollow parody of a comic actor, deploying his techniques of gesture and facial expression in ways that are not amusing but merely grotesque. A more detailed picture of comic technique is offered by an anti-theatrical commentator, William Prynne, writing in the early 1630s. Although he analyses theatrical performance in order to excoriate it, Prynne's description of the succession of '*ridiculous antique, mimicall, foolish gestures, complements, embracements, smiles, nods, motions of the eyes, head, feete, hands, & whole intire body which Players vse, of purpose to provoke their Spectators to profuse inordinate laughter*' (1633: 877) summarizes neatly the range of gestures and movements that a comic actor might deploy, conventions that had become part of the traditions of comic performance.

Flecknoe's comment underscores the fact that the leading actors of the King's Men were required to excel in both tragic and comic performance. As noted above, Burbage's known roles include Jonson's Volpone and Subtle, while Taylor played Face in *The Alchemist*, Mosca in *Volpone*, Truewit in *Epicoene* and Mirabel in *The Wild Goose Chase*. Similar versatility was required of supporting players. For example, the longstanding hired man Curtis Greville plays a range of roles demanding comic, tragic and tragicomic modes of performance: his largest known role is the sweaty, unctuous goldsmith Mountain in *The Soddered Citizen*; his role as the actor Latinus in *The Roman Actor* demands him to perform parts within the inset plays – notably that of the miser in 'The Cure of Avarice'; and his roles as the Third Merchant in *Believe as You List* and the courtier Iseas in *The Swisser* also demand comic timing and the ability to deliver lines with an ironic edge.

The company also included comic specialists, however, such as Robert Armin, John Shank, Thomas Pollard, William Rowley and William Robins. One important tradition of comic performance was established within the repertory by William Kemp, who left the Chamberlain's Men in 1599. Kemp is thought to have played Lancelot Gobbo in *The Merchant of Venice*, Costard in *Love's Labour's Lost*, Peter in *Romeo and Juliet*, Bottom in *A Midsummer Night's Dream* and Dogberry in *Much Ado About Nothing* (see Wiles 1987: 73–103). His characters manipulate and deform language through puns, wordplay and malapropism; much of their comedy derives from moments at which plain-speaking men of lower social status are brought into contact with the practices and pretensions of the elite. Through them, Kemp created a template for comic performance that lingered within the repertory of the King's Men for over thirty years.

In contrast, some of the roles created for his immediate successor, Armin, have a different flavour (Wiles 1987: 144–58). There are professional court fools – such as Touchstone in *As You Like It*, Feste in *Twelfth Night* and the Fool in *King Lear* – who voice a satiric perspective that is more wry and knowing than that of Kemp's characters. Some of Armin's lower-status characters, such as Abel Drugger in *The Alchemist*, also present a pathos that is rarely invoked by Kemp. Yet the popularity of plays such as *A Midsummer Night's Dream*, *Love's Labour's Lost*, *The Merchant of Venice*, *Romeo and Juliet* and *Much Ado About Nothing* in the early seventeenth century means that Armin would have had to take over at least some of Kemp's old roles, and Kemp-style clown roles recur in the figures of the Gravedigger in *Hamlet*, Pompey Bum in *Measure for Measure*, Frog in *The Fair Maid of Bristow* and the clowns of *Othello* and *Antony and Cleopatra*. Richard Preiss aptly notes 'a corporate investment in sustaining convention' and argues that Armin's combination of roles 'suggests an attempt to suspend two performance codes under one performer' (2014: 184). Armin not only plays Armin, but Armin-playing-Kemp. When Armin was in turn replaced in the mid-1610s by John Shank, a veteran comic actor whose anarchic style probably recalled that of Kemp, the ghosting of comic roles in the performances of the King's Men would have become yet more complex.

Shank's roles are usually small and revolve around set-piece scenes, meaning that he rarely appears in the lists of the principal actors in Fletcher's plays of the 1610s and early 1620s, and he appears in only four of the seven actor-lists that survive for plays performed by the King's Men between 1626 and 1632.[18] He is required to deploy traditional clowning techniques such as slapstick, the use of non-metropolitan dialects or distinctive forms of language such as punning, malapropism or archaism; moreover, his appearances are often self-contained set-pieces that have little impact on the main narratives or concerns of the plays in which they appear. In Clavell's *The Soddered Citizen*, Shank's character, Hodge, has just one scene, in which he delivers a message and is physically abused and humiliated by his master, Brainsick, played by another comic specialist, Thomas Pollard. In *The Picture*, Shank's serving-man, Hilario, is more integrated into the plot but he is most prominent in a theatrically allusive set-piece that could easily be extracted as a separate skit. In an attempt to amuse Sophia (John Honeyman) in the absence of her husband Mathias (Joseph Taylor), who is away fighting for the King of Hungary, Hilario appears '*with a long white hayre and beard, in an anticke armour*', his entrance heralded by the harsh tones of a sow-gelder's horn (2.1.85SD). He pretends to bring news of Mathias, which he delivers in mock-Spenserian doggerel – 'Blow lustily my

Lad', he tells the boy who accompanies him, 'and drawing nigh a / Aske for a Lady which is clep'd *Sophia*' (2.1.91–2). In its stand-alone quality, its theatrical self-awareness, its use of gesture and its presentation of the comic character's capacity to transgress linguistic norms, the scene presents a classic clown routine. Appropriately enough, the performance is a disaster. Sophia penetrates his disguise and banishes him from her house and – more importantly – her table for making light of Mathais's absence.

Shank was not the only comic specialist to appear with the company after Armin's death. A series of King's Men plays of the early and mid-1620s feature roles apparently written for the actor-dramatist William Rowley: Bustofa in Fletcher's *The Maid in the Mill* (1623), the Fat Bishop in Middleton's *A Game at Chess* (1624), Cacafogo in Fletcher's *Rule a Wife and Have a Wife* (1624), Tony in Fletcher's *A Wife for a Month* (1624) and Belgarde in Massinger's *The Unnatural Combat* (1624–5). All of these roles exploit the actor's physical bulk and his 'persona based on guileless plain-speaking', as David Nicol calls it (2012: 72), but his roles are often more complex and have greater narrative function than those of Shank.

Yet more complex are the roles of Thomas Pollard. Although he appears to have specialized in comic roles, they are characterized not by slapstick, the use of dialect or malapropism, in the manner of Kemp or Shank, but by rapid shifts from one emotional state to another and the representation of decayed or debauched glamour. They are also substantial and demanding roles. The drunken gentleman Brainsick in *The Soddered Citizen* is the second-largest role in that play; the profane Falstaffian priest Berecinthius in *Believe as You List* is the third largest. Other roles, such as the gallant Pinac in *The Wild Goose Chase*, the volatile Lieutenant in Fletcher's *The Humorous Lieutenant*, the conceited Spanish prince Pharamond – played by Pollard in the late 1630s revival of *Philaster* and, probably, at an earlier date, too – and the courtier Ubaldo in *The Picture* are only the fifth or sixth largest overall, but rank third or fourth in terms of the adult male roles that were available to him.[19]

The contrast between the typical roles of Shank and Pollard can be seen if we return to *The Picture*. Ubaldo is part of a debased and diseased double act with another courtier, Elliard Swanston's Ricardo. On the orders of the jealous queen Honoria (John Thompson) Ubaldo and Ricardo attempt to corrupt Sophia by convincing her that Mathias has betrayed her at court. Having drawn lots for the privilege of assailing her first, they work on her in tandem – Ricardo tells Ubaldo, 'I'll not part with / My share in the atchieuement; when I whistle, / Or hemme fall off' (3.6.5–7). The extended series of substitutions, as each man whistles or clears his throat to signal that it is his turn, depends upon the comic timing and collaboration of Pollard and Swanston, and the ability of each actor to manipulate tone. Pollard may have been remembered as a 'comedian' – as Wright terms him – but his skill-set was almost as varied as that of the company's other leading players. Comic roles in the plays of the King's Men thus present a range of performance possibilities and personae, encompassing the physical comedy, linguistic deformation and plain-speaking of the traditional clown role, the wry resignation of Armin's fools or the broader range of techniques that informed the performances of Pollard, Burbage, Taylor or Lowin.

Apprentices

The most unstable and shifting component of the company was the group of actors who played female and juvenile male roles.[20] Boy actors were apprenticed to sharers, often but not always to a sharer who was also a member of a livery company of the City of London, such as the Grocer John Heminges, the Goldsmith John Lowin or the Weaver John Shank. The ages at which they were apprenticed appears to have been roughly in line with that of apprentices in London generally – the average

age was around fourteen, but some boys were younger and some older. Of the King's Men's apprentices, William Trigg later claimed that that he had been only thirteen when he was apprenticed, Richard Sharpe and Robert Pallant Junior were both fourteen (Kathman 2005: 233–4, 226–7) and Thomas Holcombe was probably sixteen or seventeen.[21] The shortest term to which an apprentice in the King's Men was bound in surviving records was seven years, in line with the minimum term specified in a statute issued in 1562; the longest was ten years (see Kathman 2004a; 2005). The 1562 statute stated that apprentices should not be freed before they were twenty-four; however, in practice, as David Kathman notes, it was 'not uncommon' for apprentices in London to be freed a couple of years earlier (2004a: 4). Apprenticeship in the King's Men again reflects this broader practice. For example, Sharpe was due to finish his apprenticeship in February 1624, at the age of twenty-two; he had been freed and was a sharer in the company by 20 December that year (Bentley 1941–68: 1.14–15). John Honeyman was sworn in as a Groom of the Chamber, a sign that he had graduated from his apprenticeship, on 15 April 1633, when he was twenty years old (Nicoll and Boswell 1931: 360).

Some boys appear to have played female roles until late in their apprenticeships, depending, it seems, on their physiques and physical development. The final phase of an apprenticeship may also have seen the boy player move closer to adult status. I have found a scrivener's record of a bond drawn up between Christopher Beeston of Queen Anna's Men and one of his apprentices, James Jones, on 2 March 1616, which specifies that Jones is 'putt Apprentice' to Beeston for 'six yeares [...] the master Covenanting to fynd his & allowe his Apprentice for the last yeare of the tearme two shillings euery week & meat drinck lodging & apparel all the tyme & all the said last yeare'.[22] Beeston himself probably began his career as an apprentice with the Chamberlain's Men, and it is likely that the bond also reflects the practice of the King's Men. The reference to the boy's salary of two shillings per week during the last year suggests that the advanced apprentice was moving towards the role of a hired man with the company, and that he was not simply viewed as disposable once he stopped playing female and juvenile roles. In fact, of the boys with the King's Men whose names and careers can be traced – which may be a fraction of the total – at least seventeen progressed to adult careers as actors, and some went on to considerable prominence.[23]

Although most of the boy actors are frustratingly undocumented, the evidence that survives allows us to reconstruct aspects of the careers of some individual boys and to get a sense of their varied skills. For example, the 1623 edition of *The Duchess of Malfi* (Figure 3) names only the boy actors who appeared in the early 1620s revival of the play, but we also know something about their counterparts in 1613, when it was first performed. George Birche was bound to Heminges as an apprentice on July 1610, and he is almost certainly the 'Richard Birche' who played Lady Politic Would-Be in *Volpone* and Doll Common in *The Alchemist* in the revivals of these plays around 1616–18 (Kathman 2004a: 8–9, 21; 2005: 232–3; Riddell 1969: 295). Another boy, Richard Robinson, was probably apprenticed to Richard Burbage – whose widow, Winifred, he later married – a couple of years before Birche's arrival. In 1611 he played the Lady in Middleton's *The Second Maiden's Tragedy*. This is a relatively small role – the Lady has 158 lines, of which twenty-two are spoken by her ghost (King 1992: 106). However, it is demanding in terms of the requirements that it makes on the boy player in terms of the management of cosmetic effects and costume changes (see Stevens 2013: 132) and his ability to manipulate the emotions of spectators.

This emotive power is required especially in the scene in which the Lady, threatened with sexual violence from the Tyrant, kills herself in a locked chamber while characters offstage insistently knock upon the door. Juliet-like, she addresses the knife, telling it, 'thow art my servaunt now [...] art now preferd / vnto the service of a resolute ladie / one that knowes how to imploye thee, and scornes death / as much as some men feare it' (Middleton 1909: ll. 1350–4). This is a striking moment of independence for Robinson. As Scott

McMillin (2004) and Evelyn Tribble (2009) have explored, boy actors often appear to have been supported in performance by scripted interactions between their characters and those of experienced colleagues. This scene almost parodies these training structures: the leading actor who played Govianus is onstage, but he cannot support Robinson's performance because Govianus has fainted in the face of the pressure that the Lady puts on him to kill her.

Judging by their other roles, therefore, each of these talented boy players would have brought different qualities to a character such as the Duchess of Malfi or Julia, the Cardinal's Mistress – pathos and resolution, perhaps, from Robinson, or a muscular energy from Birche. Robinson and Birche are also among the boys that Shakespeare and Fletcher would have had available to them when they were writing plays such as *Henry VIII* and *The Two Noble Kinsmen*, and it is tempting to speculate on the contrasting skill-sets that they might have brought to characters such as Queen Katherine and Anne Bullen, and Emilia and the Jailor's Daughter. I will return to this generation of boy players in Chapter 2, when I consider in detail the casting of roles in *Othello* and *The Alchemist*.

Intriguingly, the actors who played the Duchess and Julia in the revival of 1620–3, Richard Sharpe and John Thompson, may also have presented two contrasting versions of femininity. The roles that Sharpe took on during his brief period of prominence as an adult player in the late 1620s and early 1630s suggest that he was unusually charismatic and versatile. One role in particular, the virtuous but psychologically vulnerable gentleman Witworth in *The Soddered Citizen*, demonstrates the qualities that may have made him successful as the Duchess. Witworth and his lover, Modestina (William Trigg), are persecuted by her unscrupulous father, Undermine (John Lowin). In one of the scenes between the lovers Sharpe is required to present Witworth's mental disintegration over the course of around 140 lines as he responds to a doctored letter that gives him the impression that Modestina has 'never' – rather than 'ever' – loved him, and refuses to believe that these are not her words. He finally declares 'Ile waste, pyne, dye, / And reape sweete sollace, in the *Agonie*' (Clavell 1936: ll. 1435–6). Although Witworth succumbs where the Duchess resists, an actor for whom the role of Witworth was designed would ably present her various responses to psychological torment.

Thompson was a different kind of performer. He had an unusually long run of female roles, from an unnamed part in Fletcher's *The Pilgrim* in 1622 to Panopia in Wilson's *The Swisser* in 1631, and his roles are remarkably similar. He plays queens, princesses, noblewomen and city daughters, in comedies, tragedies and tragicomedies, in roles that are often extensive and occasionally – in *The Swisser* – very small, but all of these women share a set of characteristics: they are charismatic and imperious, many of them are physically vigorous and they are often required to sing. In a performance of *The Duchess of Malfi* in the early 1620s, therefore, an authoritative and imposing performance by Thompson as Julia could have made for an appealing contrast with a more subtly shaded performance by Sharpe as the Duchess.

The casting of female roles in *The Picture* also points to the different strengths that the boy actors may have brought to their roles. Thompson's role in *The Picture*, the tempestuous queen Honoria, who attempts to seduce Mathias (Joseph Taylor) and disgrace Sophia (John Honeyman), is typical of his imperious mode. In contrast, the other boys of the cast, Honeyman, William Trigg and Alexander Gough, are required to display more versatility in their recorded roles. Gough, for instance, plays the scheming maidservant Acanthe in *The Picture*, the bumptious page Fewtricks in *The Soddered Citizen*, the poignant victim of sexual violence, Eurinia, in *The Swisser* and the witty Lillia-Bianca in the revival of *The Wild Goose Chase*.

By the late 1630s, the roster of boys available to the King's Men had shifted once more, and the available evidence again suggests the extent to which their performance styles and specialisms may have varied. Roles are attributed to four boy actors in the manuscript casting notes for *Philaster* (Figure 4): Bellario – apparently a youth but revealed in the play's final stages to be a young woman, Euphrasia – was played by 'Charles', the princess Arethusa was played by 'Wat', Gallathea was played by 'White' and Megra by 'Thomas'. 'White' has not yet been traced. 'Thomas' is probably the actor who played a Lady who is given the speech prefix '*Thom*' in the 1655 printed edition of Carlell's *The Passionate Lovers*, performed by the King's Men around 1638 (Carlell 1655: D8r, F3v).[24] He might be tentatively identified with Thomas Bedford, who was a member of a group of actors performing on the Continent in 1644–6 that included some former King's Men and described himself in a lawsuit of 1665 as 'aged 44 yeares or thereabouts'.[25] This would mean that he was born around 1621 and would have been nearing the middle of his apprenticeship in 1638 if he had been bound at the age of fourteen.

More securely identified are 'Charles' and 'Wat', the famous Restoration performers Charles Hart and Walter Clun. Wright claims that '*Hart* and *Clun,* were bred up Boys at the *Blackfriers;* and Acted Womens Parts', adding that '*Hart* was *Robinson*'s Boy or Apprentice: He Acted the Dutchess in the Tragedy of *the Cardinal,* which was the first Part that gave him Reputation' (1699: 3). 'Robinson' may be Richard Robinson or the comic actor William Robins, also known as Robinson; we do not as yet have other information about either as a trainer of boy actors. Kathman has discovered that Hart was baptized on 11 December 1625 as the son of William Hart, a minor actor who was a hired man with the King's Men around 1636–7 (2005: 241). Thus, if Hart's apprenticeship followed the pattern of others, he may have been apprenticed in 1638–9, when he was thirteen or fourteen, and have been nearing the peak of his career in female roles when he appeared in James Shirley's tragedy *The Cardinal*, which was licensed on 25 November 1641 (Bawcutt 1996: 210).

Although Wright offers less information about Walter Clun, I have found further evidence of his links with the King's

Men in the shape of a baptism record at St Giles, Cripplegate, dated 13 December 1639: 'John sonne of the reputed father Walter Clun Player, base borne of y^e: body of Elizabeth Thornes singlewoman. borne at y^e: doore of Mrs Shancks als ffffitts in Whitecrostreete Widdow'.[26] This record suggests that Clun – for whom no baptism record has yet been traced – was of an age to father a child, or to be thought to have fathered a child, in late 1639. It also provides a clue about the nature and date of his apprenticeship, as 'Mrs Shancks als ffffitts' is Winifred Shank Fitch, widow of John Shank. Shank was buried at St Giles, Cripplegate, on 27 January 1636, so it is likely that Clun was apprenticed to him in the early to mid-1630s.

The later careers of Hart and Clun suggest that even as boy players they may have had contrasting presences and specialisms onstage (see Highfill, Burnim and Langhans 1973–93: 7.147–53; 3.366–7). Hart played leading roles in comedies and tragedies, including Horner in Wycherley's *The Country Wife* (1675) and Mark Anthony in Dryden's *All for Love* (1677); John Downes comments on his 'Grandeur and Agreeable Majesty' (1708: 16) as Alexander in Nathaniel Lee's *The Rival Queens* (*c.* 1677), suggesting a vivid stage presence that may have been equally effective in *The Cardinal* thirty years earlier. Clun, in contrast, became a specialist in comic roles, playing Falstaff, Subtle in *The Alchemist* and Smug the Smith in *The Merry Devil of Edmonton* in the short period between the restoration of the commercial stage in 1660 and his untimely death in 1664. He may have brought a distinctive physical energy to his roles as early as the 1630s, but his casting as Arethusa in *Philaster* is a reminder that the leading boy players of the King's Men were generally required to move between different kinds of roles and styles of performance. While some boys may have had a marked specialism, the majority were required to develop a more varied set of techniques that may have served them better as they transitioned to adult male roles.

As the preceding discussion suggests, we can learn something of the performance styles of individual boy actors by comparing their recorded roles. Some more general commentary also survives about the impact of these performers on spectators. In her romance *Urania*, Lady Mary Wroth describes a male observer who is unmoved by the sight of his former lover wooing another man in these terms: 'there hee saw her with all passionate ardency, seeke, and sue for the strangers loue, yet he vnmoueable, was no further wrought, then if he had seene a delicate play-boy acte a louing womans part, and knowing him a Boy, lik'd onely his action' (1621: I2v). Wroth takes us behind questions of whether a performance is 'natural' – she does not argue that the performance of the 'play-boy' is unconvincing in itself, but instead suggests that a spectator's knowledge that what they see is not a woman but a boy empties it of affect, leaving them merely to admire the actor's technique.

Other commentators appear to fear, in contrast, that the boy actor's performances might be not merely pleasing but actively alluring. In a tract titled *Christ's Combat and Conquest*, Thomas Taylor writes of the playhouse:

There you shall see men wearing womens apparell, and perhaps women mens: There you shall see men trauelling of child, as one said of *Nero* beeing an actor in a Tragedie, to which his part called him; and all kind of adulterous behauiours, and such shameful gestures and actions, as the light of nature hath descried and condemned. What shall I speake of that lewd and wicked dauncing of young men, in the habit and gestures of women, like *Herodias:* which what an incentiue of lust it is, may easily be conceiued in *Herods* example: and the poyson of amatorie kissing of beautifull boyes, is vnto lust as fire to flaxe, or oyle to fire. And least you should thinke I did wrong the*m* in calling these places the deuils schooles, *Cyprian* doth no lesse, accounting the Stage-player (teaching boyes to bee effeminate, by instructing them how to play the women, and to expresse wanton gestures) to bee the deuills Vsher.

(1618: M5v)

Like many anti-theatrical writers, Taylor appears both to worry that the theatre blurs the boundary between man and woman, and that there might be something alluring or erotic about such blurring. Like them, he also frames his discussion of Jacobean theatre through allusions to the dramatic traditions of ancient Rome, collapsing temporal and cultural differences in his strident critique of the visual spectacle presented by an apparently pregnant youth or the actions of dancing or kissing. His close paraphrase of Saint Cyprian's strictures, which appear in a letter in which Cyprian advises his friend Eucratius to excommunicate a retired actor who is training boys to act (see Cyprian 1984: 1.53), also suggests that Taylor is aware of the practice and procedures of theatrical apprenticeship.

A yet more jaundiced perspective is offered in Francis Rous's moralizing tract, *The Diseases of the Time*, which describes the 'Representation of Women by Men' onstage as 'a most dangerous and pestilent Spectacle' (1622: O10v). Unlike Thomas Taylor and many other anti-theatrical writers, he does not quote classical authorities, saying,

> I need not goe to the old Law for proofe, but only appeale to new and lamentable experience, and desire the confession of them that know the times, whether the shape of a woman hath not made masculine loues, and whether the maide hath not procured loue to the boy. I am loth to speak of that wherof the very speech is lothsome, but it may not bee that sinnes should haue priuiledge to prosper, because they are lothsome to be mentioned, but euen because they are lothsome they should the more terribly be reprooued. But I will goe a middle-way betweene saying all and nothing, and wish that there were not so much merchandize of Play-boyes, nor so much counterfeiting intisement to that trafficke.
>
> (O10v)

Rous's critique is intriguing in part because he half-acknowledges the tangle that he gets into when he tries to both speak and not speak of transgressive desire; he articulates a pervasive anxiety that the 'spectacle' of transvestite performance might have power over both male and female spectators because it presents them with alternative objects of attraction. What is more unusual, however, is the way in which he tackles the commodification of such desire within the playhouse, identifying the commercial dynamic at the heart of the commercial stage in his attack on the 'merchandize of Play-boyes' – in which it is not entirely clear if 'merchandize' is acting as a verb or noun – and his use of the word 'traffic' to describe the acquisition, training and commercial exploitation of boy actors.

This 'merchandize' is the subject of commentary from the King's Men themselves. In 1635, in the midst of a dispute over shares in the Globe and Blackfriars playhouses, John Shank claimed that he had

> his owne purse supplyed the company for the service of his Majesty with boyes as Thomas Pollard, Iohn Thompson deceased (for whome Hee payd 40^{li}) your suppliant hauing payd his part of 200^{li} for other boyes since his comming to ye Company, Iohn Honiman, Thomas Holcome and diuerse others & at this time maintaines 3 more for the sayd service.[27]

Holcombe was in fact apprenticed to Heminges on 22 April 1618 for eight years; as Kathman suggests, Shank's statement about his acquisition suggests that the sharers 'split the expense of obtaining talented boys, no matter to whom these boys were bound' (2004a: 10). The large sums that Shank mentions are rendered plausible by the fact that the apprenticeship of another boy who performed with the King's Men in the 1630s, Stephen Hammerton, was valued at approximately £30 (Kathman 2004a: 14). The practices of theatre industry do not seem to have been out of kilter with the more general financial exploitation of adolescent boys with the apprenticeship system. However, the fact that these boys were required to perform for paying audiences adds an additional dimension to the ways in which they were commodified. Furthermore, as I will explain in Chapter 3, the 'traffic' in actors was not restricted to the company's apprentices but also encompassed leading players.

*

When John Webster wrote that the actor 'addes grace to the Poets labours: for what in the Poet is but ditty, in him is both ditty and musicke' (2007: 483), he identified a crucial aspect of the work of the King's Men: the transformation of text through the addition of movement, gesture and the individual actor's voice. This chapter has sought to flesh out the contexts in which this transformation occurred, from the institutional structures of apprenticeship to the shifting assignment of key roles within the plays. In the rest of the book, I put this material into closer dialogue with the repertory itself, pursuing in different ways the interplay between text and performance in the plays performed by the company to successive generations of spectators.

This chapter has avoided discussing Shakespeare's plays in detail, setting them aside in order to focus on other sources that provide more direct evidence of the practices of the King's Men. In doing so, I have been able to trace a set of connections between actors and roles, and to assess some of the evidence that survives to document practices such as casting and apprenticeship. I have also begun to consider the ways in which the different roles played by a single actor might inform one another, either from the point of view of the spectator whose responses are shaped by the ghosts of an earlier performance, or from the perspective of the theatre historian who can use them to build up a more rounded view of an actor's abilities and training.

In the chapters that follow, which return to Shakespeare's plays, I adopt a more speculative approach, considering not only examples of casting that are attested by external evidence but also the range of effects in performance that might have been created if particular actors were cast in certain roles. The few scattered assignments of Shakespearean roles, noted in the discussion above, are easy to summarize: Burbage was linked by early modern commentators with Richard III, Hamlet, Othello and King Lear; Taylor with Hamlet and Iago; Lowin with Falstaff and Henry VIII; Swanston with Othello and, less securely, Richard III. Beyond this information, which is skewed heavily towards the tragedies and histories, we are dependent on more fragmentary evidence, or on informed speculation. There is evidence – explored below – that Lowin played Iago in the earliest performances of *Othello*, and Burbage played Pericles, but even the assignment of Prospero to Burbage, or that of Touchstone, Feste and the Fool in *King Lear* to Armin is based on conjecture, albeit conjecture that is based on informed assessments of the structures of the King's Men and the capabilities of its performers. With these caveats in mind, I turn to the first 'Interlude', and the court season of 1612–13.

Interlude: Playing the Court, 1612–13

The court season of 1612–13 is the last with which Shakespeare is likely to have been involved in person, and it offers a glimpse both of the final stages of his career and the ways in which the company's repertory was developing. The season was shaped by these multiple patronage contexts and by two events of immense political importance – the death of the heir to the throne, Prince Henry, on 6 November 1612 and the marriage of his sister Elizabeth to the German prince Frederick, Elector Palatine, on 14 February 1613. On 20 May 1613, Shakespeare's old colleague John Heminges was paid for two sets of plays. The first set was performed before Henry, Elizabeth and Frederick:

> fowerteene several playes viz one playe called Pilaster, One other called the Knott: of Fooles, One other Much Adoe abowte nothinge, The Mayeds Tragedy, The merye Dyvell of Edmonton, The Tempest, A Kinge and no Kinge The Twins Tragedie The Winters Tale, Sr Iohn Falstafe, The Moore of Venice, The Nobleman, Caesars Tragedye And one other called Love Lyes a bleeding[1]

The second set, consisting of 'a badd beginininge makes a good ending, One other called ye Capteyne, One other the

Alcumist. One other Cardenno. One other The Hotspurr. And one other called Benidicte and Betteris', was attended by the king himself.

Shakespeare maintained his place at the heart of the repertory of the King's Men, but this position was beginning to be challenged. He appears to be represented by nine performances: *Much Ado About Nothing* (performed twice and recorded the second time as 'Benidicte and Betteris'), *The Tempest*, *The Winter's Tale*, 'Sr Iohn Falstafe' (which may be *1* or *2 Henry IV* or *The Merry Wives of Windsor*), *Othello* (recorded as 'The Moore of Venice', as it had been in 1604–5), *Julius Caesar* ('Caesars Tragedye'), his lost collaboration with John Fletcher, *Cardenio* ('Cardenno'), and *1 Henry IV* ('The Hotspurr'). The next most performed playwright is Fletcher, with *Cardenio* and five performances of plays written with Francis Beaumont: *Philaster* (performed twice and recorded the second time under its subtitle, 'Love Lyes a bleeding'), *The Maid's Tragedy*, *A King and No King* and *The Captain*. Jonson is represented by *The Alchemist*; the list also features a popular play of unknown authorship, *The Merry Devil of Edmonton*, and four plays that are now lost, *The Knot of Fools*, *A Bad Beginning Makes a Good Ending*, *The Twins' Tragedy* and *The Nobleman*. The last two plays had also featured in the court season of 1611–12, and both were entered in the Stationers' Register by Edward Blount on 15 February 1612, where they are attributed to 'Niccolls' and Cyril Tourneur respectively; either they were never printed or no copies have survived.[2]

Like the season of 1604–5, the 1612–13 court season featured established favourites – *Much Ado About Nothing*, *Othello*, *Henry IV*, *The Merry Wives of Windsor* and *The Merry Devil of Edmonton* – alongside more recent works. A significant change since 1604–5 was the acquisition of the indoor Blackfriars playhouse, which was used by the King's Men in tandem with the Globe from late 1609 or early 1610, when a virulent outbreak of plague in London finally subsided. Although Gerald Eades Bentley influentially argued in 1948 that the King's Men immediately created separate Globe and Blackfriars repertories, this view has been challenged and qualified by later scholars (see Gurr and Karim-Cooper 2014). There is, in fact, little evidence of plays being designed for exclusive performance at either playhouse before the mid-1630s, and it is instead better to think in terms of 'combined practices', to use Sarah Dustagheer's valuable term (2017: 6–10).

This is not to say that the company did not exploit the capabilities of their new playhouse. *The Maid's Tragedy*, for example, makes use of the dark, candlelit Blackfriars by staging two pivotal scenes in bedchambers – the bridal night of Evadne and Amintor, with her devastating announcement that she is the King's mistress; and Evadne's murder of the King. Other examples, explored in Chapters 2 and 4 respectively, are *The Alchemist*, set in the Blackfriars precinct itself, and *The Tempest*, which has often been associated with the new opportunities opened up by indoor performance. A more generalized impact on the performance practices of the King's Men around 1612–13 can also be traced. The Blackfriars was known for its music, and the company appear to have been eager to exploit this tradition. It is noticeable that a number of plays of this period – *Cymbeline*, *The Winter's Tale*, *The Tempest*, *Cardenio*, *The Captain* and *The Nobleman* – had music or settings composed for them by the court musician Robert Johnson (Cutts 1955; Theobald 2010: 104–5, 328–34).[3] These settings may originally have been created for court performances and then adopted for commercial performances, or vice versa.

Performance records from this period suggest the importance to the repertory of the tragicomedies written by Shakespeare around 1609–11: *Cymbeline*, *The Winter's Tale* and *The Tempest*. *Cymbeline* and *The Winter's Tale* were both seen by Simon Forman at the Globe in spring 1611, while *The Winter's Tale* and *The Tempest* were performed at court that autumn (see Appendix). They were joined by a set of popular plays by Beaumont and Fletcher that share their generic fluidity: *Philaster* (1609–10), *The Maid's Tragedy* (1610–11) and *A King and No King* (1611). All of these plays feature in the 1612–13 list, alongside *Cardenio*, a new play written by Shakespeare and Fletcher. Although *Cardenio* is lost, it demonstrates some of the literary interests that the younger playwright brought to the collaboration. Its apparent source, Cervantes's *Don Quixote*, was already a favourite with Fletcher, who could probably read Spanish; he and Beaumont drew on *Don Quixote* in two plays written for the Children of the Queen's Revels around 1607–8, *The Coxcomb* and *The Knight of the Burning Pestle*, some years before the publication of Thomas Shelton's translation in 1612.[4]

In Cervantes's story, which the playwrights would have had to untangle from the other plot-threads in *Don Quixote*, Cardenio and Luscinda grow up together, fall in love and are then separated. Cardenio thinks that Luscinda has betrayed him by marrying his friend Fernando; he flees and wanders the Sierra Morena in a maddened state. The other part of the narrative concerns Dorotea, seduced and abandoned by Fernando, who disguises herself as a boy to pursue her lover when she discovers that his marriage to Luscinda has been broken off. Cervantes's narrative draws its central characters into pastoral exile, where the lovers are eventually reunited and reconciled. This part of the narrative also features the inset story of the 'curious impertinent' Anselmo, who encourages his best friend, Lothario, to seduce his wife to test her virtue, with tragic consequences. That story is turned to comic ends in *The Coxcomb* – itself performed at court by the Children of the Queen's Revels in 1612–13 – and to tragic ones in Middleton's *The Second Maiden's Tragedy*, licensed for the King's Men on 31 October 1611 (Middleton 1909: xxi).

We do not know quite how Shakespeare and Fletcher dramatized this story. In 1727, Lewis Theobald claimed that his play *The Double Falsehood* – which presents the Cardenio narrative in an adapted form – was based on a work by Shakespeare, but this claim is still disputed (see Freehafer 1969; Theobald 2010; Stern 2011; Carnegie and Taylor 2012). It is, however, easy to see why Cervantes's story would appeal to Fletcher, Shakespeare and the King's Men. In addition to sharing its source with *The Second Maiden's Tragedy*, it speaks especially strongly to *Cymbeline* and *Philaster*. It shares with those plays a tragicomic narrative structure – one that may also have been thematized in the lost play *A Bad Beginning Makes a Good Ending* – and a storyline in which the relationship between a pair of lovers is threatened and finally reconfirmed. Furthermore, the tale of Cardenio and Luscinda has marked affinities with that of Posthumous and Innogen in *Cymbeline*: both couples are brought up together, fall in love and are separated when the man thinks that his lover has betrayed him. The threat of sexual violence also lurks within both narratives, in Cloten's pursuit of Innogen and in the assault that Dorotea resists when she pushes her would-be rapist off a cliff. Shakespeare had used the motif of the woman who cross-dresses as a boy to pursue her lover as early as *The Two Gentlemen of Verona*, but the ways in which the Cardenio story, *Cymbeline* and *Philaster* use the motif within a tragicomic narrative featuring real violence and – in the case of Cardenio and *Cymbeline* – actual death, gives these stories a distinctive flavour.

The connections between these plays also raise questions about casting and its impact on performance. Almost all of the leading male roles in the 1612–13 repertory fall into two groups: first, mature or older men, such as Othello, Prospero in *The Tempest*, Leontes in *The Winter's Tale*, Jacomo and the Father in *The Captain*, Peter Fabell in *The Merry Devil of Edmonton*, Brutus in *Julius Caesar* or Benedick in *Much Ado About Nothing*; and, second, very young men characterized by their immaturity, such as Posthumous in *Cymbeline*, the title role in *Philaster*, Arbaces in *A King and No King* and Amintor in *The Maid's Tragedy*. It has often been assumed that Philaster, Arbaces and Amintor – all of which are very large roles – were played by Richard Burbage.[5] It is worth recalling, however, that Nathan Field, who joined the King's Men around 1615–16 and performed leading roles alongside Burbage, was associated with *Philaster* by William Cavendish, Duke of Newcastle, in *Wit's Triumvirate* (1635). When Phantsy claims that his meditation on love is reminiscent not of Burbage or Alleyn but 'Field in *Love Lies a Bleeding*', it is likely that he has in mind the play's brooding title role (Cavendish 1975: 4.4.600). Given that Field also played Bussy D'Ambois and Face, the largest role in *The Alchemist*, during his short career with the King's Men, there is nothing implausible about his playing that part. Moreover, there was not much time for Field to pick up the role of Philaster after Burbage's death because he outlived him by less than eighteen months, so he probably inherited it from another performer.

It is possible, therefore, that roles such as Posthumous, Philaster and Cardenio were designed for an actor other than Burbage. It is noticeable that William Ostler, who joined the King's Men around 1609, appears second in three of the five actor-lists that survive for this period – those for *The Captain*, *Bonduca* and *Valentinian* – and fourth in the other two, for *The Alchemist* and *The Duchess of Malfi*. His role in Webster's play, Antonio, is its fourth largest, and with 448 lines it is only a little shorter than Burbage's more showy role of Ferdinand, which has 476 (King 1992: 115–16).[6] Ostler is also the only actor other than Burbage and Shakespeare to be singled out for praise in John Davies's *The Scourge of Folly* (?1611), where he is described as '*the Roscius of these times*' (H1v). Did the King's Men adjust some of their casting patterns in order to accommodate Ostler, taking some of the pressure off Burbage as he tackled roles such as Prospero and Leontes? An exploration of the 1612–13 court season from the combined perspective of repertory design and casting suggests that Ostler's contribution to the King's Men between 1610–14, and his creative input into the plays of Shakespeare, Jonson and Beaumont and Fletcher, bears further consideration.

2

Collaboration, Competition and Candlelight: *Othello* and *The Alchemist*

One of the most popular plays of the King's Men was Shakespeare's *Othello*. As we have seen, it was the first play of the 1604–5 court season and its recorded performances stretch into the 1630s (see Appendix). When the play was first performed, Burbage's performance in the title role is likely to have transfixed Globe audiences. John Webster's comment that the leading actor 'charmes our attention', and his instruction, 'sit in a full Theater, and you will thinke you see so many lines drawne from the circumference of so many eares, whiles the *Actor* is the *Center*' (2007: 483), seems made for this play, in which Othello 'charms' Desdemona with his stories of hardship and adventure, and wins over the Venetian Senate with his measured and lyrical account of their romance. The power of Burbage's performance in the play's later stages is specifically invoked in John Fletcher's elegy, which refers to 'the greeu'd Moore', the term 'grieved' suggesting that the actor was able easily to invoke the qualities of sympathy or pity that Aristotle and many early modern commentators though crucial to tragedy.[1]

A few years later, in September 1610, during a prolonged outbreak of plague in London, *Othello* was performed in Oxford alongside a new play, *The Alchemist*. Jonson's play joined *Othello* at the heart of the repertory of the King's Men, maintaining its popularity into the late 1630s.[2] Among the spectators at Oxford was Henry Jackson of Corpus Christi College, who wrote a letter in Latin to his friend 'G.P.' with observations on both plays. Although Jackson does not mention Burbage by name, his description of the 'masked scoundrel [...] who impiously and extravagantly defiled the Scriptures so as to place the Anabaptists' feigned sanctity before the spectators to be derided' (Elliott et al. 2004: 2.1037) appears to allude to the actor's performance as Subtle. As we saw in Chapter 1, another early spectator wrote Burbage's name against Subtle's in the character-list for *The Alchemist* in his copy of the first folio edition of Jonson's plays, and wrote Subtle's name against Burbage's in the actor-list (see Figures 5–6).[3]

Burbage's performances were central to the success of both plays, but in the following decades the centrality of Othello and Subtle was unsettled. By the mid-1630s, Burbage's successor as the leading actor of the King's Men, Joseph Taylor, was not playing Othello and Subtle, but these characters' antagonists, Iago and Face. This chapter traces the processes that led to this reversal and its impact on both plays by looking first at what James Wright called the 'Master Parts' in these plays, their internal and structural characters and their shifting casting, and then at the material factors that conditioned performance at the two playhouses of the King's Men: the Globe and Blackfriars. It attributes changes in the casting of the plays to two factors: first, the dependence of *Othello* and *The Alchemist* on narratives that create both collaboration and competition between the actors of the King's Men; and, second, the increased prominence of the Blackfriars playhouse in the 1630s and the impact of candlelight on the performance of an actor wearing blackface make-up.

Othello is a tragedy set in Venice and, later, Cyprus, while *The Alchemist* is a London comedy that draws on the conventions of farce, but these differences mask some sustained thematic, structural and dramaturgical similarities between these plays. Both deal with alterity – race in *Othello*, criminality in *The Alchemist* and gender in both plays – in ways that are calculated to challenge the assumptions of their early audiences. They also share some aspects of their material production, such as the use of cosmetics to signify racial or national identity. While the use of blackface make-up in the portrayal of Othello has been central to an important strand of criticism in Shakespeare's play (see Callaghan 2000; Vaughan 2005; Karim-Cooper 2006: 165–74; Thompson 2011: 97–118; Smith 2013), the use of cosmetics in Surly's disguise as the Spanish gentleman – signalled in Subtle's reference to his 'scurvy, yellow, Madrid face' (4.3.31) and Lovewit's comment that Surly has 'ta'en the pains / To dye your beard and umber o'er your face' (5.5.51–2) – has been less often noted (see Lublin 2011: 105–6).

Othello and *The Alchemist* both offer two outsize roles – Iago and Othello in *Othello* and Face and Subtle in *The Alchemist* – creating friction between these characters and, potentially, the leading actors who perform them.[4] Simultaneously, however, the plays also demand strength in depth, making significant demands on boy players and offering striking roles for supporting players, from Roderigo in *Othello* to the gulls in *The Alchemist*. In what follows, I will use the information that survives to document the casting of *Othello* and *The Alchemist* to build up a more complete picture of their performance than would be possible if either play was analysed separately.

In the Preface to this book I quoted Ian Smith's essay on materiality and performance in *The Merchant of Venice*, which 'proceeds from an initial inquiry largely identified with the theatre historian's research' (2016: 170) – that is, exploring the material conventions that were used to present black characters – to explore questions relating to race, embodiment and subjectivity. This chapter also considers the uses of blackface on the early modern stage, but it takes as its starting point another theatre-historical question – who played this role? Drawing connections between the casting of plays and the material conditions of their performance, it demonstrates the ways in which company-focused readings of Shakespeare's plays open up new critical perspectives on their narrative and dramaturgical structures. In the process, it argues that the 1630s were a crucial time in the performance history of Shakespeare's play, a moment of origin for casting and performance practices that are still with us in the early twenty-first century.

Collaboration and Competition

Shakespeare and Jonson both open their plays with disputes that threaten violence, creating moments at which spectators must struggle to understand where they are, who the characters are and precisely why everyone is so angry. 'Tush', cries Roderigo in the opening lines of *Othello*, 'never tell me, I take it much unkindly / That thou, Iago, who hast had my purse / As if the strings were thine, shouldst know of this' (1.1.1–3). Iago immediately ups the scene's rhetorical heat, responding with a much stronger oath than Roderigo's feeble 'tush': ''Sblood, but you'll not hear me. / If ever I did dream / Of such a matter, abhor me' (1.1.4–5). It eventually becomes clear that the cause of Roderigo's anger is the marriage of Desdemona to Othello, and the exchanges that follow establish Iago as the play's corrupt heart, the man who voices harshly, jestingly, the racism that other white characters cloak in civility, who makes explicit the more subtle misogyny of others. It is an uncompromising vehicle for the actor who plays *Othello*'s largest role, one in which all other characters are positioned as his rhetorical and intellectual inferiors. However, when Othello himself appears in Act 1, Scene 3, he offers another model of both masculinity and performance, setting against Iago's unruly energy the grandeur of the leading player. Iago's corruption of Othello is also an attempt of one style of performance to supplant another, one in which other varieties of performer – the supporting player who plays Roderigo, the boys who portray Desdemona and Emilia – are collateral damage.

The Alchemist similarly begins with obscenity and the threat of violence, as Face and Subtle confront each other – Face wielding a sword and Subtle a glass vial – and Doll attempts to keep the peace. The opening lines plunge us into the midst of the quarrel:

FACE
   Believe't, I will.
SUBTLE   Thy worst. I fart at thee.
DOLL
   Ha' you your wits? Why, gentlemen! For love –
FACE
   Sirrah, I'll strip you –
SUBTLE   What to do? Lick figs
   Out at my –
FACE   Rogue, rogue, out of all your sleights.
DOLL
   Nay, look ye! Sovereign, General, are you madmen?
                                                                    (1.1.1–5)

Intricately woven obscenities meet and clash across and within the verse lines that Face and Subtle share, while Doll's first two lines carve out their own space by presenting complete pentameter lines. The opening of *The Alchemist* is a dazzling showcase for three evenly matched performers – two leading actors and one boy – but it also, like *Othello*, places these characters, and their performers, in a battle not only of wit but also of performance technique.

Shakespeare and Jonson enjoy the queasy energy that is provoked when the implicit competition between performers is thematized within the structures of tragedy and comedy respectively. Looking at patterns of casting in the two plays helps us to consider the additional charge that might have been created when the roles in these plays were embodied by particular actors. The earliest cast of *Othello* is likely to have featured most if not all of the players in the list of the 'principall Tragœdians' in Jonson's *Sejanus* (1603) – Richard Burbage, William Shakespeare, Augustine Phillips, John Heminges, William Sly, Henry Condell, John Lowin and Alexander Cooke – with the possible exception of Shakespeare and the addition of the comic specialist Robert Armin and boy actors such as John Rice and, possibly, William Ecclestone.[5] The cast may also have included two other actors who do not feature in Jonson's list: the hired man John Sincler, who forms an engaging comic double-act with Sly as a pair of playgoers in the induction to the King's Men's version of John Marston's *The Malcontent*, also performed around 1604; and Lawrence Fletcher, who appears in the 1603 royal patent and a list of the men to whom payments were due as the King's 'Players of Interludes', which was drawn up in 1607.[6]

Burbage must have played Othello in these early performances, and a combination of internal and external evidence suggests that John Lowin played Iago. Lowin was twenty-eight in 1604, in line with Iago's statement 'I have looked upon the world for four times seven years' (1.3.312–13), and the role was still haunting him in the late 1620s and early 1630s. In Lodowick Carlell's *The Deserving Favourite* (c. 1629), for instance, Lowin's character, Iacomo, who shares Iago's fondness for insinuating direct address to the spectators, is repeatedly referred to as 'honest' by himself and others, in an echo of 'honest' Iago. At the end of one soliloquy he declares, 'My villany shall Vertue be in show, / For all shall thinke me honest *Iacomo*' (1629: G2r). The character's name also recalls another Shakespearean character, *Cymbeline*'s Iacomo, himself a tragicomic debasement of Iago, and another role that Lowin may have played.[7] Given his position as the company's specialist comedian, Armin is very likely to have played the Clown, but for the casting of other roles we are dependent on conjecture.

More information has survived about the casting of *The Alchemist*. It was accompanied in the 1616 folio edition of Jonson's *Works* by a list of the 'principall Comœdians':

Richard Burbage, John Heminges, John Lowin, William Ostler, Henry Condell, John Underwood, Alexander Cooke, Nicholas Tooley, Robert Armin and William Ecclestone (1616: 3K3v). Cooke died in 1614, while Ecclestone had departed for Lady Elizabeth's Men by 29 August 1611, when he was among the actors who bound themselves financially to the impresario Philip Henslowe (Greg 1907: 18–19, 111). It is therefore probable that the actor-list represents the cast of the play 'in the yeere 1610', as the folio's heading implies. It does not specify the casting of individual roles, but some information is provided elsewhere. Drugger's question, 'did you never see me play the fool?' (4.7.69), suggests that he was played by Armin, and the early seventeenth-century owner of a copy of the folio, mentioned above, annotated both the actor-list and the separate character-list with the names of actors (see Figures 5–6). These annotations attribute roles as follows:

> Subtle: 'Richard Burbadge'
> Face: 'Nat: Feild' (i.e. Nathan Field)
> Doll: 'Richard Birch'
> Dapper: 'John Vnderwood'
> Lovewit: 'Bently' (i.e. Robert Benfield?)
> Sir Epicure Mammon: 'John Lowin'
> Surly: 'Hen: Condell'
> Ananias: 'Nich: Tooley'
> Kastril: 'Will: Eglestone'

The annotations probably represent the cast of a revival of *The Alchemist* before July 1618, when George Birche, whose name appears to be mistakenly noted by the annotator as 'Richard', was due to complete the eight-year term of his apprenticeship (Kathman 2004a: 8). The earlier limit is established by the appearance of Nathan Field, who does not appear to have joined the King's Men until 1615 or 1616.[8]

The annotator's failure to write in any roles against the names of Armin, Cooke, Heminges or Ostler also suggests that they recalled a performance in the later 1610s. Cooke

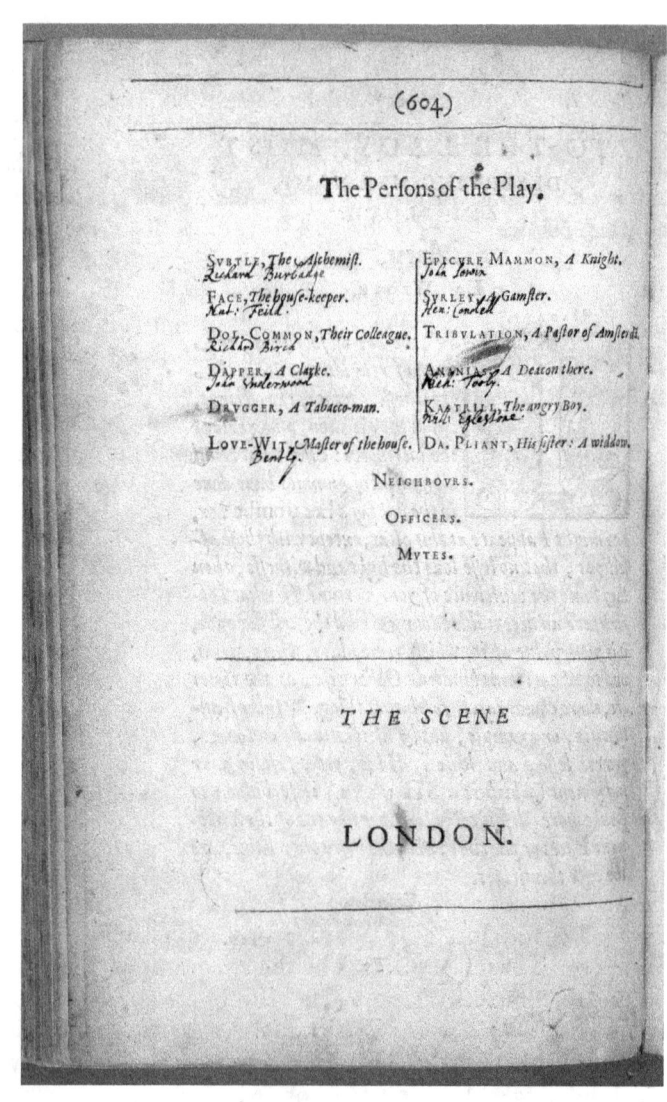

FIGURE 5 *'The Persons of the Play', in* The Alchemist, *with manuscript annotations, in* The Workes of Benjamin Jonson *(London, 1616), 49968, The Huntington Library, San Marino, California.*

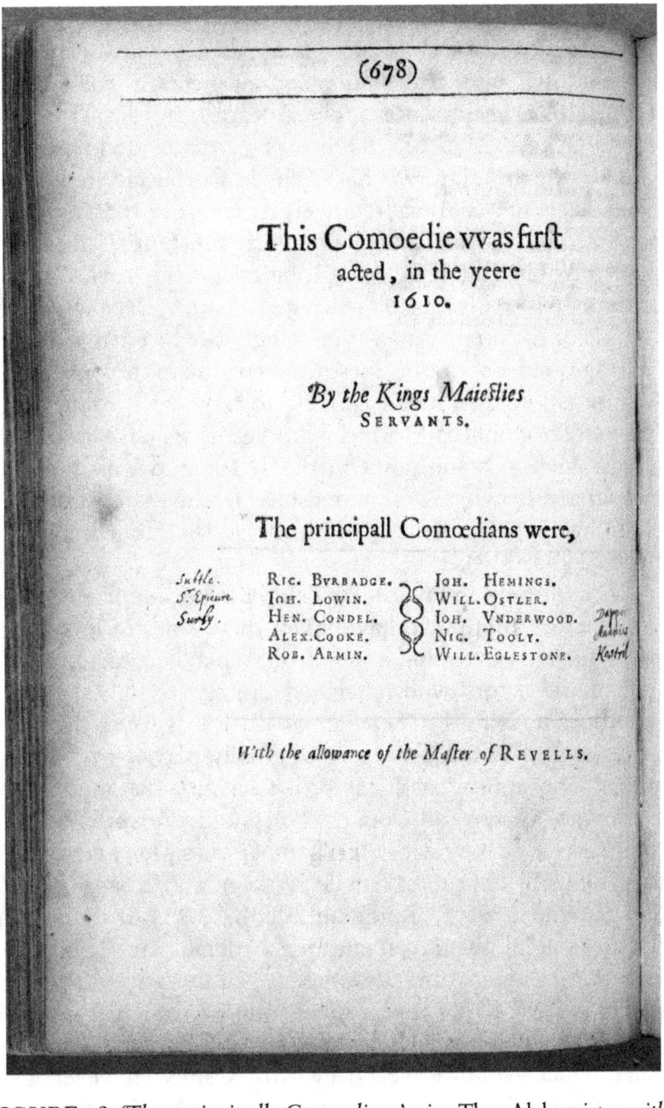

(678)

This Comoedie vvas first
acted, in the yeere
1610.

By the Kings Maiesties
SERVANTS.

The principall Comœdians were,

Subtle. RIC. BVRBADGE.   IOH. HEMINGS.
Sr Epicure IOH. LOWIN.   WILL. OSTLER.
Surly. HEN. CONDEL.   IOH. VNDERWOOD. *Dapper*
  ALEX. COOKE.   NIC. TOOLY. *Anbitio*
  ROB. ARMIN.   WILL. EGLESTONE. *Kastril*

With the allowance of the Master of REVELLS.

FIGURE 6 'The principall Comœdians', in The Alchemist, *with manuscript annotations, in* The Workes of Benjamin Jonson *(London, 1616), 49968, The Huntington Library, San Marino, California.*

and Ostler both died in 1614, followed by Armin in 1615. Heminges lived until 1630, but appears to have retired or scaled down his performance commitments in the early to mid-1610s. He does not appear in any actor-lists for plays of the King's Men after Jonson's *Catiline* (1611), and is said by the annotator to have played Corbaccio in *Volpone* (Riddell 1969: 293), a relatively small role that he might have retained while giving up more substantial ones. It is thus possible that Field and Robert Benfield – who arrived around 1614–16 – joined the King's Men to replace Ostler and Cooke, or to compensate for Heminges's reduced appearances on stage. The annotator does not record who took over from Armin as Drugger, but it is likely to have been John Shank, the veteran comic performer who seems to have joined the King's Men at some point in the 1610s and was a witness to Richard Cowley's will, alongside Heminges and Burbage's elder brother, Cuthbert, in January 1618 (Honigmann and Brock 1993: 112).

With the exception of Benfield, Birche and Field, all of these actors could also have taken these roles in the earliest performances, meaning that Tooley, playing Ananias, was one of the actors whose 'feigned sanctity' caught Jackson's attention at Oxford in September 1610. It is likely that Face, Lovewit and Tribulation were originally played by the three actors who appear in the actor-list but not the annotations: Heminges, Ostler and Cooke. Tooley and Cooke both began their careers as boys with the Chamberlain's Men and together they played the leading female roles in *2 The Seven Deadly Sins* around 1597–8 (Kathman 2004b; 2011). It is therefore fun to imagine them teaming up as Ananias and Tribulation, and such casting would also make sense in terms of the order in which these actors appear in the folio's actor-list. It is usually assumed that Heminges, who appears second in that list, played Face, which would leave Lovewit for Ostler. However, given Ostler's prominence in the company between 1610 and 1614, it may be more likely that he played Face, leaving Heminges to play Lovewit, who is important in terms of his status and the scale of his intervention in the later stages of the play but has relatively few lines.

Neither *Othello* nor *The Alchemist* demand large numbers of boy actors. *The Alchemist* has only two female roles (Doll and Dame Pliant); *Othello* has three (Desdemona, Emilia and Bianca), plus a role for a young musician referred to as 'Boy' in his speech prefixes in the quarto (Shakespeare 1622: F4r–v). However, Doll, Desdemona and Emilia are all demanding roles, and each would provide opportunities and challenges for the boy actors who were assigned them. John Rice and Richard Robinson are the leading candidates for these roles around 1610. As I described in Chapter 1, Robinson played the role of the Lady in Middleton's *The Second Maiden's Tragedy* in 1611; the technical demands of that part suggest that nothing in *Othello* would have been beyond him, but it is perhaps harder to imagine him as Doll in *The Alchemist*.

It is also intriguing to consider the contribution of Rice – who was probably apprenticed to one of the King's Men around 1603–4, at the age of thirteen or fourteen (Kathman 2015: 249–50) – to the play's early stage-life. He may have lacked the experience to play Desdemona or Emilia in the very first performances of *Othello*, but he became one of the company's most prominent boy actors. In 1607 he delivered a speech at a banquet of the Merchant Taylors' Company (Kathman 2015: 249), and on 31 May 1610 he appeared in a water pageant written by Anthony Munday, mounted on the Thames to celebrate the investiture of James's older son, Henry, as Prince of Wales. Appearing alongside Richard Burbage, who played Amphion, Rice played Corinea of Cornwall, '*a very fayre and beautifull Nimphe* [...] *suited in her watrie habit yet riche and costly, with a Coronet of Pearles and Cockle shelles on her head*' (Munday 1610: C1v).

By 1611, Rice had left the King's Men for Lady Elizabeth's Men, possibly on the conclusion of his apprenticeship (Greg 1907: 18–19, 111). However, he was probably available for the Globe performance of *Othello* on 30 April 1610 and the Oxford performances of both plays in September 1610, and the fact that his role as Corinea required him to deliver a 220-word speech while '*riding on a Whale*' (C2r) suggests that little in *Othello* or *The Alchemist* would have daunted him. If Rice played Desdemona, his casting as a '*very fayre and beautifull Nimphe*' in Munday's pageant might suggest that he brought to the role a more decorous and conventional femininity than a boy like George Birche, who excelled as Doll and Lady Pol. Yet if he played Emilia, this very quality may have given an additional edge to the role, especially in the performance of Emilia's outburst against Othello and her defiance of Iago in the play's final scene.

A similar interplay between different modes of femininity may have informed the performance of *Othello* and *The Alchemist* in the late 1620s and early 1630s, when both were revived. *Othello* was performed at Blackfriars on 22 November 1629, when the Master of the Revels, Sir Henry Herbert, claimed £9 16s. from the takings for his winter benefit (Bawcutt 1996: 169).[9] At this time, two of the most prominent boy actors in the King's Men were the sixteen-year-old John Honeyman and the slightly older John Thompson. They take the largest female roles in Philip Massinger's *The Roman Actor* (1626), Lodowick Carlell's *The Deserving Favourite* (*c.* 1629) and Massinger's *The Picture* (1629), and it seems likely that they played Desdemona and Emilia in *Othello*. But which actor would have been assigned which role? The parts that they took in one of these plays, *The Picture*, offer more than one possibility. Honeyman's role, Sophia, is complex and demanding. She confronts successively an allegation that her husband, Mathias (played by Joseph Taylor), has been unfaithful to her, the depredations of two sleazy courtiers, Ubaldo and Ricardo (Thomas Pollard and Elliard Swanston) and the fact that Mathias has used a magical portrait to test her own ability to remain chaste. The psychological and technical challenges of the part are epitomized by the series of soliloquies that Massinger gives her during the crucial scenes at the end of Act 3 and the beginning of Act 4 (3.6.8–28, 3.6.126–61, 4.2.1–25). Sophia comes to the point of betraying Mathias before eschewing revenge and instead punishing Ubaldo and Ricardo. 'Haue I no spleene / Nor anger of a woman?' she asks, 'shall he build / Vpon my ruins and I vnreueng'd / Deplore his falshood?' (3.6.149–52). Thompson's role, that of the imperious queen Honoria, who pursues Mathias and sets Ubaldo and Ricardo on Sophia, is in some respects less technically challenging, but he also has a complex scene at the end of Act 4 in which Honoria is forced to reassess her behaviour and repent, and he appears to be required to sing a seductive '*song of pleasure*' from offstage as part of her attempted seduction of Mathias (3.5.25SD).

Honeyman and Thompson's other roles thus offer different possibilities for their casting in *Othello*, and the problems are compounded because we do not know precisely what version of the text was performed in 1629. The text published in the folio edition of Shakespeare's plays in 1623 requires Desdemona to sing the 'Willow' song in Act 4, Scene 3 while Emilia 'unpins' her, but the quarto, published a year earlier in 1622, omits the song. It is not unlikely that the scene was regularly amended depending on the singing abilities of the boy who was available. Casting Thompson as Desdemona would enable the King's Men to perform the folio version which, as Clare McManus notes, 'deliberately brings the performance into jeopardy in a high-wire act of exceptional confidence in the skills of both the singing boy and the laboring boy, who must unpin Desdemona in the time it takes to sing the ballad' (2015: 108). If Thompson played the role in a fashion similar to that demanded by his other roles, his would have been a notably imperious and imposing Desdemona. Such a performance could give additional weight to Desdemona's appearance before the Venetian Senate, with her forthright declaration 'I did love the Moor to live with him' (1.3.249) and her demand to be allowed to accompany him to Cyprus. It might also complicate the effect of later moments in the play, especially the presentation of Othello's violence towards Desdemona in Act 4, Scene 1, and the murder itself – potentially, the moment at which she briefly revives would register more powerfully in the context of Thompson's established track record of playing assertive characters such as Honoria. Conversely, an actor who could play convincingly Sophia's mental turmoil, such as Honeyman, would also handle effectively the demands of Desdemona's role, perhaps excelling in portraying her wry humour and resignation in lines such as 'I cannot weep, nor answers have I none / But what should go by water' (4.2.105–6). Moreover, a less effective vocal performance in the 'Willow' song might give an additional edge to the scene if spectators knew that an Emilia played by Thompson could sing it better.

By 1 December 1631, when the King's Men revived *The Alchemist* at Blackfriars, Honeyman had ceased to play female roles, and was in a period of transition during which he was given relatively minor male roles such as Sly in John Clavell's *The Soddered Citizen* (c. 1630), the First Merchant in Massinger's *Believe As You List* (1631) and the Young Factor in the revival of Fletcher's *The Wild Goose Chase* (1623). Thompson was still playing female roles, taking the parts of Miniona in *The Soddered Citizen* and Panopia in Arthur Wilson's *The Swisser* (1631). Other female roles in *The Soddered Citizen* and *The Swisser* are played by two further boy actors, Alexander Gough and William Trigg. However, reviving *The Alchemist*, which has one outstanding female role, apparently well suited to Thompson's strengths, and youthful male roles, such as Kastril and Dapper, that might be played by Honeyman, might have been a way for the King's Men to reduce the pressure on their temporarily depleted cast of boys.

We are accustomed to considering the shifts in casting that would have occurred as boy actors ceased to play female roles. It has often been assumed that the casting of leading roles was more static, but the evidence that survives presents a more complex picture. Wright assigns the roles of Sir Epicure Mammon to Lowin and Face to Taylor, giving Iago to Taylor and Othello to Swanston (1699: 4). He probably drew on the memories of his father, Abraham, who attended plays and made notes on their characters and plots around 1640. Abraham commented of *Othello*: 'A very good play both for lines and plot, but especially ye plot. Iago for a rogue and Othello for a iealous husband 2 parts well pend. Act: 3 ye scene beetwixt Iago and Othello, and ye 1 sce: of ye 4 Act beetween ye same shew admirably ye villainous humour of Iago when hee persuades Othello to his ielousy.'[10] Given his interest in the roles of Iago and Othello, it is likely that he remembered who played them and discussed the performances with his son, and there is no reason to think that James Wright's information is inaccurate.

Taylor probably acquired the roles of Face and Iago at different times. When Field died within eighteen months of Burbage in 1619–20, both of the leading roles in *The Alchemist* became available, and Taylor appears to have preferred the role of Face over that of Subtle. Lowin appears to have played Sir Epicure Mammon until the 1630s; and Hugh Clarke, who played leading roles in the late 1630s and early 1640s. So it is unclear who would have played Subtle in Burbage's place. Potential casting options across the 1620s and 1630s include: William Ecclestone, Nicholas Tooley and John Underwood, who appear prominently in the Fletcherian actor-lists of the early 1620s, but who all died in 1623–5; Thomas Pollard, who takes comic leads in a number of plays of the 1620s and 1630s; Swanston, who does not appear to have moved into leading roles until the late 1630s and early 1640s; and Hugh Clarke, who played leading roles in the mid- to late 1630s.[11]

The picture is somewhat clearer for *Othello*. Piecing together the evidence we have gives us two Othello/Iago pairs: Burbage and Lowin (1603–19) and Swanston and Taylor (1630s or early 1640s). But this cannot be the whole story. Swanston did not join the King's Men until around 1623, and the ways in which dramatists such as Carlell exploit audience's familiarity with Lowin's performances as Iago suggest that he retained the role until the early 1630s. It seems likely, therefore, that Taylor originally inherited Burbage's role as Othello, playing him opposite Lowin's Iago. It is noticeable, in this context, that a similar Taylor/Lowin pairing appears in *Believe as You List*, discussed in detail in Chapter 3, in which the doomed Antiochus, played by Taylor, is pursued by the implacable and enigmatic Titus Flaminius, played by Lowin. Echoes of *Othello* may also be exploited in *The Picture*, performed in repertory with *The Deserving Favourite* (in which Lowin's Iago-like Iacomo appears) and *Othello* in 1629. Taylor's character, Mathias, unreasonably suspects that his wife Sophia might be unfaithful to him and demands 'ocular proof' in the shape of a magic portrait of Sophia that will turn from 'white, and red' to 'yellow' if she is 'with all violence courted but vnconquered', and finally 'all blacke' if 'The fort by composition, or surprise / Is forc'd or with her free consent surrenderd' (1.1.180–5). Massinger reconfigures Shakespeare's treatment of jealousy and race, but both plays place Taylor at the heart of a potent network of English anxieties about sex, skin colour and female agency.

Later in the 1630s, however, something appears to have changed, and the casting of leading roles in *Othello* shifted again, perhaps as part of the same overhaul of roles described in Chapter 1. It is not unlikely that Lowin, who would have been nearly sixty in the mid-1630s, would have given up the demanding role of Iago; Taylor, in turn, would have handed over Othello to Swanston, perhaps around the time of the court performances of *Richard III* and *Bussy D'Ambois* in 1633–4, in which Swanston appears to have played the leading roles. We do not know how casting decisions were made within the King's Men, but the evidence that survives for *Othello* and *The Alchemist* suggests something more complex than the idea that actors took clearly defined 'lines' within companies, which were inherited wholesale by their younger colleagues. This model, proposed by Thomas Whitfield Baldwin in the 1920s, has been challenged by a number of later scholars (see Howard 1985). Looking closely at the evidence for casting patterns within the repertory of the King's Men further suggests that it is flawed. Instead of inheriting Burbage's 'line', Taylor appears to have chosen to play Face rather than Subtle when Field's death gave him the opportunity. Moreover, the casting of plays was less stable over a long period than the idea of the 'line' suggests because actors may have ceased playing some roles as they aged – as Taylor himself appears to have stopped playing Bussy D'Ambois, another role inherited from Field, in the early to mid-1630s.

If the performances of actors such as Taylor or Swanston were 'ghosted' by the memories of their earlier roles and the performances of their roles by other actors, this process was complex. Rather than inhabiting Burbage's shadow, Taylor appears to have performed a bricolage of roles originally performed by different actors, and if his roles shifted at certain points, so did the associations between his roles. For example, if *The Picture* remained in the repertory of the King's Men as Taylor transitioned from playing Othello to playing Iago, the associations provoked by his performance as Mathias would have changed. Mathias's jealous paranoia, and his desire to gain proof of his wife's chastity or infidelity, may link him with Othello, but the underhand means through which he goes about testing Sophia may have been brought to the fore if spectators recalled a recent performance as Iago.

Competition, Collaboration and the 'Master-Parts'

Thus far, I have set out evidence that the casting of both *The Alchemist* and *Othello* shifted during the early seventeenth century, but I have not addressed the question of why Taylor might have wanted to play Iago and Face over Othello and Subtle. This question will be addressed over the next two sections of this chapter, the first focusing on the qualities of these leading roles, and the second on the impact of the material conditions of performance on *The Alchemist* and *Othello*.

As we have seen, Fletcher attempted to capture something of Burbage's impact as Othello by describing this character as 'the greeu'd Moore', a term that links his performance with the tragic emotions of pity and fear identified by Aristotle. In a recent essay, Dennis Austin Britton has explored the workings of pity in *Othello* via Shakespeare's engagements with his Italian source texts, Cinthio's novella in *Gli Hecatommithi* and Ariosto's *Orlando Furioso*, and the interactions of both of these works with the conventions of romance. Britton argues that 'Shakespeare contaminates Cinthio's novella with *Orlando Furioso* in order to introduce into his play a type of pity that is typically elicited by romances – romances often allow characters to pity others whose racial and religious identities are different from their own' (2018: 47). The pity generated within romance is, he suggests, 'a crucial emotion for helping the English audience experience tragic pity and for feeling the complexity of Italian attitudes about race' (47). It is this quality of pity to which Fletcher appears to respond, and I am interested in how the casting and performance of *Othello* might have worked with and against the generic structures that Britton identifies.

Shakespeare begins to position Othello as the subject of this engaged pity when he appears before the Senate in the play's third scene. In his account of the circumstances in which he and Desdemona fell in love with one another, Othello emphasizes her emotional response to his tales of his former hardships: she weeps (1.3.157–9) and describes her own emotions: 'She swore in faith 'twas strange, 'twas passing strange / 'Twas pitiful, 'twas wondrous pitiful' (161–2). At the end of Othello's speech, the Duke takes over Desdemona's reported role in modelling an appropriate emotional response, declaring, 'I think this tale would win my daughter too' (172). Othello epitomizes the techniques of the leading actor, drawing power from his position at the centre of the Globe audience's attention and from his very status within the playing company.

Yet Burbage's Othello was 'grieved' in more ways than one, the term referring in early modern English not only to vexation and mental turmoil but also to harassment and oppression, the quality of having been wronged and the affliction of pain or disease (*OED* grieved, *adj.*). All of these senses are raised by the ways in which Iago works on Othello, in a set of interactions that affect both the characters and the actors who play them. A decisive moment, singled out for praise by Abraham Wright, is typical of their effect:

IAGO
   Is't possible? my lord?
OTHELLO
   Villain, be sure thou prove my love a whore,
   Be sure of it, give me the ocular proof,
                              [*Catching hold of him*]
   Or by the worth of man's eternal soul
   Thou hadst been better have been born a dog
   Than answer my naked wrath!
IAGO   Is't come to this?
OTHELLO
   Make me to see't, or at the least so prove it
   That the probation bear no hinge nor loop
   To hang a doubt on, or woe upon thy life!
IAGO
   My noble lord –
OTHELLO
   If thou dost slander her and torture me
   Never pray more, abandon all remorse;
   On horror's head horrors accumulate,
   Do deeds to make heaven weep, all earth amazed,
   For nothing canst thou to damnation add
   Greater than that!
IAGO   O grace! O heaven forgive me!
   Are you a man? have you a soul or sense?
   God buy you, take mine office. O wretched fool
   That lov'st to make thine honesty a vice!
   O monstrous world! Take note, take note, O world,
   To be direct and honest is not safe.
   I thank you for this profit, and from hence
   I'll love no friend, sith love breeds such offence.

OTHELLO
  Nay, stay, thou shouldst be honest.
IAGO
  I should be wise, for honesty's a fool
  And loses that it works for.
OTHELLO   By the world,
  I think my wife is honest, and think she is not,
  I think that thou art just, and think thou art not.
  I'll have some proof. Her name, that was as fresh
  As Dian's visage, is now begrimed and black
  As mine own face. If there be cords or knives,
  Poison, or fire, or suffocating streams,
  I'll not endure it. Would I were satisfied!
IAGO
  I see, sir, you are eaten up with passion.
  I do repent me that I put it to you.
  You would be satisfied?
OTHELLO   Would? nay, and I will!
                                          (3.3.361–96)

Most of this exchange appears in the quarto and folio texts, but the quarto lacks Othello's longest speech (386–93), meaning that Iago's last two speeches appear as one speech.[12] It is not entirely clear whether the folio text represents an expansion of the quarto or the quarto an abridgement of the folio (see McMillin 2001: 8–11). However, the inclusion of the speech in the folio version gives Othello a greater share of the exchange and a more complex response to Iago's provocation; without it there is a clear shift halfway through this section of the dialogue, Iago taking over from Othello as its driving force. Moreover, if the speech is omitted, it takes with it the only explicit reference to Othello's race in the entire exchange.

This is not an exchange in which Iago exploits his intimate relationship with the audience, established through soliloquy and aside. Instead, it deploys a scenic structure described by Charles Lamb in the early nineteenth century, when he criticized what he called 'scolding scenes', 'where two people talk themselves into a fit of fury, and then in a surprising manner talk themselves out of it again'. Lamb thought that such scenes appealed to an audience because they called on them to sit in judgement on this 'war of words', 'they are the legitimate ring that should be formed round such "intellectual prize-fighters"' (1811: 301). Something of this dynamic is evident in *Othello*, and it is noticeable that Lamb's image of prize-fighters invokes similar questions of violence and domination as an image that has dominated later commentaries on the play. As Lois Potter points out, reviewers often liken the interactions between Othello and Iago to a bullfight, with Othello as the beleaguered bull and Iago as the matador (2002: 3). Yet what interests me in particular here is the structure of the exchange, and the physical and verbal interactions between the characters and (thereby) the actors.

Throughout, different demands are made of the two actors. Othello moves through aggressive fury to an attempt to placate Iago – the exchange pivots on the key utterance, 'Nay, stay' (3.3.384) – and then to distressed confusion. Iago's comment, 'I see, sir, you are eaten up with passion' (394), indicates the emotional turmoil that the Othello-actor is intended to convey. Iago mines a seam of affronted loyalty – particularly in the abrupt questions and exclamations of his longest speech (376–83) – and the Iago-actor must find a way of making the performance both plausible for Othello and histrionic for the knowing spectators. Othello's speeches have a more obvious rhetorical patterning – for instance, the alliteration on 'On horror's head horrors accumulate' (373), the use of anaphora in 'I think my wife is honest, and think she is not. / I think that thou art honest, and think thou art not' (387–8), and the simile of 'as fresh / As Dian's visage' (389–90) – but Iago's very plainness is calculated.

Through such exchanges, the play confronts the tragic protagonist with his actorly 'other', and these dramaturgical techniques would also have been inflected by the personal and physical dynamics that existed between performers. In the original performances of 1603–4, Lowin – who was eight years younger than Burbage – was newly arrived in the company, and Iago's destruction of Othello may have been yet more devastating as a result of this disparity in age and status, the upstart newcomer challenging his established rival. Yet Lowin may have dominated physically. Burbage does not appear to have been a small man, but Lowin was noted for both his height and physical bulk, which inflect a number of his known roles. In Fletcher's *The Wild-Goose Chase*, for instance, Lowin's Belleur is described as the 'tall fat fellow' (3.1.121), while Andrucho in Wilson's *The Swisser* (1631) is told 'thy great Beard and Bulke / Will grace the Gallows well' (1904: 3.2.112–13). James Wright assigns Lowin the part of Falstaff (1699: 4) and John Downes that of Henry VIII (1708: 24), and it is highly likely that Jonson had his physique in mind when he created Sir Epicure Mammon. Lowin's physically imposing and deceptively solid Iago was thus played off in early performances against Burbage's emotional Othello.

After 1619, an older Lowin was paired with Taylor. These men occupied similar positions in the company's hierarchy, and the physical interaction between performers may also have shifted. No portraits survive of Taylor, but there is a continuity in the way in which characters that he appears to have played are described. In Fletcher and Massinger's *The Sea Voyage* (1622), the part that Taylor probably played, Alberto, is described as being of 'middle stature, and of brown complexion' (4.1.37), while Pedro in Fletcher's *The Pilgrim* (1622) is '[b]oth yong, and handsome; / Only the Sun has bin too saucy with him' (1.2.61–2).[13] Subtle's reference to Surly's 'scurvy, yellow, Madrid face' (4.3.31) may have taken on a different quality when Taylor played Face, and although the actor's 'brown complexion' may not have registered if his face was artificially blackened with cosmetics, the relatively slight build of his Othello may have intensified the power of Lowin's Iago over him.

In the later 1630s, when Taylor played Iago and Swanston played Othello, the relationship between the actors may have approximated for the first time the one that has dominated the play's later tradition. Potter notes that '[m]ost productions have traditionally showed a large, powerful but rather static Othello playing opposite a lighter, more mercurial Iago' (2002: 3). We do not know what Elliard Swanston looked like, but seventeenth-century commentators invoke both a vivid physical presence and a certain vocal power. Thomas Shadwell describes Swanston as a 'brave roaring Fellow' with the ability to 'make the stage shake' (1676: 14), while Edmund Gayton evokes the stateliness, gravity and command that he was able to portray in roles such as Bussy D'Ambois (1654: E1r). It is likely, therefore, that the powerful Othello/mercurial Iago pattern was established in the 1630s, demonstrating the importance to stage history of thinking not only about the initial performances of plays but their seventeenth-century successors.

If the role of Othello accords with the qualities that Shadwell and Gayton thought necessary to the leading man – bravery, stateliness, gravity and command – Iago presents something rather different. The late seventeenth-century commentator Charles Gildon writes: 'I'm assur'd from very good hands, that the Person that Acted *Jago* was in much esteem for a Comoedian, which made *Shakespear* put several words, and expressions into his part (perhaps not so agreeable to his Character) to make the Audience laugh, who had not yet learnt to endure to be serious a whole Play' (1694: 88–9). Gildon tells the story to explain what he sees as a lapse of taste on Shakespeare's part, yet he rightly identifies the affinity between Iago and comic roles of the period, to which scholars have also drawn our attention (see Potter 2002: 4; Hankey 2005: 6). In fact, *Othello* depends on a more complex interaction between comic and tragic modes than Gildon acknowledges, and – as we saw in Chapter 1 – actors such as Burbage, Lowin and Taylor succeeded in roles that went beyond the specialisms of the Restoration comedians with whom he was familiar. *Othello* pits an actor drawing on all of the affective resources of tragic performance with one who is, in contrast, required to deploy comic techniques, yet it also depends on having performers in each role who could turn their talents in other directions.

An additional perspective on this interplay between characters and roles can be seen if we return to *The Alchemist*. Jonson's play opens – as we have seen – with its own sardonic, debasing take on the 'intellectual prize-fighting' described by Lamb, albeit with the important difference that Doll takes an active part in the exchanges between the members of the 'venture tripartite'. As noted above, we do not know which actor played Face in the original performances in 1610, but two alternatives present themselves: John Heminges and William Ostler. Born in 1566, Heminges was two years older than Burbage; the two men had been close collaborators since at least the mid 1590s. If Heminges played Face, the tensions between the characters may have been rendered more playful or simply more complex by his longstanding relationship with Burbage. In contrast, the much younger Ostler had begun his career with the Children of the Chapel around 1600, when he was probably aged around eleven to thirteen; he had only recently joined the King's Men when they performed *The Alchemist* for the first time. If he played Face, the confrontations between the characters would have taken on something of the charge of those between Othello and Iago when *Othello* was first performed in 1603–4, the newcomer manipulating and ultimately destroying his older colleague. A similar quality informed the performance of these roles in the later Jacobean revival, when Nathan Field – who had also begun his career with the Chapel company and had recently performed with rival companies such as Lady Elizabeth's Men – took over the role of Face.

This overview of the 'master parts' in *Othello* and *The Alchemist* offers a series of possible answers to the question of why Taylor might have preferred to play Iago and Face over Othello and Subtle. Fletcher's elegy suggests the extent to which Othello was identified with Burbage, and the long shadow cast by the older man on his successors. Taylor may not have been able to avoid playing Othello when he first joined the King's Men, but the death of Field offered him an alternative to playing Subtle, just as Condell's retirement may have allowed him to play Mosca rather than Volpone. Yet Iago, Mosca and Face share internal characteristics that may have made them more attractive to Taylor. Each is the largest role in the play in which it appears, and each establishes a distinctive relationship with spectators through techniques such as soliloquy or asides. These are Protean figures, offering a range of opportunities for an actor to demonstrate his skill and versatility, and they drive the plots of their respective plays. The appeal of these roles may also be explained by the competition inherent to each play – each gains the upper hand over a supposedly senior figure, if only temporarily. Yet – as I will argue – we should not underestimate the physical contexts of performance, and one of the factors that made the King's Men distinctive: their use of two playhouses.

Candlelight

Othello was originally a Globe play, and aspects of its dramaturgy both exploit and resist the wide-scale expansiveness of the open-air theatre. Othello's bravura speeches in Act 1, Scene 3 must have reverberated in the large space of the Globe, creating something of the effect described by Webster in 'An Excellent Actor'. In the same scene, the play teases its audience with the possibility of staging a full-scale battle with the Ottoman forces, the Duke telling Othello, 'Valiant Othello, we must straight employ you / Against the general enemy Ottoman' (1.3.49–50). However, that threat is dismissed offstage, in the 'desperate tempest [that] hath so banged the Turks / That their designment halts' (2.1.21–2), and what *Othello* actually gives spectators from this point onwards is an increasingly claustrophobic series of private interactions, propelled and sustained by the queasy intimacy of Iago's soliloquies and asides. Perhaps unsurprisingly, the play seems to have become a staple of the Blackfriars repertory after 1608. It was published in 1622 with the title-page claim '*As it hath beene diverse times acted at the* Globe, and at the Black-Friers, by *his Majesties Servants*', and performances are recorded at the Blackfriars in the 1630s (see Appendix). In such performances the effects that I have just described would have been reversed, the opening scenes would have pushed against the small indoor space, whereas later ones would have seemed calculated to exploit its dark and huddled environment.

The Alchemist appears to have been written with the Blackfriars in mind. It is set in London during a time of plague, and it gains something of its power from the fact that the playhouse – a room in the Blackfriars precinct – is made to represent not an exotic locale, but a room in the Blackfriars precinct. Much of the play's theatrical vitality derives from its physical action – the rapid back-and-forth of characters onto, off and through the stage – its attention to sound (from Doll's plea in the opening scene, 'Will you have / The neighbours hear you? Will you betray all? / Hark, I hear somebody' [1.1.7–9], to the loud bang with which the alchemist's laboratory explodes offstage in Act 4, Scene 5), its linguistic excess and its attention to details of clothing and to props such as the gingerbread with which the unfortunate Dapper is gagged. All of these factors appear to be tailored to the claustrophobic atmosphere of the Blackfriars, which had a relatively small stage, crowded by boxes on either side and often occupied not only by actors but also by the most wealthy – or pretentious – members of the audience, who paid extra to sit on stools there (Wickham, Berry and Ingram 2000: 514). Yet, for any play to be a truly successful part of the repertory of the King's Men it would have to be capable of performance at the Globe. It is in fact possible that the performance that Sir Humphrey Mildmay saw on 18 May 1639 (Bentley 1937: 69) may have been outdoors, as the King's Men appear to have used the Globe from around April or May. In performance at the Globe, the 'house' that Face and Subtle exploit becomes more securely fictional; in the larger space of the open-air playhouse on the Bankside, across the river from the Blackfriars, the role of fantasy in keeping the play's precarious narrative afloat is brought to the fore.

In 1619, when Taylor inherited the role of Othello from Burbage, the King's Men did not maintain separate repertories in their two playhouses. As I will explore in further detail in later chapters, some of the plays of their most important dramatists continued to receive their first performances at the Globe as late as the early 1630s. By the mid-1630s, however, things may have been changing. The prologue to William Davenant's *News from Plymouth*, licensed for the Globe on 1 August 1635 (Bawcutt 1996: 193), claims that '*each Spectator knows / This House, and season, does more promise shewes / Dancing, and Buckler Fights, then Art, or Witt*' (1673: 1). A similarly condescending attitude towards the Globe and its audiences appears in a prologue written around 1640 for James Shirley's *The Doubtful Heir*, which grumbles about being at the Globe:

> Our Author did not calculate this Play
> For this Meridian; the Banckside, he knows,
> Are far more skilfull at the Ebbes and flows
> Of water, than of wit [...]
>   you that can contract your selves, and sit
> As you were now in the *Black-Fryers* pit;
> And will not deaf us, with leud noise and tongues,
> Because we have no Heart to break our Lungs,
> Will pardon our vast Stage, and not disgrace
> This Play, meant for your persons, not the place.
>   (1653: A3r)

Such comments suggest that by the mid-1630s some dramatists and spectators felt that the Blackfriars was superior to the Globe, and new plays were written with one or the other playhouse in mind, even if playwrights' intentions for their plays were at times ignored. This shift may have had implications for the performance of plays such as *Othello* and *The Alchemist*, and it is worth considering the potential impact of the rise of the Blackfriars on Shakespeare's play in particular.

It is not that *Othello* did not adapt well to the Blackfriars, but its success there may have come at a price, and the role of Othello may have become less prized when the Blackfriars became the more prestigious of the King's Men's playhouses. In particular, the effects of candlelight on artificially blackened skin may have meant that the role became more technically challenging. Recent performances at the Sam Wanamaker Playhouse at Shakespeare's Globe, designed to represent an archetypal early seventeenth-century indoor playhouse (Tosh 2018: 13–15), suggest that the material conditions of indoor playing and, in particular, the use of candlelight, pose problems for actors of colour. In Ellen McDougall's 2017 production of *Othello* the candlelight combined with the dark wood of the Wanamaker's frons and a newly stained darkwood floor to render the features of Kurt Egyiawan, playing Othello, almost invisible at times. A year later, in August 2018, a performance workshop led by Farah Karim-Cooper and Erika Lin in the same theatre as part of a Globe festival on 'Shakespeare and Race', with Ayanna Thompson and Kim F. Hall as respondents, sought to explore the problem of candlelight's effect on actors of colour in more depth. Interviewed ahead of the event, Karim-Cooper commented that '[u]sing the same lighting and stage design as you do for white actors puts actors of colour at a disadvantage. There is a danger with traditionally dark, tragic, stage settings, that actors of colour merge into the background' (quoted in Sawer 2018).

Although it has been less studied in relation to stage practice, this phenomenon has been widely noted in film lighting, Richard Dyer noting that '[m]ovie lighting in effect discriminates on the basis of race […] [it] relates people to each other and to setting according to notions of the human that have historically excluded non-white people'.[14] Universal lighting, as it is used at Shakespeare's Globe and, less consistently, in the Sam Wanamaker Playhouse, is not designed to light specific individuals and thereby privilege their individuality, freedom and autonomy, a tactic that Dyer describes in film lighting, but it can nonetheless discriminate against actors of colour. The

Globe workshop concluded, as McDougall's production had perhaps unintentionally demonstrated, that a combination of candlelight and dark surrounds makes the features of darker-skinned actors difficult to see, even for spectators sitting near the stage. Furthermore, such problems may have been exacerbated in the Jacobean and Caroline playhouse because the black skin of the actor playing Othello was not natural but dull and artificial.

Thus, as indoor playing became more prestigious, the relative desirability of the roles of Othello and Iago may have shifted. The development of complex black characters such as Othello, which Virginia Mason Vaughan argues was fuelled from the late 1580s by the adoption of the stage technology of blackface in place of leather or fabric masks or vizards (2005: 10–12), may itself have been facilitated by the outdoor playhouses that emerged in London in the late 1570s, their natural light allowing the actor's facial expressions to be 'read' more easily. In contrast, in an indoor playhouse, the effects of candlelight on the artificially blackened skin of the actor playing Othello would have made his facial expressions harder to read, impairing his ability to connect with spectators and inspire the tragic pity that is so crucial to the role. Playhouse conditions themselves shaped the impact of individual roles and, thereby, their value among the actors of the King's Men.

It may not, therefore, be a testament merely to the ability of the boy actor who played Desdemona at Oxford in September 1610 that Henry Jackson singled him out for praise in his description of the King's Men's performance of *Othello*. Having described the scandalous performances of *The Alchemist*, Jackson writes that

> They also held tragedies which they acted decorously and aptly. They moved (the audience to) tears in these (tragedies) not only by what they said but also by what they did. –
>
> – But indeed that Desdemona, who was slain before us by her husband, although she always pleaded her case very

well, nevertheless moved (us) more after she was murdered, when lying on the bed she appealed to the spectators' pity with her very expression. –

(Elliott et al., 2004: 2.1037–8)

We do not know the precise location of this performance, but it is likely to have been an indoor venue, reflecting practice at the Blackfriars or at court more than that at the Globe. We should therefore imagine the pale, cosmeticized face of the boy playing Desdemona shimmering as he controlled the spectators with his facial expression alone, exploiting what Karim-Cooper has called the 'arousing glister of the fair face' and the 'dramatic spectacle of [Othello's] cosmeticized blackness and the glistening white of the boy'.[15]

Jackson's comments may also indicate, however, that candlelit indoor performances privileged whiteness. The boy actor's whitened face was easier to see and 'read' than Burbage's blackened face, and this is a play in which seeing faces is important. As Ambereen Dadabhoy notes, Shakespeare's play 'turns on the epistemology of sight'; she argues that Othello himself 'embodies the limits of sight because he is the site where the gaze is confronted by opacity, necessitating interpretation' (2014: 121). In indoor performance, this 'opacity' would have been exaggerated. Othello's final speech, with its defiant assertion of his 'service' to the Christian, Venetian state and its recovery of the rhetorical panache of his appearance in Act 1 must have rung around the Globe, especially in contrast with the silence of dogged silence of Iago. But was its impact reduced at Blackfriars, where Iago could gather attention to himself, like the actor who played Desdemona, with the power of his facial expression?

In the early days of the King's Men's possession of the Blackfriars, when the status of the two playhouses was more equal, the technical difficulties of playing Othello indoors may have mattered less, especially if theatregoers were already accustomed to pitying and empathizing with Burbage's Othello. However, by the mid-1630s, as the Blackfriars became increasingly key to the King's Men's prestige, the difficulty of playing Othello and the attractions of playing Iago – his collusion with the audience, the complexity of his stage persona, his position as the driver of the plot, his eventual humiliation of Othello and the sheer size of his role – may have propelled Taylor's desire to switch. A comparison with *The Alchemist* is again instructive. The latter stages of Jonson's play hinge on questions about Face's intentions and his response to the moment of crisis when Lovewit unexpectedly returns. Face's dialogue at the start of Act 5, Scene 2 suggests that he smoothly accommodates the appearance of Lovewit, but his aside when Surly and Mammon enter – 'How shall I beat them off? What shall I do? – / Nothing's more wretched than a guilty conscience' (5.2.46–7) – and his further asides as the other gulls appear, not only suggest greater emotional turmoil but also focus spectators' attention on him. His facial expressions would also provide vital supplementary information about his newly reconfigured attitudes towards and feelings for Subtle and Doll, especially at the moment at which he tells Doll 'I am sorry for thee, i'faith', but then immediately undercuts this sympathy by promising to find her a new bawd (5.4.139–40). Face remains the focus of attention as the play ends, occupying the liminal space that the epilogue creates between character and actor, and dominating the Blackfriars stage in a way that became increasingly difficult for Othello to achieve.

*

Othello and *The Alchemist* provide a striking example of how we can use the fragmentary evidence that survives to document the casting and performance of the plays of the King's Men to open up new questions about their stage lives in the early seventeenth century. The plays weathered changes in the composition of the company, the acquisition or shifts in status of performance spaces and the demands of successive generations of playgoers, but they did not emerge unchanged. The evidence that I have explored in this chapter suggests that, rather than presenting a relatively static set of 'lines' of roles, passed in an orderly fashion from one generation of actors to the next, the repertory of the King's Men was subject to a more varied set of changes in casting. Leading actors could inherit roles from various of their predecessors, and actors might even shift roles within a play. This flexibility in casting has implications for our understanding not only of the practices that surrounded casting but also the range of responses that a spectator might have to an actor's performance, based on his current or past repertory of roles, or to that of the company as a whole. By looking beyond Burbage, this chapter has also traced the origins of some practices that still linger in the performance of these plays. The 'matador' casting of a heavy Othello and a light-footed Iago, and the dominance in performance of Iago over Othello, both appear to date not from the earliest performances of Shakespeare's play or those of the Restoration, but from the 1630s. It is not, therefore, an inevitable feature of the performance of *Othello*, but one that has its own history and origins in the specific contexts of Shakespearean performance in the neglected period between 1616 and 1660.

Interlude: Playing the Court, 1619–20

This third interlude returns to the moment of Richard Burbage's death and the recruitment of Joseph Taylor, exploring a set of plays that the Master of the Revels, George Buc, appears to have been considering for court performance during the Christmas season of 1619–20.[1] Buc's notes are preserved only in fragments, but they nonetheless list a substantial collection of plays of the King's Men: *The Captain*, *The Winter's Tale*, *The Two Noble Kinsmen*, *Volpone* (which is crossed out), *The Mayor of Quinborough or Hengist, King of Kent*, *The Maid's Tragedy*, *Hamlet*, *The Tragedy of Hieronimo*, *Philaster, or Love Lies a Bleeding*, an unidentifiable 'Comedy' and tragedy, *The Knight of Malta* and *2 Henry IV* ('[Seco]nd part of Falstaff'). *2 Henry IV* appears to be described as '[not p]laid y^{eis} 7. yeres', a possible allusion to the court season of 1612–13, when 'Sr Iohn Falstafe' was performed (Chambers 1925: 481–2). Along with the performance history of some of the other plays, such as *The Knight of Malta*, which must have been played after 22 April 1618 when one of its principal actors, Thomas Holcombe, was apprenticed to John Heminges (Kathman 2004a: 10), this suggests that Buc made his notes in 1619–20.

It is noticeable that the King's Men did not retire plays in which Burbage is known to have played leading roles, such as *Hamlet*, *The Spanish Tragedy* and *Volpone*. Moreover, the list reflects the late Jacobean consolidation of the repertory around the work of a small group of dramatists: Shakespeare, represented by *The Winter's Tale*, *Hamlet*, *The Two Noble Kinsmen* and *2 Henry IV*; Fletcher, represented by *The Maid's Tragedy*, *Philaster*, *The Knight of Malta* and *The Two Noble Kinsmen*; Jonson, represented by *Volpone*; and Middleton, represented by *The Mayor of Queenborough*. Thomas Kyd's *The Spanish Tragedy*, listed by Buc as *The Tragedy of Hieronimo*, was a long-standing favourite; first performed around 1587, it may have been acquired by the company in the 1590s (Syme 2013). The scraps also list *The Scholar Turned to School Again*, *The False Friend* and 'The Cambridge Playe of Albumazar and Trinculo', all of which may also have been in the repertory of the King's Men. It may seem odd that the King's Men would perform Thomas Tomkins's university drama *Albumazar*, but – as I will describe below – they were later commissioned to perform William Cartwright's Oxford play, *The Royal Slave*. It is therefore possible that the idea of commissioning a commercial playing company to perform an academic play had its roots in the earlier period, and that the repertory of the King's Men was even broader than has generally been thought.[2]

One problem that we face in reconstructing this court season is the fact that we do not know whether Nathan Field lived through it. He was alive in May 1619, when the King's Men were issued with a new set of royal livery, but he had died by 2 August 1620, when his sister, Dorcas Rice, was granted administration of his estate (Bentley 1941–68: 1: 72; Honigmann and Brock 1993: 231). It is notable, however, that Buc's lists include *The Two Noble Kinsmen*, a play that would be well suited to two actors – Taylor and Field – who were exact contemporaries, had worked together in Lady Elizabeth's men, and were known for both comic and tragic roles. The inclusion of *The Knight of Malta*, which Field co-authored with Fletcher and Massinger, may further suggest that Field was alive when the lists were drawn up. This play features three large leading roles: the young probationer knight Miranda (531 lines), the older, morally dubious knight Mountferrat (459 lines) and the forthright Danish knight Norandine (417 lines), who does not accept full knighthood because he refuses to give up drink and women.[3] When the play was originally performed in 1618, these roles are likely to have been played by Field, Burbage and Lowin respectively; while Taylor could easily have picked up the role of Mountferrat in 1619, it is less easy to see why the King's Men would want to revive it and play it at court if they had since lost another of its leads.

Complex questions are also posed by *2 Henry IV* and *Volpone*. Burbage played the lead in Jonson's play and it is likely that it was taken over by Lowin, to whom it is assigned by James Wright (1699: 4), in place of Sir Politick Would-Be, his original role in the play (see Riddell 1969: 292–3). Taylor probably inherited the role of Mosca from Condell, who appears to have retired from playing around 1619. Field played Voltore before Burbage's death and is likely to have retained that role. Wright also says that Lowin played Falstaff, but it is less clear when he acquired that role or who played it before him. Leading candidates for the original Falstaff are William Kemp, who left the Chamberlain's Men in 1599, or Thomas Pope, who died in spring 1603, just before Lowin himself joined the company (Shakespeare 2002: 78–9). It is even possible that Pope inherited the role from Kemp, passing it in turn to Lowin. The role of Prince Henry – which could easily have been played by Field or Taylor – may also have become available at this time, either through Burbage's death or Condell's retirement.

In this context, the inclusion of *Hamlet* and *The Spanish Tragedy* in Buc's lists may mark Taylor's claim to the status of the King's Men's leading player. '[Y]oung Hamlett' and 'old Hieronimo' are cited by Fletcher as key Burbage roles in his elegy, and the same pair of roles are invoked by William Cavendish, Earl of Newcastle, in *Wit's Triumvirate*, in which

Clyster imagines the impact 'if Burbage's soul had newly revived Hamlet and Jeronimo again'.[4] Did the King's Men seek to pay tribute to Burbage in their selection of plays, or to demonstrate their ability to reconstitute themselves around a new leading man? We do not know how similar Taylor's Hamlet was to Burbage's, but at the very least the substitution of a new voice, face and body in the role would have unsettled spectators' understanding of the character, as the fifty-year-old Burbage was succeeded by a man who was nearly twenty years younger. '[Y]oung Hamlett' was rejuvenated, while the performance of 'old Hieronimo' relied to a greater degree on the performance of age. If Taylor indeed took on the roles of Hamlet and Hieronimo in 1619, he would immediately have demonstrated both his virtuosity and his ability to play roles across a spectrum of ages.

Buc's lists thus mark a key point of transition in the history of the King's Men, from Burbage to Taylor, and combining them with other surviving information about the casting of the plays again suggests the complexity of the ways in which roles were passed from one actor to another. Like the material discussed in Chapter 2, the list also suggests the importance of the period between 1616 and 1660 to the stage-lives of Shakespeare's plays. Although we are accustomed to think of Burbage as the great, incomparable star of the Shakespearean stage, it is striking to note that the Hamlet remembered in the Restoration was not Burbage but Taylor. James Wright claims that Taylor 'Acted *Hamlet* incomparably well' (1699: 4), while John Downes treats Taylor as if he were the first actor to play the role when he describes its descent to Thomas Betterton: 'Sir *William* [Davenant] (having seen *Mr. Taylor* of the *Black-Fryars* Company Act it, who being Instructed by the Author *Mr. Shaksepeur* [sic]) taught Mr. Betterton in every Particle of it' (1708: 21). In 1619, Taylor's performance must have been 'ghosted' by that of Burbage, but he appears to have left his own mark on the role. The Restoration Hamlet had its roots in this second Hamlet, not the first.

3

Painful Adventures: *Pericles* and the 'Traffic' of the Stage

A peculiar but arresting insight into the stage-life of one of Shakespeare's most popular plays is offered by an anecdote in a 1630s jest-book, *The Book of Bulls*:

> [T]Wo Gentlemen went to see *Pericles* acted, and one of them was moved with the calamities of that Prince that he wept, whereat the other laughed extreamely. Not long after the same couple went to see the Major of Qinborough [*sic*], when he who jeered the other at *Pericles* now wept himselfe, to whom the other laughing, sayd, what the Divell should there bee in this merry play to make a man weep. O, replied the other, who can hold from weeping to see a Magistrate so abused?
>
> The Jest will take those who have seene these two plaies.
> (Anon 1636: f9r–v)

The jest juxtaposes Shakespeare and Wilkins's *Pericles*, originally performed nearly thirty years earlier, with another longstanding favourite from the repertory of the King's Men, Middleton's *The Mayor of Queenborough, or Hengist, King of Kent*. The plays appear to have been selected because they present such generic and emotional extremes, and a 'right' and 'wrong' response is provided for each play. The 'Magistrate' with whom the second gentleman sympathizes is Simon the tanner, who becomes Mayor of Queenborough, Kent, in a spectacular rise to prominence that mirrors and parodies that of the Saxon invader Hengist. The scene recalled here appears at the start of Act 5, when Simon is gulled by a company of 'cheaters' impersonating travelling players, one of whom throws meal in his face and steals his purse. Simon's comic humiliation is presented in a very different fashion from the 'calamities' of Pericles, who is propelled around the Mediterranean by fate, circumstance and extreme weather, first losing and then finally being reunited with his wife and daughter. The jest as a whole analyses both the ways in which spectators might immerse themselves in the dramatic fiction and the ways in which they might resist it.

I will come back to this jest, and the paradoxical responses of the two gentlemen, later in this chapter, but I want to return for a moment to the idea of 'traffic' that I touched on in Chapter 1. As we have seen, in his critique of the use of boy actors on the Jacobean stage, Francis Rous refers to the 'merchandize of Play-boyes' and 'counterfeiting intisement to that trafficke' (1622: O10v). It is worth spending a little time with the term 'traffic' in order to set up some of the key concerns of this chapter. In early modern English, it referred to the activity of trade and the transportation of goods and people. The fact that a 'traffic' was a synonym for a prostitute links it to what was later termed 'human traffic', 'human trafficker' being a term used in the context of the Atlantic slave trade as early as the eighteenth century (*OED*, traffic, *n.*; *OED*, human trafficker, *n.*). Rous's use of the term seems to encompass the range of early modern meanings of the term 'traffic', from trade to servitude and sexual exploitation.

The 'traffic' to which Rous refers was not confined to boys, however, but also extended to other actors. Holger Schott Syme has explored in a recent essay the ways in which the King's

Men drew on other companies to renew themselves in the early years of James's reign (2019a: 239–40), and the acquisition of Joseph Taylor shortly after Richard Burbage's death in 1619 is another example of their power to 'traffic' in leading men as well as boys. This practice is reflected in a warrant issued to Taylor and John Lowin in May 1633 that gave them the right to 'choose, receaue & take into yo*u*r Company any such Actor or Actors belonging to any of the licensed Companyes w*i*thin & about the Citty of London' on the grounds that

> the late decease, infirmity & sicknes of diuerse principall Actors of his M*aj*esties Company of Players hath much decayed & weakened them, soe that they are disabled to doe his M*aj*esty service in their quality, vnlesse there bee some speedy order taken to supply & furnish them with a convenient number of new Actors.[1]

Circumstances in 1633 may indeed have been tough for the King's Men. The death of the rising star Richard Sharpe in January 1632 appears to have hit the company hard, and a longstanding hired man, William Mago, also died in the same year. The reference to 'decease, infirmity & sicknes' suggests, moreover, that a range of bodily ailments may have prevented actors from performing regularly. It is not clear whether the warrant represents a break with earlier methods of recruitment, the formalization of an informal practice or the continuation of an established tradition. However, it underscores the links between the 'traffic' in players and the company's status as the king's 'servants', who were issued with royal livery on an annual basis. As Urvashi Chakravarty notes, 'the languages of livery engaged, resisted, and problematized fictions and depictions of free service and consensual labor' (2012: 366). The King's Men's ability to use their status as royal servants to press others into service underlines the workings of these contradictions in real life.

The word 'traffic' also has a wider resonance in the context of the early modern theatre industry, bringing together a number of its activities. Rous refers to the trafficking of actors, and the responses of the two playgoers in the joke about *Pericles* and *The Mayor of Queenborough* remind us that spectators also played a part in these exchanges, but the act of making plays could also be termed 'traffic'. 'I am not known unto the open stage, / Nor do I traffic in their theatres' (1.2.50–1), the poet Ovid tells his father in Ben Jonson's *Poetaster*, performed by the Children of the Chapel around 1601, while Thomas Heywood in *An Apology for Actors* refers to 'they whose pennes haue had the greatest trafficke with the Stage' (1612: B3r). The transaction between playing company and audience that takes place when a play is performed is also 'traffic', as in the reference of the Prologue in Shakespeare's *Romeo and Juliet*, originally performed by the Chamberlain's Men around 1595, to 'the two hours' traffic of our stage' (12). The 'gentlemen' in *The Book of Bulls* engage with the 'traffic' of the King's Men, and in the process they enter into a set of commercial, aesthetic and emotional transactions that the jest both exploits and parodies.

It is a coincidence, but a satisfying one, that the entry for '*traffique*', glossed as 'bargayning', in Robert Cawdry's glossary of difficult words, *A Table Alphabetical* (1609), appears directly before those for '*tragèdian*', 'a maker, or player of a tragedie', '*tragedie*', 'a solemne play, describing cruell murders and sorrowes' and '*tragicall*', 'cruell, sorrowful like a tragedie' (1609: I5r). Accidental as it may be, Cawdry's juxtaposition of 'traffic' with terms relating to the workings of dramatic genre point us towards a further use of the term in Janet Clare's recent book, *Shakespeare's Stage Traffic*, which explores 'the matter and practice of plays [that] were trafficked amongst playwrights and amongst communities of spectators', the 'histories, narrative patterns, and dramatic scenarios [that] were circulated on stage with little regard to origins or originality' (2014: 1). Her book is part of a broader trend within scholarship that considers in detail the intricate ways in which texts and performances interact. Further examples include Louise George Clubb's exploration of the 'interchange and transformation of units, figures, relationships, actions, *topoi*, and framing patterns', which combine to form what she calls a 'theatregram' (1989: 6), and the study of the various forms of interaction between material and performative elements within plays that scholars have termed 'intertheatricality' (see Bratton 2003: 37–8; Harris 2009: 69; West 2013).

This chapter extends these approaches to consider the trafficking of plays, narratives and actors that characterize the extended stage history of *Pericles*. It visits *Pericles* at four different moments: its earliest performances in 1607–8; a revival of 1619, when it appeared in repertory with John Fletcher and Philip Massinger's *The Custom of the Country*; a revival of 1631, when it appeared alongside both *The Custom of the Country* and Massinger's *Believe as You List*; and its appearance in *The Book of Bulls* in 1636, around the time of the composition of Thomas Killigrew's *The Princess* (*c.* 1635–6). It argues that *Pericles* and these three later plays, all of which draw heavily on its narrative and characters, both embody and critique the King's Men's 'trafficking' of plays, narratives and actors. These plays traverse the Mediterranean, buffeting their characters from country to country and dramatizing the threats that this involuntary travel poses to their personal liberty, health and bodily integrity. They deal with pressing ethical questions relating to imperialism, encounter, servitude and, especially, slavery, and they do so within an institutional framework in which actors were circulated, commodified and consumed by spectators.

1607–8: *Pericles*

From the moment of its first performance around 1607–8, *Pericles* was not merely popular, but a byword for theatrical success. A 1609 pamphlet, *Pimlico, or Run Redcap*, describes a crowd of cut-throats who are as busy and noisy as the crowd at a new play, 'So that I truly thought all These / Came to see

Shore, or *Pericles*' (Anon 1609: C1r), while the prologue to Robert Tailor's *The Hog Hath Lost his Pearl*, performed by a group of apprentices at the Whitefriars playhouse in 1613, concludes by saying '*if it prove so happy as to please, / We'll say 'tis fortunate like* Pericles' (1614: A3v). It was quickly adapted as prose fiction, in the shape of *The Painful Adventures of Pericles Prince of Tyre, Being the True History of the Play of Pericles*, published in 1608 by George Wilkins, Shakespeare's apparent collaborator in the play. Even this non-dramatic version acknowledges the place of the King's Men in the play's popularity, as Wilkins 'intreat[s]' his readers 'to receiue this Historie in the same maner as it was vnder the habite of ancient *Gower* the famous English Poet, by the Kings Maiesties Players excellently presented' (1608: A3r).

Pericles was designed as a star vehicle, being one of a sequence of plays of this period featuring outsize leading roles that look as if they were designed for Richard Burbage. Pericles is by far the largest role in *Pericles*, with 570 lines; Gower, in second place with 310 lines, does not appear in the main narrative of the play, and the third largest role is Marina, who has only 154 lines (King 1992: 249–51). Similar structures appear in Shakespeare and Middleton's *Timon of Athens* (*c*. 1607) and *Coriolanus* (*c*. 1609–10). Timon has 867 lines, followed by Apemantus with 251 lines and Alcibiades with 157; Caius Martius in *Coriolanus* has 872 lines, followed by Menenius with 579 lines and Volumnia with 316 (King 1992: 239–40, 236–8). These roles exploit to the full the power that the individual performer might gain as he stood on the Globe stage, the focus of spectators' attention, yet each play also complicates and undermines that position. Timon withdraws himself from the final scenes of the play that takes his name, which refuses to provide a grand finale; he dies offstage and is memorialized in a nihilistic epitaph that refuses mourning and concludes with the lines '*Pass by and curse thy fill, but pass and stay not here thy gait*' (5.5.70). Caius Martius is ingloriously killed by a group of conspirators and his antagonist Aufidius then '*stands on him*' (5.6.131SD). Pericles retreats from view after the apparent death of his wife and daughter, 'in sorrow all devoured', vowing 'Never to wash his face nor cut his hairs' (4.4.25, 28), leaving his daughter to take his place at centre-stage in the play's final act.

The demands that *Pericles* places on its leading players are underscored by its treatment of the hardships that Pericles and Marina undergo and its constant recourse to the common early modern pun on 'travel' and 'travail'. The play's initial uses of these terms cluster around geographical travel: Hellicanus, for example, advises Pericles to 'go travel' to avoid King Antiochus's wrath (1.2.104), while Thaliard declares that he has 'understood / Your lord has betook himself to unknown travels' (1.3.33–4). Yet Pericles' 'travels' increasingly become his 'travails', as his own body and the bodies of those he loves are subjected to various kinds of effort and endurance. In the Act 3 Prologue, Gower describes the moment during the storm at which Thaisa goes into labour: 'The lady shrieks and, well-a-near, / Does fall in travail with her fear' (3.0.51–2). Pericles himself refers to 'my queen's travails' (3.1.14), emphasizing the play's treatment of childbirth as a form of hardship or labour. Yet the act of sexual intercourse could itself be described as 'travail', as Bolt punningly suggests in Act 4 when he claims that the brothel might attract 'of every nation a traveller' by advertising Marina for sale (4.2.105). Collectively, then, the uses of 'travel' and 'travail' in *Pericles* gather together the various forms of translocation, strain and hardship that its characters undergo.

Another aspect of the play's language crystallizes the threat posed to Marina in the later stages of the play. In the opening scene, Pericles describes himself as 'son and servant to [Antiochus's] will' (1.1.24), and he similarly imagines himself bound to Hellicanus when he describes him as 'Fit counsellor and servant for a prince, / Who by thy wisdom makes a prince thy servant' (1.2.61–2). This discourse eventually rebounds on Marina. Gower refers to Marina's 'unholy service' when he describes her entry into the Mytilene brothel (4.4.50), and images of service and travel/travail coalesce when the Bawd asks Lysimachus of Marina, 'Is she not a fair creature?' and he replies, 'Faith, she would serve after a long voyage at sea' (4.6.39–41). Summing up her plight to Pericles, Marina declares that 'time hath rooted out my parentage, / And to the world, and awkward casualties, / Bound me in servitude' (4.6.83–5). The play never quite articulates the fact that its central female character is sold into sexual slavery, but the repetition of euphemisms like 'servitude' and 'unholy service' serve both to express and cloak the ways in which its characters are trafficked.

It is thus appropriate that the title-page of the first edition of *Pericles* does not focus solely on Pericles himself; instead, it describes the play as 'THE LATE, And much admired Play, called Pericles, Prince of Tyre. With the true Relation of the whole Historie, aduentures, and fortunes of the said Prince: As also, the no lesse strange, and worthy accidents, in the birth and life, of his daughter *MARIANA* [*sic*].' Marina's declaration that she 'ne're before invited eyes, / But have been gazed on like a comet' (5.1.76–7) encapsulates the quality of the play in performance, in which the actors playing father and daughter are subjected to attention that is potentially curious, sympathetic and prurient. Like the gentlemen of the jest quoted at the head of this chapter, spectators are encouraged to weep, but the play also confronts, in its tough-minded treatment of the brothel scenes, the kind of spectator who might be expected to 'laugh extremely'.

Pericles makes significant demands not only on the actor who plays Pericles, but also on the boy player who performed the role of Marina – perhaps John Rice, William Ecclestone or Richard Robinson. Spectators' enjoyment of the encounter between father and daughter in the play's final scenes may have been fuelled not only by the fulfilment of the expectations built up by the narrative of a happy reunion, but also by the way in which two familiar performers are brought together. If Marina's role was not doubled, this would have been the first time that they had shared a stage, lending the meeting of the estranged father and daughter an odd undertone of familiarity that may have heightened its emotional impact. However, if the actor who played Marina also played Antiochus's daughter – the most plausible piece of doubling if he was required to take two speaking roles – the scene may have had a different quality. The reunion of Pericles and Marina radically inverts the dynamics of the earlier one scene, but the ghost of Antiochus's daughter nonetheless may have haunted it. In its original early Jacobean moment, therefore, *Pericles* presented a showcase for the star actor that nonetheless left space for the boy actor to make his mark. Moreover, the play's thematic interest in travel, travail and sexual servitude point to all of the varied meanings of the term 'traffic' with which this chapter is concerned.

1619: *The Custom of the Country*

The death of the first Pericles, Richard Burbage, occurred shortly after that of another Jacobean celebrity, Anna of Denmark, queen consort of James I. Writing to Dudley Carleton on 19 March, John Chamberlain elided the death of queen and player: 'the quenes funerall is put of to the 29th of the next moneth, to the greate hinderance of our players, which are forbidden to play so long as her body is aboue ground[:] one speciall man among them Burbage is lately dead, and hath left they say better than 300[1] land'.[2] Anna was eventually buried on 13 May, her funeral having been postponed until sufficient funds could be raised to support its expense, and the King's Men appear to have been permitted to play again, without Burbage. On 19 May the company was issued with a livery list in which Burbage's successor, Joseph Taylor, was listed last; on the following day, however, Taylor is likely to have been at the centre of attention, performing the role of Pericles as part of a high-profile farewell to the departing French ambassador.[3] The King's Men's performance of the play in the 'kinges greate Chamber' was accompanied by other festivities in the 'greate chamber', 'pryuy chamber' and 'bedd Chamber' of the recently deceased queen.[4] One invitee, Philip Herbert, Earl of Pembroke, was overcome by the situation, writing that night to Viscount Doncaster, 'even now all the company are at the play, which I being tender harted could not endure to see so soone after the loss of my old acquaintance Burbadg'.[5] For Herbert, and perhaps for some of the other spectators, it would have been 'painful' indeed to see another actor undertake Pericles' adventures.

Not long after the court performance of *Pericles*, Taylor took one of the leading roles in Fletcher and Massinger's *The Custom of the Country*, a play that takes aspects of the narrative and locations – notably that of the brothel – of the earlier play and reworks them in an ironic vein. *The Custom of the Country* was probably designed to capitalize not only on interest in its main source, Cervantes's *Los trabajos de Persiles y Sigismunda*, which was entered in the Stationers' Register on 22 February 1619 and published later that year, but also on the potential of the newly reconfigured King's Men. Taylor appears at the head of the list of the principal actors printed in the 1679 folio, alongside John Lowin, Nicholas Tooley, John Underwood, Robert Benfield, William Ecclestone, Richard Sharpe and Thomas Holcombe (Beaumont and Fletcher 1679: M2r). Yet unlike *Pericles*, in which Taylor would have been a central attraction, *The Custom of the Country* features two large roles for leading adult players; like *Othello*, it presents a duo rather than a solo star turn. Taylor probably took the second largest role, the romantic lead Arnoldo, who has 406 lines, while the largest, that of Arnoldo's witty, blunt and morally suspect brother, the significantly named Rutillio, who has 501 lines, is likely to have been taken by Lowin.[6]

Fletcher and Massinger's play makes significant demands on its leading boy players. It includes four important female roles: Hippolita, who pursues Arnoldo (the play's third largest role, with 300 lines); Zenocia, Arnoldo's betrothed and later wife, who is placed in Hippolita's household as a slave (the play's fourth largest role, with 281 lines); Guiomar, who saves

Rutillio at a crucial point in the narrative and eventually marries him (the play's fifth largest role, with 275 lines); and the bawd Sulpitia. In this it reflects *Pericles*, which also has four prominent female roles: Marina, Thaisa, Dionyza and the Bawd. Candidates for these roles include Sharpe, then aged eighteen, and Holcombe, aged around nineteen. As we saw in Chapter 1, Sharpe played the Duchess in *The Duchess of Malfi* around this time. He also appears in the actor-lists for a series of Fletcherian plays in which he played female roles: *The Mad Lover* (1616), *The Knight of Malta* (1618), *The Loyal Subject* (1618), *The False One* (1619), *The Humorous Lieutenant* (1619), *The Laws of Candy* (1620), *The Little French Lawyer* (1620), *Women Pleased* (1620), *The Island Princess* (1621), *The Double Marriage* (1622), *The Prophetess* (1622) and *The Lovers' Progress* (1623). Holcombe's career is less well documented, but he appears in the actor-lists for *The Knight of Malta*, *The Queen of Corinth* (1618), *The Little French Lawyer*, *Women Pleased* and *The Prophetess*, and he played the Provost's Wife in *Sir John Van Olden Barnavelt* in August 1619 (King 1992: 38). Another boy actor, Nicholas Crosse, was apprenticed to Heminges on 25 May 1614; he played Barnavelt's Wife in *Barnavelt*, and I have found a later, unflattering, reference to him when he was nearing the end of his ten-year term, in the shape of an entry in the parish register of St Olave, Bermondsey, which records that 'Nicholas the Reputed son of Nicholas Crosse Staggeplayer of the body of Ann [blank] out of the Cagge [i.e. cage, or local prison] at battoll bridge' was baptized on 17 September 1623.[7]

Like *Pericles*, *The Custom of the Country* depicts involuntary or enforced travel, repeatedly invoking the travel/ travail pun and underscoring its connections with human and sexual trafficking. A betrothed couple, Zenocia and Arnoldo, flee from an unnamed country where the Governor, Clodio, enforces a *droit de seigneur* that allows him to usurp the place of the groom and sleep with any bride on her wedding night. Like that of *Pericles*, the narrative of *The Custom of the Country* has its origins in an act of sexual predation. Fletcher and Massinger could have increased this similarity had they chosen, given that in *Persiles y Sigismunda*, the new bride, Transilla, does not flee the governor but her husband's family, as the 'custom' in that story is that 'her husbands brothers, or (in default of such) the neerest kinsfolkes come to gather flowers in that garden where her husband onely should have entrance' (Cervantes 1619: E5v). However, the dramatists eschew this narrative and instead imitate *Pericles* by opening their play with the sexual misdemeanours of a ruler. In another echo of *Pericles*, in which Marina is carried off by pirates, Zenocia and Arnoldo are attacked by privateers off the coast of Lisbon. Zenocia is captured and given as a slave by one of their number, Leopold, to Hippolita, an Italian noblewoman who tries to woo Arnoldo for herself. Arnoldo's brother, Rutillio, who has accompanied the lovers, gets into a fight with a local nobleman, Duarte, and, thinking that he has killed him, takes refuge first in the house of Duarte's mother, Guiomar, and then in a male brothel. The sexual threat faced by Marina is thus displaced onto Rutillio, who is first delighted and later exhausted by his employment.

When the narrative reaches Lisbon, another discourse, which has driven the earlier action but remained unspoken, emerges, that of slavery. The year 1619 saw not only the death of Richard Burbage but also a more significant event: the transportation of the first recorded cargo of enslaved people from Africa to the English colony at Jamestown, Virginia.[8] There are no direct allusions to Virginia in *The Custom of the Country*, but scholars such as Carolyn Prager (1988) and Amanda Bailey (2013: 97–116) have highlighted the urgency with which the play engages with issues of bondage and subjugation that were increasingly pressing as England's colonial aspirations intensified. *The Custom of the Country* reworks the language of service of *Pericles*, but it does so in ways that directly invoke the human bondage that is submerged in the earlier play. Duarte refers casually to slavery when he distains 'Young Don Alonzo, the great Captaines Nephew', saying, 'I looke downe upon him /With such contempt and scorne, as on my slave' (2.1.86, 91–2). When Zenocia is captured and taken by Leopold as 'spoile', she declares that 'No slavery can appear in such a forme, / Which with a masculine constancy, I will not / Boldly looke on and suffer' (2.2.50–2). As the play goes on, the language of slavery is increasingly used to describe erotic traffic and travail, in line with the 'unholy service' evoked in *Pericles*. The bawd Sulpitia promises to 'redeem' Rutillio from the 'slavery' of captivity, and he promises her his 'service'.

When *Pericles* and *The Custom of the Country* were performed in repertory in 1619, the forceful connections that Fletcher and Massinger draw between travel, travail, servitude and slavery would have had the capacity to rebound on Shakespeare and Wilkins's play, holding up to scrutiny the various forms of economic and sexual trafficking that are veiled by the conventions of romance. Moreover, the casting of individual actors across the two plays – for instance, the same player as Marina and Zenocia, or the Bawd and Sulpitia – would reinforce the connections between them. Simultaneously, long-term playgoers may have been reminded of the earlier actors who played Maria and the Bawd, and the longstanding traffic in boy players on which the theatre industry depended. The combined impact of the two plays was to link the stage traffic of the plays of the King's Men inexorably with human bondage, royal abuse and sexual exploitation. These connections were to be sustained and extended over the following decade, as *Pericles* and *The Custom of the Country* became staple plays in the Caroline repertory of the King's Men, and the basis of further new works.

1631: *Believe as You List*

Pericles and *The Custom of the Country* were both current on the stage in the late 1620s and early 1630s. *The Custom of the Country* was revived at the Blackfriars on 22 November 1628, when the Master of the Revels, Sir Henry Herbert, was granted a winter 'benefit' of £17 10s. (Bawcutt 1996: 167), and at court on 24 October 1630.[9] *Pericles* was performed at the Globe on 10 June 1631, when Herbert was given a 'gratuity' of £3 10s. by the King's Men 'upon the cessation of the plague' (Bawcutt 1996: 173). The success of these plays was in contrast to the apparently disastrous performances by the King's Men of Jonson's *The New Inn* in 1629; the title-page that accompanied *The New Inn* when it was published described it as 'neuer acted, but most negligently play'd, by some, the Kings Seruants, And more squeamishly beheld, and censured by others, the Kings Subiects' (Jonson 1631). The popularity of *Pericles* at this time clearly irritated Jonson; in an 'Ode to Himself' printed after *The New Inn*, he attributes the continued success of Shakespeare and Wilkins's play to the same lack of discernment among spectators that led to the rejection of his own work:

> No doubt some mouldy tale,
>   Like *Pericles*, and stale
> As the shrieve's crusts, and nasty as his fish-
>   Scraps, out every dish
> Thrown forth and raked into the common tub,
>   May keep up the play-club;
>   There sweepings do as well
>   As the best ordered meal.
> For who the relish of these guests will fit
> Needs set them but the alms-basket of wit.
>
> (ll. 21–30)

This was not the only allusion to *Pericles* around this time. James Shirley's dramatic adaptation of *The Arcadia*, performed by Queen Henrietta Maria's Men in 1632, incorporates a reference to *Pericles* when Pamela asks Dametas, 'What haste does tire you?' and he replies, 'Tire me, I am no woman, keepe your tires to your selfe / Nor am I *Pericles* prince of *Tyre*' (1640: B4v). The allusion invokes a complex form of nostalgia, as

Philip Sidney's reanimated Elizabethan romance exploits the ongoing life of a Jacobean play. *Pericles* may have been nearly thirty years old, but it had a significant impact on the theatrical culture of the early 1630s.

In dialogue with both *Pericles* and *The Custom of the Country* was a new play, Massinger's *Believe as You List*. It was originally submitted to Herbert in January 1631 as a play about a pretender to the identity of King Sebastian of Portugal. Sebastian died in Morocco in 1578, at the conflict known to the English as the Battle of Alcazar, but persistent rumours circulated that he had survived, and four different pretenders to his identity emerged over the following decades, posing a challenge to Spanish dominance of the Iberian peninsula. Herbert refused to licence Massinger's play 'because itt did contain dangerous matter, as the deposing of Sebastian king of Portugal, by Philip the <Second,> and ther being a peace sworen twixte the kings of England and Spayne' (Bawcutt 1996: 171–2). The 'peace' was a treaty signed between England and Spain in November 1630, which meant that plays dealing with Spanish material were both topical and risky. Undeterred, and apparently unwilling to waste the effort that he had put into the play, Massinger changed its setting, relocating it from turn-of-the-century Europe to the ancient world; in the process, he transformed Sebastian into Antiochus III, the conqueror of Lower Asia, and the Spanish Empire into the Roman Republic. Some of the earlier setting survives in the names of places and characters that have been crossed out in the manuscript, including Dom Sebastian (1927: ll. 634, 1127, 2662), 'Hermit' (l32), 'kinge Hiero' (1213) and Venice (1173). Herbert does not appear to have objected, and he licensed *Believe as You List*, its earlier title being lost, on 6 May (Bawcutt 1996: 172).

In addition to its use of the name Antiochus, *Believe as You List* has sustained structural parallels with *Pericles*, focusing on the physical and mental strain that involuntary travel and subjection place on its central figure. It also extends the associations of stage traffic with bondage, subjection and sexual exploitation, and it adds to the mix a metatheatrical concern with the status of the leading actor himself. The movements of Antiochus are even more constrained than those of Pericles. After announcing himself at Carthage, he is forced to flee to Bithynia, and is then taken to Callipolis, Syracuse and, finally, the Greek island prison Gyaros. In its original form, the play must have drawn much of its power from its focus on the desire of the Portuguese to regain their independence from Spain, while the revised version anatomizes the pressures faced by client states in the face of Rome's dominance of the ancient Mediterranean. Both versions of *Believe as You List* thus depicted the might of a colonial power, and its trafficking in the lives of those who have been subjected to it.

While none who encounter Antiochus doubt the truth of his claim, both the Carthaginian Senate and the Bithynian King Prusias are intimidated by Titus Flaminius, and Prusias eventually hands him over to the Romans. Antiochus is then subjected to various trials aimed at persuading him to deny his identity before he is paraded through the street of Callipolis, dressed and manacled as a slave, and imprisoned in the Roman galleys. In the final act, he is reunited with his old Roman friends Marcellus and Cornelia, but, even though Marcellus believes Antiochus's claims, he is unable to do more than have the former king transferred from the galleys to a prison. *Believe as You List* thus converts the tragicomic narrative structures of *Pericles*, complete with its repeated moments of recognition and the revelation of identity, into something that leans closer to tragedy but ultimately refuses tragic catharsis.

Other patterns within *Believe as You List* also point towards its interactions with *Pericles*. Like *The Custom of the Country* in 1619, this new play is able to speak back to *Pericles* and to shape the perspectives of 1630s playgoers towards it. The playhouse manuscript of *Believe as You List* includes annotations that allow us to reconstruct some of its casting. The play's largest roles were taken by Taylor, who played Antiochus (680 lines), and Lowin, who played Titus Flaminius (597 lines); the third largest role, the profane flamen

Berecinthius, was taken by Thomas Pollard (237 lines), and Robert Benfield played the fourth largest role, Marcellus (100 lines) (King 1992: 111–12). None of the five female roles are attributed in the manuscript. The largest is that of the Courtesan (105 lines), followed by Cornelia (100 lines) and the Queen of Bithynia (28 lines); there are also two smaller roles, a Lady attending the Queen and Zanthia, a servant to Cornelia, who is described as a 'Moore' in dialogue, stage directions and speech prefixes (Massinger 1927: ll. 2631SD, 2761, 2765SP). As described in Chapter 1, the company's boy actors in 1631 included John Thompson – who is likely to have played the singing role of the Courtesan – Alexander Gough and William Trigg. Like the revival of *The Alchemist* in the same year, described in Chapter 2, the production of *Believe as You List* – with its important but relatively limited female roles – may have helped to bridge a gap after John Honeyman graduated to male roles.

Like *The Custom of the Country*, *Believe as You List* focuses on a duo of two outsize leading roles for Taylor and Lowin; however, *Believe as You List* otherwise has casting patterns similar to *Pericles*, requiring most of its cast to double relatively small roles across its successive locations. Both *Believe as You List* and *Pericles* are structured around an extended series of encounters between the protagonist and this shifting cast of characters, but *Believe as You List* adds a new dimension by pitting Taylor's Antiochus against Lowin's Titus Flaminius. Where Shakespeare and Wilkins deploy the metatheatrical frame of the chorus, in the shape of Gower, Massinger exploits the idea that both Antiochus and Titus Flaminius are aware that they are acting out roles, giving an additional edge to their confrontations, which are framed not only as encounters between characters but between actors. Titus Flaminius declares in Act 3, Scene 1,

> I am on the stage
> and yf now in the scæne imposd vpon mee
> soe full of change, nay a meere labirinth

of politic*que* windinges I showe not my selfe
a Protean actor varijnge everie shape
with the occasion, it will hardlye poyze
the expectation.

(Massinger 1927: ll. 1201–7)

In the extremity of his tortures in Act 5, Antiochus similarly frames his experience in theatrical terms:

where lyes the scæne now?
thowgh the hangeinge of the stage were congeald gore
the Chorus flintye executioners
and the spectators, yf it coulde bee, more
inhumane then flaminivs, the cue gieven
the principall actor's readie.

(2608–13)

Antiochus alludes to the traditional performance of tragedy with black hangings on the stage (Gurr 2006; Stern 2016: 489–90), a practice that had probably lapsed by the 1630s, and the classical figure of the chorus, presenting his current predicament as a debasement of both. He and Titus Flaminius draw on two aspects of the leading player's skill-set: his ability to stand at the centre of attention as the 'principall actor' and his 'Protean' ability to vary his style to fit the demands of his role. Moreover, Massinger draws on Lowin's previous villain roles – such as Iago, Domitianus Caesar in Massinger's *The Roman Actor* and Iacomo in Carlell's *The Deserving Favourite* – in presenting Titus Flaminius as a scheming, self-conscious machiavel, and he exploits Taylor's track record as the tragic lead in *Othello*, *Hamlet* and *The Roman Actor*. In presenting the subjection of the tragedian, moreover, *Believe as You List* plays metatheatrical games with the ways in which leading actors appear to have been trafficked by the King's Men, a practice that is given royal sanction in the 1633 warrant.

Believe as You List deconstructs the figure of the leading actor on which plays such as *Pericles* centre, and it both exploits and rejects the emotions of spectators. Pericles subjects himself to both physical discipline and a traumatic encounter with nature and fate in the aftermath of Marina's supposed death. The stage directions for the dumbshow state that he '*makes lamentation, puts on sackcloth, and in a mighty passion departs*' (4.4.22SD), and Gower comments,

> He swears
> Never to wash his face, nor cut his hairs.
> He puts on sack, and to sea he bears
> A tempest, which his mortal vessel tears,
> And yet he rides it out.
>
> (4.4.27–31)

In contrast, Antiochus's identity is stripped away from him as he is buffeted not by storms but by the human agency of Titus Flamininus. In the most symbolic action of the play, the former king's subjection to Rome, his loss of realm and individual liberty is rendered visible through costume. Where Pericles' 'calamities' are marked by his traumatic refusal to cut his hair or wash his face, those of Antiochus are given more symbolic form in the shaved head and costume of the galley-slave. The moment is carefully prepared in a brief exchange between Flaminius and Sempronius that offers an implicit challenge to spectators not to be moved by Antiochus's appearance:

FLAMINIVS
   haue you forc'd on hym
   the habit of a slaue?
SEMPRONIVS
   yes, and in that
   pardon my weakenesse, still there does appeare
   a kinde of maiestie in hym.
FLAMINIVS
   you looke on it
   with the eies of foolishe pittie that deceiues you.

SEMPRONIVS
> this way Hee comes, and I beleeue when you see hym
> you'll bee of my opinion.
>
> (1927: ll. 2313–21)

Antiochus then enters, 'his head shaude in the habit of a slaue' (2322SD), and Massinger gives him a long speech in which both character and actor can engage spectators' sympathies. Especially powerful is the moment at which Antiochus draws attention to the symbolism of his costume, asking,

> is it not sufficient
> that the lockes of this once royall head are shau'd of
> my glo[r]ious robes changd to t[h]is slavishe habit
> this hande that graspd a scepter manaclde,
> or that I haue bene as a spectacle
> exposde to publicq*ue* scorne
>
> (ll. 2335–40)

Images of Antiochus as ruler, slave and actor are fused in this speech. Not only does he refer to himself as 'a spectacle', but the description of his change of costume recalls the references to players being 'stript of their borrowed apparell' (Primrose 1625: 2H1r) at the end of a play that appear in some anti-theatrical commentaries. Subjected to travel, travail, servitude and, eventually, slavery, Antiochus embodies the complex ways in which the plays of the King's Men expose the forms of trafficking on which they are nonetheless dependent.

1635–6: *The Princess*

As a regular playwright for the King's Men for over twenty years, Massinger was well placed to understand intimately the structures within the company. Yet a similarly potent response to *Pericles* and to the stage traffic of the King's Men appears in *The Princess*, written by the courtier-playwright Thomas Killigrew around 1635–6, and it is to that play, which also offers an intriguing new perspective on the text of *Pericles*, that I turn in the final section of this chapter.

The anecdote in *The Book of Bulls* strongly suggests that *Pericles* was current on the stage around 1636; these performances may have helped to inspire the composition of Killigrew's *The Princess*, even though its premiere may have been delayed until the playhouses reopened after a severe outbreak of plague in October 1637. *The Custom of the Country* was also part of this matrix of influence, and Fletcher and Massinger's play helped to mark further changes in the personnel of the King's Men when a new prologue and accompanying epilogue for it were written by an unidentified dramatist '*For my sonne Clarke*', that is, Hugh Clarke (Beaumont and Fletcher 1647: 2D1r). Clarke joined the company around 1636 in another example of the King's Men's 'trafficking' in leading actors, one that may have been facilitated by the 1633 warrant itself. Although Killigrew is often perceived as the kind of dramatist whose plays were designed for the Blackfriars, *The Princess* is far more vigorous and exuberant than the work of Carlell or some of the Blackfriars plays of Davenant and, later, Shirley. It is not hard to imagine this sprawling, hyperactive romance in performance at the Globe alongside *The Custom of the Country* or *Pericles*, and – like the earlier plays – it offers an important perspective on the structures of the King's Men and the concerns with travel, travail, servitude and slavery to which their repertory so constantly returned.

The play's casting patterns themselves suggest that it may offer a fresh viewpoint on the matter of the earlier plays. In contrast with *Pericles*, which centres on a single star turn, or *The Custom of the Country* and *Believe as You List*, which are organized around Taylor/Lowin duos, *The Princess* offers a more ensemble structure. The largest role is the play's comic lead, the elderly Lieutenant in the band of pirates who are crucial to the play's representation of the slave economy of the ancient world, who has 513 lines.[10] The late 1630s annotations of actors' roles in *Philaster* discussed in Chapter 1 (Figure 4) suggest that John Lowin (then aged around sixty) or Thomas Pollard (aged around forty) would have been available to play him. A group of younger men – Virgilius (439 lines), Facertes (419 lines) and Cilius (356 lines) – dominate much of the play's action. Given the shifting casting of Bussy D'Ambois and Philaster in the early 1630s, explored in Chapter 1, it may be unlikely that one of these roles was taken by Joseph Taylor (aged around fifty), especially given the availability of actors such as Clarke and Theophilus Bird (both aged around thirty) or Elliard Swanston (probably in his mid-thirties). Like Clavell's *The Soddered Citizen*, this may be a play that was intended to reduce the load on Taylor. Alternatively, he may have begun to perform less in the mid- to late 1630s; it is noticeable that the annotator of the *Philaster* cast-list does not assign him a role. The largest female role is Facertes' sister Cicilia (304 lines), followed by Sophia (146 lines), the bawd Olympia (131 lines) and the Neopolitan gentlewoman Paulina (102). Stephen Hammerton's apprenticeship to William Waverley, Merchant Taylor – which appears to have been the mechanism through which he moved from the Children of the Revels to the King's Men in late 1631 or early 1632 – was not due to end until 5 December 1639, so he is likely to have taken one of the leading female roles (Kathman 2004a: 14). Another may have been taken by Walter Clun, who appears to have been apprenticed to John Shank at some point before the latter's death in January 1636.[11]

Like *Believe as You List*, Killigrew's play dramatizes the subjection of other states to Rome, presenting an unhistorical narrative in which the lives of Virgilius and Sophia – fictional children of Julius Caesar – are intertwined with those of the children of the King of Sicily, Facertes, Cicilia and Lucius. Facertes, Cicilia and Lucius have been separated after a battle, the death of their father and Rome's conquest of

Sicily. For much of the play Lucius appears to have been lost, but he turns out to be Cilius, who has been brought up by the commander-turned-pirate Terresius under a false name. In the words of Alfred Harbage, who is one of the few scholars to have given the play any sustained attention, the play's characters are 'jostled through many militant encounters up and down many storm-racked coasts' before 'they are brought miraculously together for a climactic conflict followed by a climactic reconciliation' (1936: 106). Yet underlying the heightened narrative of *The Princess*, which is poised on the point of self-parody throughout, are a set of more serious concerns that deal with the questions relating to stage 'traffic' that I have been exploring in this chapter, and the issues of travail and servitude that inform both the matter of the King's Men's plays and the structures of the company itself.

The relationship between *The Princess* and *Pericles* is even closer than those of the earlier plays. Not only does *The Princess* deal in depth with the mechanisms through which young women are trafficked around the Mediterranean, on which *Pericles* touches in its representation of Marina in the Mytilene brothel, but it also directly reworks some crucial scenes of Shakespeare and Wilkins's play. Unlike *Pericles*, it is explicit in its use of language of slavery; indeed, the play even opens with the word 'Slaves', as the Lieutenant beats off his fellow pirates in order to claim Sophia for himself (Killigrew 1664: A3r). Both Sophia and Cicilia are faced with the prospect of their sale into servitude, Killigrew dramatizing the Neapolitan slave-market in a scene that strongly recalls the Mytilene market in *Pericles*, and the language of slavery also inflects the play's treatment of the 'love at first sight' convention that propels its narrative, in an echo of *The Custom of the Country*. Institutional and erotic subjection are brought together when Virgilius sees Cicilia at the market and falls instantly in love with her, thinking that she is an enslaved person from Greece and not knowing that she is the sister of his friend Facertes. He later tells Facertes, 'I am a slave to a slave, and to hers my Fate is bound', to which his friend – not knowing that he is talking about his own sister – responds 'All this for a slave!' (C4r–v). Nigro, a Sicilian general and Facertes' foster-father, makes a case for the overarching political force of this discourse when he tells Terresius, 'I have no joy now left; for I have seen all my Masters family ruin'd; and Our Countrey sold to slavery' (H1r). Because its focus runs far beyond one central figure, *The Princess* is able to offer a detailed critique of the political factors that shape the slave economy that it presents.

As we have seen, *Believe as You List* offers a carefully structured response to the narrative, performative and generic structures of *Pericles* that responds most powerfully to the figure of Pericles himself. In contrast, *The Princess* draws heavily on two scenes in which Pericles does not feature – the Mytilene slave-market (4.2) and Marina's 'conversion' of Lysimachus (4.6) – suggesting that Killigrew was more interested in Marina's travails than those of her father. This in itself marks a shift in the reception of *Pericles* within the repertory of the King's Men: in the possible absence of Taylor, Killigrew creates an ensemble piece in which the ambivalent figure of the Lieutenant is challenged for prominence not by one antagonist but by a group of three younger men.

In the opening scene, Sophia manages to persuade the Lieutenant not to sexually assault her, but her effect on him is continually liable to wear off. 'Now do I begin to find, I was a fool', he later comments, 'and this wench a talker' (Killigrew 1664: B3r). Killigrew appears to be responding cynically to the idea that women might negotiate or negate the sexual threat posed by men, but this impression is undercut in his treatment of Cilius's own lust for Sophia later in the first act. Where Marina's encounter with Lysimachus puts her in genuine danger, the outcome of Cilius's meeting with Sophia is predetermined when he '*gazes upon her*' (B3v) at the beginning of the sequence, before he has even spoken to her, and falls in love with her instantly:

CIL[IUS]
  Lieutenant, is that the Prisoner, you spoke of?
LIEU[TENANT]
  Yes Sir.
CIL[IUS]
  Thou liest.
LIEU[TENANT]
  Sir.
CIL[IUS]
  I tell thee, its false, its here the Prisoner stands.

(B3v)

Cilius's sudden infatuation with Sophia is not signalled solely in his words, but in a gesture specified by Killigrew in the stage direction, '*Touches himself*', which appears in the margin against the final line quoted here. It suggests that Cilius underlines the switch of perspective and his adoption of the identity of the 'prisoner' by touching his chest on the words 'its here'.

Although Killigrew frames his sequence differently from the one he found in *Pericles*, the exchange between Cilius and Sophia that follows imitates closely the pattern established by Shakespeare and Wilkins:

CIL[IUS]
  Fair one, what Country boasts these Beauties?
SOPH[IA]
  Sir, I can answer for my self, But for those Beauties, you speak of, let them find a friend, I have misfortunes enough to busie my time, and I find it business enough to make it appear fit to live: The thoughts of beauty, are fit for those that have fortunes like their faces, and if mine be like my fortune, (as a friend I counsel you) not to let your eyes dwell longer here, for its a dangerous habitation, Not safe to me, that am native there, and I should mourn more for your dangers,

> then mine own, for I know how to be just, but I could never find, how to be fortunate.
>
> CIL[IUS]
>
> A Curse find him, and all pass'd Plagues be but stor'd for him, that would seek to deface that Temple, and what ere your modesty can urge.—— [*He kneels to her.*] Thus I'll pay my duty, for I know, such a worship can be no new thing to the Deity, that's shrowded in their eyes.
>
> SOPH[IA]
>
> If you kneel, I must kneel too, for the guilt is no less to take a worship where it is not due, then to pay it. [*She kneels likewise.*]
>
> CIL[IUS]
>
> But if the guilt be equal, pray refuse not to receive an unfeigned one.
>
> SOPH[IA]
>
> I dare not rise, while you kneel; for although the fault be equal, yet civility makes this fitter. [*They both rise.*]
>
> CIL[IUS]
>
> I'll not dispute; for know, should you command, through sin, I'de serve you; and therefore you may be confident, I'll obey you, when you command me shun it; and here, with shame, I confess, I came prepar'd with lust, hungry with sin, and look'd to have met a sacrifice to me.—But I have found the power, and now return as from the Altar, struck with holy despairs, and shall feed on what I have already fed my eyes and ears with.
>
> (B3v–B4r)

Killigrew exploits the audience's memories of the similar exchange between Lysimachus and Marina in *Pericles*; casting may have underscored the similarity between the two scenes, especially if Lysimachus was also played as a young, inexperienced man. Moreover, it is not unlikely that in the mid-1630s the same actors played Lysimachus and Cilius, Marina and Sophia, and Boult and the Lieutenant. If so, spectators may have been cued by both the narrative and the physical presence of individual performers to 'read' Killigrew's scene, and his treatment of slavery and erotic subjection, through that of Shakespeare and Wilkins. Thus, by revisiting the structures of *Pericles* through dialogue and gesture, Killigrew also exploits the qualities of their own stage-life, restaging Shakespeare and Wilkins's play through narrative and embodied means.

There is, however, a complexity to the relationship between *Pericles* and *The Princess* that mirrors the textual problems of *Pericles* itself. Two versions of *Pericles* were printed to capitalize on its early popularity: a poorly printed and possibly corrupt dramatic text and a non-dramatic adaptation, Wilkins's *The Painful Adventures of Pericles, Prince of Tyre*, which has often been thought to preserve elements of a lost original version of the play.[12] Intriguingly, the exchange between Cilius and Sophia preserves elements of both *Pericles* and the *Painful Adventures*. Cilius's second speech closely parallels Lysimachus's 'a curse upon him, die he like a thief / That robs thee of thy goodness!', which appears in the play-text (4.6.110–11). However, Cilius's confession of his original intentions in the final speech quoted above has more in common with Lysimachus's words in *The Painful Adventures*, 'I hither came with thoughtes intemperate, foule and deformed, the which your paines so well hath laued, that they are now white' (H3v–H4r), than the latter's shiftier statement in the play of *Pericles*: 'Had I brought hither a corrupted mind, / Thy speech had alter'd it. [...] For me, bethoughten that I came / With no ill intent' (4.6.99–100, 104–5).

The action of kneeling and rising, which Killigrew annotates in stage directions placed in square brackets in the left-hand margin of the printed page, also features in *The Painful Adventures*, in which Wilkins says that Marina utters her persuasive words 'vpon her knees' and Lysimachus 'lift[s] her vp with his hands' (H3v), rather than the play-text. Killigrew turns a gesture that combines sympathy with an element of physical control into one of mutuality; his version of the exchange similarly turns a moment of genuine jeopardy into one in which the threat of sexual violence is displaced onto the comic figure of the Lieutenant, whose role parallels that of Boult in *Pericles*. Does Killigrew's play preserve something of the way in which the scene in *Pericles* was performed in the early to mid-1630s? The quarto text of *Pericles*, which had been reprinted in 1630 and 1635, was readily available to him when he was composing *The Princess*, but the *Painful Adventures* had not been printed since 1608 and may have been inaccessible. It is possible, therefore, that Killigrew drew on his memories of *Pericles* in performance, and on a version of the play that never saw print.

*

This account of the stage-life of *Pericles*, and the plays that it both inspired and accompanied, has brought together the various forms of 'traffic' on which the activities of the King's Men were based. Through multiple responses to and revisions of *Pericles*, the dramatists of the King's Men trafficked narratives that held up for scrutiny the trade in goods and bodies that fused commercial and sexual exploitation, in which the English increasingly participated as the seventeenth century wore on. Simultaneously, these narratives and their theatrical presentation depended on the company's other forms of trafficking. Acquired through apprenticeship or enlistment from other troupes, its actors helped to create and cement connections between the narratives that they presented. Simultaneously, the plays exploit actors' own states of servitude – to a monarch, to a paying public – to add an additional emotional charge to the subjection of figures such as Antiochus in *Believe as You List*. Spectators such as the ones in *The Book of Bulls* also participated in this traffic, both sustaining and critiquing the company's theatrical wares. As Jonson points out on the title-page of *The New Inn*, 'the Kings Seruants' were dependent upon the 'the Kings Subiects' and their ability both to behold and censure.

Pericles also provides a important example of the way in which Shakespeare's plays were not only kept alive through their performance by later generations of King's Men but also enabled the dramatic innovations of the dramatists that followed in his footsteps. Looking at Shakespeare through the extended repertory of the company of which he was once a member serves to deconstruct present-day hierarchies within the Shakespearean canon, in which *Pericles* is often placed in a marginal position. For seventeenth-century playgoers, actors and writers, *Pericles* was as important a component of 'Shakespeare' – the theatrical institution – as *Hamlet* or *Othello*.

Interlude: Playing the Court, 1633-4

This interlude moves forward into the reign of Charles I, and a changed court in which the new queen consort, Henrietta Maria, exercised considerable influence over cultural life. While the extent of the patronage activities of James's queen, Anna of Denmark, has been underestimated because few of her household's papers survive, the Caroline court saw a greater integration of royal patronage.[1] Some performances by the King's Men took place at Denmark House, the queen's court, and Herbert also notes that Henrietta Maria attended performances of Lodowick Carlell's *The Spartan Ladies* and Philip Massinger's *Cleander* at the Blackfriars playhouse in April–May 1634 (Bawcutt 1996: 188). Moreover, the survival in Edmond Malone's transcriptions of some of Henry Herbert's notes on the performance of plays before the king and queen add another dimension to the evidence, as Herbert frequently makes observations on the contexts of performance and responses to them. The plays performed by the King's Men between 17 November 1633 and 8 April 1634 comprised *Richard III*, *The Taming of the Shrew* ('Likt'), *The Woman's Prize, or The Tamer Tamed* ('Very well likt'), *The Loyal Subject* ('very well likt by the king'), *Cymbeline* ('Well likte by the kinge'), *The Faithful Shepherdess* ('in the clothes the Queene had given Taylor the year before of her own pastorall'), *The Guardian* ('well likte'), *The Winter's Tale* ('likt'), *The Wits* ('Well likt.'), *Bussy D'Ambois* and 'The Pastorall' (probably *The Faithful Shepherdess*) (Shakespeare 1821: 3.233–4; see Bawcutt 1996: 184–8).

The 1633–4 court season demonstrates the continued importance of the plays of Shakespeare and Fletcher to the King's Men, but it also shows some new developments with the repertory. Shakespeare is represented by four plays: *Richard III*, *The Taming of the Shrew*, *Cymbeline* and *The Winter's Tale*. Karen Britland has argued that the revival of *Richard III* may have been a response to Henrietta Maria's reputed involvement in plots surrounding two of her brothers, King Louis XIII and Gaston d'Orléans, noting that the play 'famously dramatizes the results of a usurping brother's tyranny and might well have served as a warning to the English queen not to become embroiled in her family's problems' (Britland 2006: 133). *The Winter's Tale* was, of course, an established favourite at court, but its selection alongside *Cymbeline* suggests that the company were drawing on the tragicomic and pastoral elements of their established repertory. It is noteworthy, in this context, that Massinger's *The Guardian*, licensed by Herbert on 31 October 1633 (Bawcutt 1996: 184), also draws on these generic and dramaturgical models, most notably in the scene in which Iolante is celebrated as a May Queen in the forest.

I will discuss the revival of *The Taming of the Shrew* alongside one of Fletcher's four plays, *The Tamer Tamed*, below. Fletcher was also represented by *The Loyal Subject*, *The Faithful Shepherdess* and *Cleander*, which was a thorough revision by Massinger of *The Wandering Lovers*, originally licensed for the King's Men on 6 December 1623 and performed at court on 1 January 1624 (Bawcutt 1996: 147–8).[2] *Cleander* was licensed on 7 May 1634, six days before the Blackfriars performance attended by the queen (Bawcutt 1996: 188). Massinger had a run of ill-received plays in 1631–2, apparently as a result of an argument over the direction of Caroline drama with Thomas Carew (see Beal 1980), and the success of *The Guardian* and *Cleander* was presumably welcome to both playwright and company.

The other new plays demonstrate a fresh trend within the repertory: the employment of dramatists with links to the court, such as Lodowick Carlell and William Davenant. Carlell held a number of court offices that mostly related to hunting: he was a royal huntsman, keeper of the royal hounds, gentleman of the bows and groom of the privy chamber (Sanders 2004). Davenant's first connection with the court came when he was employed as page to Frances Howard, Duchess of Richmond – for whom *The Winter's Tale* was performed at court on 18 January 1624 – and by the mid-1630s he was moving in the circles around the queen (Edmond 1987: 27–30, 44–62; Bawcutt 1996: 149; Bailey 2009: 132–74). Both men had a track record with the company. Carlell's tragedy *Osmond the Great Turk* was performed by the King's Men in 1622 (Bawcutt 1996: 137) and his tragicomedy *The Deserving Favourite* was printed in 1629 'As it was lately Acted, first before the Kings Maiestie, and since publikely at the *BLACK-FRIERS*. By his MAIESTIES seruants'. *The Spartan Ladies* is now lost; the publisher Humphrey Moseley entered it in the Stationers' Register in 1646 (Eyre 1913–14: 1.245) and included it in an advertisement for 'Books I do purpose to Print very speedily' (Middleton 1657: a10v), but it appears never to have been issued. Davenant had already written two plays for the King's Men: *The Cruel Brother*, licensed on 12 January 1627, and *The Just Italian*, licensed on 2 October 1629 (Bawcutt 1996: 165, 168).

The performance of plays by Carlell and Davenant underlined the connections between the King's Men and the court that are also visible elsewhere in the 1633–4 season, most strikingly around the performance of *The Faithful Shepherdess*. In a letter of 9 January 1634, George Garrard told Thomas Wentworth, Earl of Strafford, that the queen 'feasted the King at *Somerset-house*, and presented him with a Play, newly studied, long since printed, *the Faithful Shepherdess*, which the King's Players acted in the Robes she and her Ladies acted their Pastoral in the last Year' (Knowler 1739: 1.177). The 'Pastoral' was *The Shepherds' Paradise*, written by Walter Montagu for performance by the queen and a group of female courtiers in January 1633. Joseph Taylor appears to have been involved with this performance, too: John Pory gossiped to John, Viscount Scudamore, on 3 November 1632 that Montagu had been paid the enormous sum of £2,500 by the king and queen for *The Shepherds' Paradise*, adding that 'M[r] Taylour the Player hath also the making of a knight given him for teaching them [i.e. the queen and her ladies] how to act the Pastorall'.[3] Taylor did not receive a knighthood, but the costumes used in the court performance of *The Faithful Shepherdess* on 6 January 1634 may have been part of his reward for his help with *The Shepherds' Paradise*. Given the apparent physical size of actors such as John Lowin, it is probable that the costumes were altered and reconfigured before the King's Men's performance. Nonetheless, the costumes were recognizable to at least some spectators, lending the King's Men's performance of *The Faithful Shepherdess* the quality of a palimpsest and setting up an implicit competition between the female courtiers and the male players. We do not know if the King's Men were allowed to use these costumes on the commercial stage. In 1637 William Laud, Archbishop of Canterbury, requested that the costumes used in the Oxford and court performances of *The Royal Slave* be prevented from coming 'into the Hands and use of the Common Players abroad, which was graciously granted' (1700: 104). It is not clear, however, if Laud's request was in line with previous custom or a response to the use of the costumes from *The Shepherds' Paradise* 'abroad'.

The Faithful Shepherdess – which had been inherited from the repertory of the Children of the Queen's Revels – was a startling success for the King's Men in 1633–4. Other plays in the court season had a more troubled recent history. On 19 October 1633, having been altered to 'foule and offensive matters' in *The Tamer Tamed*, Herbert sent a messenger to

'Mr. Taylor, Mr. Lowins, or any of the King's players at the Blackfryers' with an order 'to will and require you to forbeare the actinge of your play called The Tamer Tamd, or the Taminge of the Tamer, this afternoone, or any more till you have leave from me'. The King's Men obeyed the order and 'acted The Scornful Lady instead of it'. Herbert continues, 'On saterday morning followinge the booke was brought mee, and at my lord of Hollands request I returned it to the players ye monday morning after, purgd of oaths, prophaness, and ribaldrye' (Bawcutt 1996: 182). Following this altercation, the King's Men appear to have taken more care over another Fletcher play that they wanted to revive, *The Loyal Subject*, which they sent to Herbert on 16 November and he licensed it 'with some reformations' on 23 November 1633, charging them £1 for the privilege (Bawcutt 1996: 185).

Yet in December Davenant's *The Wits* also caused problems. Herbert appears to have censored terms such as *faith*, *death* and *slight* – *death* or *'sdeath* in particular being a powerful oath invoking 'God's death', i.e. Christ's crucifixion – but Davenant complained to his friend Endymion Porter, who went over his head to the king. On 9 January 1634, Charles looked over the playbook himself and, according to Herbert's report, 'went over all that I had croste in Davenants play-booke, and allowing of *faith* and *slight* to bee asseverations only, and no oathes, markt them to stande, and some other few things' (Bawcutt 1996: 186). The altercation did not hurt the play in the long run. Sir Humphrey Mildmay saw it at Blackfriars on 22 January, three days after it had finally been licensed, and it was rushed into court performance on 28 January.[4] Herbert commented, perhaps with some satisfaction, that although the play was 'Well likt' in general, 'the kinge commended the language, but dislikt the plott and characters' (Bawcutt 1996: 187). The period 1633–4 was thus marked by a series of altercations over dramatic propriety and theatrical licensing, in which the King's Men were repeatedly put under pressure.

Despite its problems on the Blackfriars stage, *The Tamer Tamed* had been rehabilitated by the time it was performed at court, and it appears to have brought with it *The Taming of the Shrew*, the play to which it acts as a mock-sequel. The responses of the courtly audience recorded by Herbert, in which Shakespeare's play was 'Likd' and Fletcher's 'very well likt', perhaps reflect the way in which *The Tamer Tamed* is presented in a prologue and epilogue apparently written at this time. The prologue addresses '*Ladies* [...] *in whose defence and right / Fletchers brave Muse prepar'd herself to fight / A battaile without blood*' (1–3), while the epilogue declares that the play's conclusion – in which Maria, Petruchio's second wife, gets the better of her husband but then submits in turn to him – is '*aptly meant / To teach both Sexes due equality; / And as they stand bound, to love mutually*' (6–7). Prologue and epilogue thus position *The Tamer Tamed* in opposition to *The Taming of the Shrew*, which stages Katherine's submission to Petruchio in her extended final speech. Where Katherine declares that a wife's role is not to 'seek for rule, supremacy and sway / When they are bound to serve, love and obey' (5.2.169–70), Maria challenges Petruchio's authority as both a means of survival and a stepping-stone to a newly reconfigured relationship between husband and wife. The interaction between Shakespeare's plays and those of the broader repertory thus indicates the ways in which older plays could be reconfigured retrospectively by newer ones, with *The Taming of the Shrew* being questioned and qualified by its mock-sequel and thereby being rehabilitated – up to a point – for the Caroline court.

4

Men, Women and Magic: Shakespeare, the Merry Devil and the Prophetess

One of most popular plays of the repertory of the King's Men is now among their least regarded. *The Merry Devil of Edmonton*, first performed around 1603, rivals any of Shakespeare's plays for its prominence within early seventeenth-century culture. Allusions to the play stretch across nearly four decades. It is referred to in Thomas Middleton's 1604 pamphlet *The Black Book* (ll. 640–1) and his 1605–6 play *A Mad World My Masters* (5.2.111–12), while the prologue to Jonson's *The Devil is an Ass*, performed by the King's Men in 1616, hopes it will be received as well as 'Your dear delight, *The Devil of Edmonton*' (22). Jonson invoked *The Merry Devil of Edmonton* again in another play written for the King's Men, *The Staple of News* (1626) (First Intermean, 25–6), and the play is mentioned in such disparate materials as the preface to the English translation of Jean Puget de la Serre's *Le Miroir qui ne flatte point* (*The Mirror Which Flatters Not*) (1639: B5v) and the satiric pamphlet *The Brothers of the Blade: Answerable to the Sisters of the Scabbard* (Anon 1641: A3r–v). There also appears to be an allusion to the Host's catchphrase, 'grass and hay', in Richard

Braithwaite's *Whimzies, or a New Cast of Characters* (1631: F7v). A non-dramatic pamphlet by Thomas Brewer, *The Life and Death of the Merry Devil of Edmonton*, was entered in the Stationers' Register in 1608 (Arber 1875–7: 3.165v); the earliest edition that survives dates from 1631. The play was revived at court in 1612–13, 1618, 1631 and 1638, suggesting its appeal to elite as well as popular audiences.[1]

This chapter explores the impact of *The Merry Devil of Edmonton* on Shakespeare and his successors as the principal dramatists of the King's Men, John Fletcher and Philip Massinger, by tracing the development of the representation of magic-working men and women within the repertory. Focusing on *The Merry Devil of Edmonton* and three other popular plays, *The Winter's Tale* (*c.* 1610–11) and *The Tempest* (*c.* 1611) and Fletcher and Massinger's *The Prophetess* (1622), it considers not only thematic elements within the plays of the King's Men but also the company's casting patterns and its use of its two playhouses.[2] It thus tells two interlinked stories. The first focuses on the relationship between the Globe, where *The Merry Devil of Edmonton*, *The Winter's Tale* and *The Prophetess* all saw early performances, and the Blackfriars, which has been strongly linked by critics with the dramaturgy of *The Tempest*. The second focuses on the relationship between the male and female magus, and between the leading actors and boy players who performed these roles.

I argue that *The Merry Devil of Edmonton* established a set of conventions for the staging of supernatural themes and the figure of the magic-worker when it was staged at the Globe around 1603. In *The Tempest*, Shakespeare reworks the figure of the male magic-worker as it appears in *The Merry Devil of Edmonton*; in *The Winter's Tale*, he reacts against its patriarchal structures by developing a woman who appears to wield magic. In doing so, he shifts the focus of magical power from the leading actor, Richard Burbage, to the boy actor who plays Paulina. Fletcher and Massinger's *The Prophetess* then responds to the combined heritage of *The Merry Devil of Edmonton*, *The Winter's Tale* and *The Tempest*, presenting in the shape of Delphia, the titular prophetess, a full-blown female magus, who exploits the space of the playhouse as capably as her male forebears.

Supernatural Space

The title-page of the first quarto edition of *The Merry Devil of Edmonton*, published in 1608, states that the play is printed '*As it hath beene sundry times Acted, by his Maiesties Seruants, at the Globe, on the banke-side*', and this proclaimed link with outdoor playing remained stable across the many editions that followed, in 1612, 1617, 1626, 1631 and 1655. The prologue printed with the play does not mention the Globe by name, but it clearly imagines the round, outdoor playhouse as its performance location. Like the prologue of Shakespeare's *Henry V*, who refers to 'this wooden O' (13), the prologue of *The Merry Devil of Edmonton* places himself at the centre of the playhouse and the spectators' attention:

> Your silence and attention, worthy friends,
> That your free spirits may with more pleasing sense
> Relish the life of this our active scene;
> To which intent, to calm this murmuring breath,
> We ring this round with our invoking spells.
> If that your listening ears be yet prepar'd
> To entertain the subject of our play,
> Lend us your patience.
> (Anon 2000: Prologue, 1–8)[3]

The prologue's words align the theatrical and magical in ways that would have been especially potent in an outdoor playhouse such as the Globe, where the circle drawn by the magician – evoked, for example, in the famous title-page of the 1616 edition of Marlowe's *Doctor Faustus* – would echo the 'round' of the theatre itself. Having introduced the 'merry devil', Peter Fabell, the prologue returns to the specific fabric of the playhouse. Instructed by a stage direction, '*Draw the curtains*', he says,

> Behold him here, laid on his restless couch,
> His fatal chime prepared at his head,
> His chamber guarded with these sable sleights;
> And by him stands that necromantic chair
> In which he makes his direful invocations
> And binds the fiends that shall obey his will.
> Sit with a pleased eye until you know
> The comic end of our sad tragic show.
>
> (34SD–41)

The prologue makes use of the physical features of the playhouse, such as the curtained space at the back of the stage from which the devil Coreb will emerge, and it draws attention to a stage property, the 'necromantic chair' that will be turned against Coreb in the following scene. It also toys with the play's genre – unlike a play such as *Doctor Faustus*, which ends in the tragedy of the sorcerer's damnation, *The Merry Devil of Edmonton* begins with the stuff of tragedy but explicitly promises its spectators that it will subsequently turn to comedy. This negotiation is itself signalled in the reference to the 'sable sleights', an allusion to the convention of hanging the stage with black drapes for the performance of a tragedy.

The Merry Devil of Edmonton offers a set of provocative contexts for thinking about the manipulation of theatrical space in *The Tempest*, and the relationship of Shakespeare's play with the Blackfriars and the Globe. It is not unlikely that Shakespeare performed in *The Merry Devil of Edmonton* in 1603, given that he was in the cast of Jonson's *Sejanus* in the same year, and it lingered in his theatrical imagination. Considering the influence of this play on Shakespeare's later work acts as a counterbalance to influential critical narratives that have privileged the relationship between *The Tempest* and the Blackfriars. These narratives have encompassed not only *The Tempest* but, in some cases, all of Shakespeare's plays from *Cymbeline* (1609–10) onwards. In August 1608, Richard Burbage's Blackfriars tenant, Henry Evans, surrendered the lease of the playhouse, and Burbage had a new lease drawn up, assigning shares in it to himself, his brother Cuthbert and a group of the actors in the King's Men, Shakespeare among them (Wickham, Berry and Ingram 2000: 514–17). In an influential essay, Gerald Eades Bentley imagines a 'conference' between the King's Men in which they considered how to use their new playhouse:

> One of their decisions, I suggest, was to get Jonson to write Blackfriars plays for them. [...] Another decision [...] was to secure for the new theatre the services of the rising young collaborators, Francis Beaumont and John Fletcher. [...] The third of these three important changes in policy [...] was, of course, that William Shakespeare should write henceforth with the Blackfriars in mind and not the Globe. [...] No competent critic who has read carefully through the Shakespeare canon has failed to notice that there is something different about *Cymbeline*, *The Winter's Tale*, *The Tempest*, and *The Two Noble Kinsmen*.
>
> (1948: 43, 44, 46, 47–8)

Aspects of Bentley's narrative are strained. While he includes *The Two Noble Kinsmen* in his list of plays that display 'something different', he omits not only *Pericles*, performed around 1607–8, before the acquisition of the Blackfriars, but also *Coriolanus*, which was probably composed during the long plague closure of 1608–9, and *Henry VIII*, premiered at the Globe in summer 1613. Moreover, Simon Forman saw *The Winter's Tale* at the Globe on 15 May 1611, suggesting that it was always required to succeed in that space, and it is almost certain that Shakespeare's other plays of the period between 1610 and 1613 were also performed there.

Andrew Gurr therefore modifies Bentley's claim, referring to *The Tempest* as 'the first play Shakespeare unquestionably wrote for the Blackfriars rather than the Globe' (1989: 92). In support of this claim, he points to the uses of music in *The Tempest* and its use of a five-act structure, describing it as 'uniquely a musical play among Shakespeare's writings' and 'the first of his plays to show unequivocal evidence that it was conceived with act-breaks in mind' (92, 93). We cannot be absolutely sure that the five-act structure of the text of *The Tempest* published in the 1623 folio – more than a decade after its first performance – was part of Shakespeare's original concept for the play. However, the play indeed has more extensive music than Shakespeare's earlier works, may require different instrumentation and makes extensive use of ambient music in ways that had been seen previously in plays performed at the Blackfriars by the Children of the Queen's Revels, such as John Marston's *Sophonisba* (c. 1605) (see Dustagheer 2017: 117–21). Moreover, these uses of music are embedded within the structures of the play to such an extent that it is difficult to image it without them.

In other respects, however, *The Tempest* juxtaposes indoor and outdoor theatre conventions. As Sarah Dustagheer points out, its opening scene, which begins with '*A tempestuous noise of thunder and lightning heard*' (1.1.0SD) and a series of altercations between a ship's crew and its passengers, brings an outdoor effect indoors in a fashion that would have been even more disturbing if the King's Men maintained the Blackfriars tradition of beginning an afternoon's entertainment with an hour of instrumental music. She imagines the effect on stage-sitting gallants, 'who found themselves [...] in the midst of the chaos of the storm scenes' (2017: 120–1). Gurr is right to link these effects with the techniques of the 'amphitheatre play of the kind Heywood was writing for the Red Bull' (1989: 102), but he underestimates their sophistication. Heywood's Ovidian adaptations of classical myth, *The Golden Age* and *The Silver Age*, are indeed full of spectacle and sound, but *The Silver Age* was sufficiently refined for it to be performed before Queen Anna at Greenwich in January 1612, when it was preferred to one of Shakespeare's plays for a combined performance by the Queen's and King's Men.[4] Moreover, *The Silver Age* has marked affinities with aspects of *The Tempest*, as Jonathan Bate points out, describing its pastoral song to Ceres as 'the closest analogue in all Jacobean drama to the agricultural benison of Prospero's masque' (1993: 260). These interactions argue that Shakespeare's fusion of indoor and outdoor playhouse conventions is more complex than Gurr suggests.

If plays such as *The Merry Devil of Edmonton* and *The Tempest* were to be successful commodities for the King's Men after 1608, they would have to be flexible enough to be performed at indoor and outdoor venues. The long line of court performances of *The Merry Devil of Edmonton* argues that it was successfully performed indoors, and there is also evidence that *The Tempest* was at home in the Globe. In 1622, a decade after the first performances of Shakespeare's play, Fletcher and Massinger wrote two plays shaped by their knowledge of *The Merry Devil of Edmonton* and *The Tempest* that appear to have been licensed for initial performance at the Globe. *The Prophetess* was licensed by the Master of the Revels, Sir John Astley, on 14 May 1622, and it was performed again at the Globe a few years later, on 21 July 1629 (Bawcutt 1996: 137, 168). Similarly, *The Sea Voyage*, the opening of which parodies that of *The Tempest*, and which draws on Shakespeare's play in its depictions of rule, female agency and sexual inexperience, was licensed by Astley for the Globe on 22 June 1622 (Bawcutt 1996: 137). These plays reinforce the connection between the dramaturgy of *The Tempest* and the Globe, and it is likely that a revival of Shakespeare's play around 1620 spurred Fletcher and Massinger's repeated interactions with it in the early 1620s, prior to its publication in the 1623 folio.

The Prophetess fuses sound effects of the kind that Shakespeare pioneered in *The Tempest* with the visual spectacle often associated with outdoor playing through Heywood's *Ages* plays or saints' plays such as *The Two Noble Ladies*, performed at the Red Bull around 1619–23, in which the future St Cyprian '*Throws his charmed rod, and his books [vnder] the stage*', whereupon '*a flame riseth*' (Anon 1930: ll. 1899–1901SD), relinquishing his magic in a gesture that echoes and reverses Prospero's plan to 'drown' his own books. The hybrid dramaturgy of Fletcher and Massinger's play is most evident in a series of scenes in which Diocles, a Roman politician who becomes the Emperor Diocletian, is first assisted and then punished by the sorceress Delphia. Delphia promises her niece, Drusilla, who is in love with Diocles, that they will watch him unseen:

> From *Ceres* I will force her winged Dragons,
> And in the air hung over the Tribunal;
> (The Musick of the Spheres attending on us)
> There, as his good Star, thou shalt shine on him.
>
> (2.1.70–4)

Accordingly, in the opening moments of Act 2, Scene 3, Delphia and Drusilla enter 'In a throne drawn by Dragons' (2.3.0SD), which probably descended from the heavens in a moment recalling the decent of Jupiter in Shakespeare's *Cymbeline*. Where Jupiter's descent has an onstage audience, in the shape of the dreaming Posthumus and the ghosts of his family, *The Prophetess* presents its spectacle for the benefit of the playhouse spectators alone. The two women hover over Diocles, unseen, and Delphia summons her 'Musick from the Spheres' (2.3.9) in order to set a favourable gloss on his execution of Aper, the 'boar' that she has prophesied Diocles will slay in order to gain power. But when Diocles displeases her later in the scene by proposing marriage to Aurelia and rejecting Drusilla, Delphia summons '*Thunder and Lightning*' to create an ill omen (2.3.130SD).

In the following scene, she attempts to manipulate Diocles further by retrospectively claiming the sound and visual effects as her own. ''Twas I', she cries,

> that at thy great Inauguration,
> Hung in the air unseen: 'twas I that honoured thee
> With various Musicks, and sweet sounding airs:
> [...]
> 'Twas I that thundred loud; 'twas I that threatned;
> 'Twas I that cast a dark face over heaven,
> And smote ye all with terrour.
>
> (3.1.142–4, 152–4)

Drusilla creates music, sound effects and spectacle that rival those of Prospero, but unlike her male counterparts she appears to use no intermediary devils or spirits. In these moments, *The Prophetess* sets up a teasing, allusive dialogue between plays, a dialogue that is sustained through narrative, dramaturgy and the uses of theatrical space. Like Shakespeare and the author of *The Merry Devil of Edmonton*, Fletcher and Massinger exploit not only the specific spaces and environments of a single playhouse but also the capacity – or necessity – for plays to move between the Globe and Blackfriars. As Roslyn L. Knutson has argued, the King's Men 'continued to construct a multi-purpose repertory playable before any audience, on any stage' (2006: 54; see also Parr 2014).

Men, Women and Magic

Returning to the prologue to *The Merry Devil of Edmonton*, it is evident that this play is interested not only in theatrical space, but also in the ways in which that space is inhabited, notably by the leading actor who plays Peter Fabell. I have already quoted more than once the description, probably by Webster, of the 'Excellent Actor' who 'charmes our attention', standing at the centre of a 'circumference of [...] eares' (Webster 2007: 483). Similar terms are employed by Evelyn Tribble in her recent account of actorly skill: '[t]he ability to produce "significant" or meaningful movement through the managed body is akin to sorcery, a reminder that the secret of both the actor and the conjurer is to manage and direct attention and affect' (2017: 25). In the figure of the speaker who 'ring[s] this round with our invoking spells', the prologue to *The Merry Devil of Edmonton* similarly aligns the theatrical and magical and maps the figure of the magician onto that of the actor. It establishes a dynamic relationship between Richard Burbage, who is highly likely to have played Peter Fabell, and Edward Alleyn, who returned to performance at the Fortune between 1600 and 1603 after a short withdrawal from playing (Cerasano 1998). The actor-playwrights William Bird and Samuel Rowley were paid for 'adicyones in doctor fostes' on 22 November 1602 (Foakes 2002: 206), and the composition of *The Merry Devil of Edmonton* in early 1603 was probably a response to both the new *Faustus* and Alleyn's performance in it. A complex form of 'ghosting' is at work here, as spectators' memories of past and current performances are invoked across plays and playhouses.

The prologue thus introduces its subject in ways that prepare us for Burbage's appearance as Fabell, describing him in ways that echo the prologue to *Doctor Faustus* but relocate the scholar-magician from Wittenberg to more homely locations: the suburbs and villages that ringed London to the north:

> In Middlesex his birth and his abode,
> Not full seven mile from this great famous city –
> That, for his fame in sleights and magic won,
> Was called the merry fiend of Edmonton.
>
> (12–15)

The Merry Devil of Edmonton begins where Faustus ends, with the expiration of the magic-worker's deal with the devil and the arrival of the latter's representative to claim his soul. Fabell even makes a speech in which he apparently regrets his supernatural dealings:

Oh, that this soul, that cost so great a price
As the dear precious blood of her redeemer,
Inspir'd with knowledge should, by that alone
Which makes a man so near unto the powers,
Even lead him down into the depth of hell,
When men in their own pride strive to know more
[T]han man should know!
For this alone God cast the angels down.
The infinity of arts is like a sea
Into which when man will take in hand to sail
Further than reason (which should be his pilot)
Hath skill to guide him, losing once his compass,
He falleth to such deep and dangerous whirlpools
As he doth lose the very sight of heaven.
The more he strives to come to quiet harbour,
The further still he finds himself from land.
Man striving still to find the depth of evil,
Seeking to be a God becomes a devil.

(Induction, 42–58)

Although I am quoting from Nicola Bennett's modern-spelling edition of *The Merry Devil of Edmonton*, at line 47 I have followed the lineation in the 1608 quarto text. Doing so creates a meaningful pause, adding to the power delivered by Fabell's contemplation of his likely fate. The author or authors of *The Merry Devil* clearly had Marlowe's *Faustus* in mind, given the way in which the speech sets up its religious framework, and its attitude towards the scholar's aspiration for forbidden knowledge. Yet Fabell's speech also prefigures the association between magic, individual subjectivity and the storm in *The Tempest*, and it may have been in Shakespeare's mind when he composed the opening scene of that play.

The Merry Devil of Edmonton then veers off in a different direction from *Faustus*. Just before he makes this apparently remorseful speech, Fabell tricks the 'spirit' Coreb into sitting on an enchanted chair; as it concludes, Coreb tries to approach

Fabell to take him to hell, but finds that he cannot move, and Fabell does not release him until he promises 'I will not touch thee / Till seven years from this hour be full expir'd' (73–4). Unlike Faustus, Fabell is able to outwit the forces of hell, meaning that he can instead continue his work as the 'servant' of the paying audience. His role as a trickster may have been amplified in later versions of the play. The *Merry Devil* pamphlet features a sequence in which Fabell convinces the devil to spare him only as long as an inch-long stub of a candle takes to burn down, only to 'put the candle out, and into his pocket', saying 'looke heere […] till this is burnt, thou maiest not claime my soule: Ile keep this safe enough from burning out and so keepe that thou lookst for safe enough' (Brewer 1631: B1r). Such a sequence would be highly effective in the candlelit Blackfriars playhouse, and it is possible that one was added.

It is notable, in this context, that Fabell's exploits with the candle are recalled in Jonson's 1626 play for the King's Men, *The Staple of News*. A metatheatrical inter-act sequence, or Intermean, features a group of female playgoers, Tattle, Mirth, Expectation and Censure, who praise the devil in another King's Men play, Jonson's own *The Devil is an Ass*, first performed in 1616. They then discuss the devil in *The Merry Devil of Edmonton*, lamenting his failure to ensnare Fabell, before discussing other aspects of the play and its performance:

CENSURE

   The conjurer cozened him with a candle's end. He was an ass.

MIRTH

   But there was one Smug, a smith, would have made a horse laugh, and broke his halter, as they say.

TATTLE

   Oh, but the poor man had got a shrewd mischance, one day.

EXPECTATION

   How, gossip?

TATTLE

> He had dressed a rogue jade i'the morning that had the staggers, and had got such a spice of 'em himself by noon as they would not away all the play time, do what he could, for his heart.

MIRTH

> 'Twas his part, gossip; he was to be drunk, by his part.

TATTLE

> Say you so? I understood not so much.

EXPECTATION

> Would we had such another part and such a man in this play!
>
> (First Intermean, 51–61)

The fact that Jonson mentioned the trick with the candle in the context of performance suggests that he associated it with the play rather than the pamphlet. He also locates the women's memories of the trick within a network of assumptions about performance, casting and stage masculinity. Given the regular revivals of *The Merry Devil of Edmonton*, it is likely that the man who played Smug the Smith was indeed one of those performing in *The Staple of News*. Part of the comedy of the sequence thus comes from the way in which it requires a group of boy actors to critique the performances of senior players. Moreover, if the role of Smug was taken in the 1620s by John Shank, one of the company's most prominent comic actors, the jibes would take on an additional edge, given that Shank trained many of the company's boys (Kathman 2004a: 37; Astington 2010: 98–100).

The dynamic relationship that Jonson sets up between *The Merry Devil of Edmonton* and *The Staple of News*, which depends not only on allusion but on the casting practices of the King's Men, suggests some of the long-term impact of the earlier play on the company's repertory. A similar relationship exists between *The Merry Devil of Edmonton* and *The Tempest*. In addition to the image of the storm, discussed above, a later speech of Fabell similarly prefigures Prospero. In the final act of *The Tempest*, Prospero famously appeals to the 'elves of hills, brooks, standing lakes and groves' and claims to have 'bedimmed / the noontide sun, called forth the mutinous winds, / And 'twixt the green sea and the azured vault / Set roaring war' (5.1.33, 41–4). Prospero's speech appropriates the words of a female magic-worker, Ovid's Medea, which are given to their original speaker in Heywood's 1611 Red Bull play *The Brazen Age* (1613: G1v). They also, however, recall Fabell's own assertion of his magical power in *The Merry Devil of Edmonton*. Addressing *in absentia* his friend and former pupil Raymond, who is meeting with little success in his attempt to win over the parents of his beloved, Millicent Clare, Fabell asks:

> And come we back unto our native home
> For want of skill to lose the wench thou lov'st?
> We'll first hang Enfield in such rings of mist
> As never rose from any dampish fen;
> I'll make the briny sea to rise at Ware
> And drown the marshes unto Stratford bridge;
> I'll drive the deer from Waltham in their walks
> And scatter them like sheep in every field:
> We may perhaps be cross'd, but if we be,
> He shall cross the devil that but crosses me.
>
> (1.2.75–84)

Fabell's boasting description of his powers is homelier than Prospero's and it lacks the latter's startling, Ovidian claim to have brought the dead to life (*The Tempest*, 5.1.48–50), but the figure that he presents of the magus holding the stage and describing his power to shape the natural world is one that is echoed in Shakespeare's play. There is an active relationship between the roles of Fabell and Prospero that would have been particularly effective when the plays were performed alongside each other, and both Fabell and Prospero were played by Burbage.

Fabell does not dominate the extant text of *The Merry Devil of Edmonton* in the way that Prospero dominates *The*

Tempest; indeed, Peter Kirwan argues with some justification that 'the Merry Devil himself is not the focus of interest, and his story effectively ends before the play proper even begins' (2015: 108). Yet Fabell's role is nonetheless the largest in the play, and one that might have considerable impact in performance if it was played by the company's leading actor. Moreover, the interaction between roles that I have been discussing is also created by the way in which both characters dabble in matchmaking and the creation of dynasties. Prospero uses his magic to stage-manage Miranda's marriage to Ferdinand, while Fabell instead uses tricks and disguises. The latter claims at the end of *The Merry Devil of Edmonton*,

> I used some pretty sleights, but I protest
> Such as but sat upon the skirts of art:
> No conjurations, nor such weighty spells
> As tie the soul to their performancy [...]
> And let our toil to future ages prove
> The Devil of Edmonton did good in love.
>
> (5.1.257–60, 268–9)

Fabell does not resign his art, but he pulls back noticeably from the infernal dealings of the opening scene, and – like Prospero – he appears to have reconsidered the impact that the use of magic may have upon his prospects for salvation.

The suggestive connections between *The Merry Devil of Edmonton* and *The Tempest* may have been especially pointed when the plays were performed alongside *The Winter's Tale* in the court season of 1612–13, a season that itself probably reflected the plays performed at the Globe and Blackfriars in the preceding months. Leontes in *The Winter's Tale* is another outsize role that is likely to have been played by Burbage, but here he is cast not as the magus but as a man manipulated and baffled by what is presented as the working of female magic. Although Leontes' role, with its 676 lines, is almost twice as large as Paulina's, hers is nonetheless the second largest in the play, with 331 lines, ahead of Camillo (293 lines), Polixenes (270 lines) and Autolycus

(237 lines) (King 1992: 244–5). Moreover, her impact is increased by the fact that most of her lines are concentrated in five sequences: 2.2, 2.3.26–130, 3.2.171–242, 5.1.1–121 and 5.3. In the hands of an actor such as George Birche, who played Doll Common in *The Alchemist* and Lady Politick Would-Be in *Volpone* around 1616–18, Paulina would have been a powerful stage presence.[5]

As a number of scholars have noted, Shakespeare presents in Paulina a revision and recuperation of the female magic-worker, in the face of stereotypical representations such as his own witches in *Macbeth* or Sycorax in *The Tempest*, who is kept offstage and labelled a 'hag' by Prospero.[6] While Paulina may in fact use subterfuge rather than magic, she nonetheless redefines the ability to apparently bring someone back from the dead – to which Prospero also refers – as what Leontes calls 'an art / Lawful as eating' (5.3.110–11). Moreover, like the 'art' of Fabell and Prospero, hers fuses the apparently supernatural with the materially theatrical, in a sequence that she both stage-manages and choreographs:

> Music; awake her; strike!   (*Music*)
> (*to Hermione*) 'Tis time; descend; be stone no more; approach.
> Strike all that look upon with marvel. Come,
> I'll fill your grave up. Stir – nay, come away.
> Bequeath to death your numbness, for from him
> Dear life redeems you.
>
> (5.3.99–103)

The 'music' to which Paulina appeals is present within the fictive world – although its source may be deliberately unclear – and the immediate environment of the playhouse, and it accompanies a series of lines in which she appears gradually to coax Hermione to move. No stage direction appears in the folio text of the play, but Hermione apparently moves after the final appeal, as Paulina then turns to Leontes and says, 'You perceive she stirs', shifting her attention to him and filtering spectators' reactions through his:

> Start not. Her actions shall be holy as
> You hear my spell is lawful. Do not shun her
> Until you see her die again, for then
> You kill her double. Nay, present your hand.
> When she was young, you wooed her; now, in age,
> Is she become the suitor?
>
> (104–9)

Paulina presents herself here, as she has done earlier in the play, as the only person who is capable of finding an appropriate match for Leontes, in the very wife that he rejected in the past. In this respect, she also echoes and appropriates the role of Fabell in *The Merry Devil of Edmonton* and Prospero in *The Tempest* as the fixer of heirs and the succession. However, she is more vulnerable than Fabell to becoming part of the marriage market herself, as Leontes hurriedly pairs her off with Camillo in the closing lines of the play.

If these plays were performed at court in 1612–13 in the order in which they appear in the Treasurer of the Chamber's account, their elite spectators could have seen *The Merry Devil of Edmonton* and *The Tempest* in consecutive performances by the King's Men and then – after performances of *A King and No King* and *The Twins Tragedy* – *The Winter's Tale*. As a group, these plays appear to have presented differing configurations of comedy and tragedy, and various versions of the diseased and recuperated family. The sequence of the 1612–13 performances may also give us pause in other respects. It reminds us that we cannot be certain that *The Tempest* was written after *The Winter's Tale*, although the perceived parallels between Prospero's retirement and Shakespeare's own presumed retirement have encouraged commentators to believe that *The Tempest* is the last 'solo' play.[7] At the very least, this performance sequence encourages us to view the relationship between these plays in terms of the shifting place of the figure of the magic-worker in the repertory of the King's Men, and to view Paulina as an important, perhaps radical, reconfiguration of it. Fletcher and

Massinger seem to have seen it as such, if the depiction of Delphia in *The Prophetess* is anything to go by.

It is, I think, no coincidence that *The Prophetess*, licensed on 14 May 1622, also appeared in the midst of a run of revivals and projected revivals of *The Winter's Tale*. *The Winter's Tale* was performed before King James on 7 April 1618 (during a court season that also featured *The Merry Devil of Edmonton*) – before being considered for court performance again around 1619–20 (see Appendix). On 19 August 1623, it was relicensed by Herbert 'on Mr. Hemmings his worde that there was nothing profane added or reformed, thogh the allowed booke was missinge', and in 1624 it was repeated at court before the Duchess of Richmond, 'in the kings absence' (Bawcutt 1996: 142, 149). It is likely that the boy actor who played Paulina at this time also played Delphia. Like Paulina, Delphia is a substantial role in terms of its size and the technical demands that it would make on an actor. Delphia's 340 lines give her the third largest role in *The Prophetess*; moreover, while the largest role in *The Prophetess*, Diocles, has 501 lines, the second largest, Maximinian (343 lines), is almost identical in size to Delphia.[8] Although – as I argue in Chapter 1 – there are few certain patterns in the casting of boy actors in the King's Men's plays, the size and status of these roles, and the fact that a boy who succeeded as Paulina would appear to be good casting as Delphia, mean that it is harder to think of reasons why they should *not* be played by the same performer. Richard Sharpe and Thomas Holcombe, who had been bound as apprentices to John Heminges on 21 February 1616 and 22 April 1618 respectively, both appear in the list of the principal actors in *The Prophetess* (Beaumont and Fletcher 1679: 4C1r), indicating that these were performers who could have carried such roles ably. Sharpe appears ahead of Holcombe in the list, suggesting that he may have taken the more prominent role in *The Prophetess*; his appearance as the Duchess in *The Duchess of Malfi* in the revival of 1620–3, discussed in Chapter 1, suggests his ability to deal with a demanding role and to command the stage.

Both Paulina and Delphia are dramatically appealing figures, combining warmth with combative wit. Delphia displays a sardonic sense of humour about her own prophetic power, wryly noting Diocles' response to her prophecy of his future glory, 'Thou shalt be Emperor, O *Diocles*, / When thou hast kill'd a mighty Boar', when she comments, 'From that time / (As giving credit to my words) hee has imploy'd / Much of his life in hunting' (1.2.34–7). Nonetheless, in both *The Winter's Tale* and *The Prophetess* the female magic-worker is threatened with the stereotype of the witch. When Paulina challenges Leontes to accept the baby Perdita as his own, Leontes brands her a 'mankind witch', a 'most intelligencing bawd' and a 'gross hag' (2.3.66–7, 106). More outrageously still, in *The Prophetess* the cynical Maximinian derides Diocles' belief in Delphia's power, arguing that that those who trust her are

> made her Purveyors,
> To feed her old chaps: to provide her daily,
> And bring in Feasts, whilst shee sits farting at us,
> And blowing out her Prophesises at both ends.
>
> (1.3.82–5)

This carnivalesque image of the witch cynically exploiting those who submit to her power runs counter to what we see of Delphia in the play, yet it hangs over the representation of the female magic-worker. Moreover, Maximinian goes on to claim that prophetesses are either frauds, exploiting their supposed power in order to feed their carnivalesque consumption and excretion, or they are tools of the devil, to whom their age makes them vulnerable:

> Old women will lie monstrously; so will the divell,
> Or else he has had much wrong: upon my knowledge,
> Old women are malicious; so is hee:
> They are proud, and covetous, revengefull, lecherous;
> All which are excellent attributes of the Divell.
>
> (1.3.109–13)

Like Leontes, Maximinian fuses accusations of witchcraft with sexual slurs; both men appear to view women who challenge any aspect of conventional femininity – whether it be through speech or other aspects of their behaviour – as transgressing sexual and religious norms. In Delphia, Fletcher thus confronts stereotypes about women – and older women in particular – and magic, picking up where Shakespeare left off and putting in the place of the ambiguous Paulina, whose magic may be nothing but performance, a genuine wielder of supernatural power.

Like Paulina, Delphia appropriates the male magic-worker tradition of Fabell and Prospero. Molly Hand describes her as 'a working woman magus who is meant to out-Prospero Prospero' (2011: 161), an insight that alerts us to the complex workings of gender and status in the figure of the magic-worker in these plays. Delphia outdoes her male rival through the sustained structural, thematic, dramaturgical and aural connections that the dramatists make between their sorceress and her predecessors. For example, in a dumbshow at the start of Act 4, Delphia recalls both Prospero and Fabell when she exercises her magic by '*circl[ing]*' the 'kneeling' ambassadors '*with her Magick rod*' and '*raises a Mist*' (4.1.19SD), exerting her authority on the very environment itself. She is perhaps more powerful than her male counterparts. While Prospero works through intermediaries such as Ariel and is dependent on his symbolic book for his power, and Fabell makes use of devils, the source of Delphia's power is never disclosed. Shakespeare splits the intention and execution of magic between Prospero, the leading actor, and Ariel, the boy player, but Fletcher and Massinger combine intention and execution in one figure, allowing the boy to exercise power over his senior colleagues.[9] These structural contrasts also extend to the ways in which the characters engage in matchmaking. Where Prospero manipulates Ferdinand and Miranda through various forms of reverse psychology, Delphia magically controls the emotions of other characters. She causes Aurelia to change in her affections from Diocles to Maximinian, and she claims to have 'forc'd' a 'discontentment' upon the sulky Maximinian in Act 3.

The Prophetess thus demonstrates how female characters, played by boy actors such as Richard Sharpe, might inhabit and control the space of the Globe, implicitly challenging the likes of Joseph Taylor and John Lowin – who probably played Maximinian and Diocles – for dominance.[10] Like Prospero or Peter Fabel, Delphia 'ring[s]' the 'round' of the outdoor playhouse with her 'inuoking spelles' and 'charmes our attention' like the leading player described by John Webster. Yet her capacity to stand at the centre of attention is not drawn merely from the appropriation of a male subject position, but from the example of Paulina, who in the final scene of *The Winter's Tale* directs the gaze and controls the narrative through her careful display of the statue of Hermione, and her stage-management of the statue's awakening.

*

The plays explored in this chapter present an especially complex form of the interactions described by Marvin Carlson and Joseph R. Roach, in which the ghostly echoes of prior and current performances are carried by both the individual roles and the actors who played them. Moreover, the conjunctions between these plays also suggest fresh ways of thinking about the relationships that existed between the roles of leading actors such as Richard Burbage, Joseph Taylor or John Lowin, and apprentice players such as George Birche or Richard Sharpe. Boy players may have been subordinate to the authority of the sharers in the King's Men, some of whom were officially their 'masters' through their binding as apprentices, but on stage they were capable of subverting the privileged positions of their elders.

More than any other in this book, this chapter has considered the role of Shakespeare as actor and writer for the King's Men as well as one of their most valuable theatrical commodities. He is likely to have taken a part in *The Merry Devil of Edmonton* when it was first performed around 1603, and although he never wrote a play quite like it, its characters, narrative structures and exploitation of both the capacities of the playhouse and the capabilities of the actor all inform his later work. Viewed thus, *The Winter's Tale* and *The Tempest* sit at the centre of a network of influence that stretches from *The Merry Devil of Edmonton* in 1603 to *The Prophetess* in 1622. Yet the patterns of revivals of these plays suggest that a linear narrative does not account for their range of interactions. At each point in their long stage-life, *The Merry Devil of Edmonton*, *The Winter's Tale*, *The Tempest* and *The Prophetess* were vigorously alive, animated through the efforts of successive generations of performers that constantly remade 'Shakespeare'.

Interlude: Playing the Court, 1636–7

This final interlude explores the court repertory of 1636–7, which shows the acceleration of some of the trends in the 1633–4 repertory, such as the prominence of Fletcher's plays and the rise of the courtier-dramatist. A list of 'Playes acted before the Kinge and Queene this present yeare of the Lord. 1636', submitted by the King's Men to the court officials records the plays that they performed between 17 November 1636 and 21 February 1637.[1] They comprise: *The Coxcomb*; *Beggars' Bush*; *The Maid's Tragedy*; *The Loyal Subject*; 'the moore of Venice' (i.e. *Othello*); *Love's Pilgrimage*; the first and second parts of *Arviragus and Philicia*; *Love and Honour*; *The Elder Brother*; *A King and No King*; 'the new play from Oxford the Royall slave'; *Rollo, Duke of Normandy*; *Hamlet*; 'the tragedie of Cesar' (noted by Henry Herbert as 'Julius Caesar'); 'the wife for a moneth'; *The Governor*; and *Philaster* (Shakespeare 1821: 3.239). The plays of Fletcher now outnumber those of his older colleague. While Shakespeare is represented in the schedule by three plays, *Othello*, *Hamlet* and 'The Tragedie of Cesar' (noted by Herbert as 'Julius Caesar'), Fletcher and his collaborators have ten: *The Coxcomb*, *Beggars' Bush*, *The Maid's Tragedy*, *The Loyal Subject*, *Love's Pilgrimage*, *The Elder Brother*, *A King and No King*, *Rollo, Duke of Normandy*, *A Wife for a Month* and *Philaster*.

As in the 1633–4 season, older plays are complemented by the work of William Davenant, who contributes *Love and Honour*, licensed by Herbert on 20 November 1634 (Bawcutt 1996: 190) and seen by Sir Humphrey Mildmay on 12 December (Bentley 1937: 66), and Lodowick Carlell, whose two-part play *Arviragus and Philicia* was fairly new when it was performed at court on Easter Monday and Tuesday 1636.[2] It appears to have been a favourite with the royal family: Charles Louis, Elector Palatine, King Charles's nephew, wrote to his mother Elizabeth, the exiled Queen of Bohemia, reporting that the king had sat for a portrait at the studio of Antony Van Dyck 'close by Blake Friers, where the Quene saw Lodwick Carlile's second part of Arviragus and Felicia acted, wch is hugely liked of every one, he will not faile to send it to your Mat^{y}'.[3] *The Governor*, performed on 16 February 1637, may be the play entered in the Stationers' Register by Humphrey Moseley amongst a group of plays mainly associated with the King's Men on 9 September 1653 as 'The Gouernor. by Sr Cornelius Formido' (Eyre 1913–14: 1.428). It is not clear, however, if this is also the tragicomedy set in Barcelona that survives in manuscript with the label 'The Governor, a tragi-comedy, 1656'.[4]

The remaining play, *The Royal Slave*, sits uneasily in the repertory. Written by William Cartwright, it was originally performed before the king, queen, Charles Louis and his brother, Prince Rupert, at Christ Church, Oxford, on 30 August 1636, with a cast of university students, opulent 'Persian habits' and elaborate scenery that made one observer comment that it was 'full of shewes & partaking of ye nature of a maske'.[5] According to William Laud, Archbishop of Canterbury and Chancellor of the University, who planned the three plays performed for the royal visit,

> the Queen liked it so well, that she afterwards sent to me to have the Apparel sent to *Hampton* Court, that she might see her own Players act it over again, and see whether they could do it as well, as t'was done in the University. I caused

the University to send both the Clothes, and the Perspectives of the Stage; and the Play was acted at *Hampton* Court in *November* following. And by all Men's confession the Players came short of the University Actors.

(Laud 1700: 104)

The King's Men were paid £30 'for their paynes in studying and acting the new Play sent from Oxford called The Royall Slaue'.[6] This sum was higher than the £20 that they were normally paid for a performance before the king, but it was lower than the £50 paid to Peter Lehuc, the propertymaker, and George Portman, the painter, the £54 paid to Etienne Nau and Sebastian la Pierre 'for themselues & twelue Dancers', or the £40 that Herbert reported had been given to Cartwright himself.[7] The King's Men prepared the play for one performance only, as they were not permitted to take it to the commercial stage. Laud reports, 'I humbly desired of the King and the Queen, that neither the Play nor Cloathes, nor Stage might come into the Hands and use of the Common Players abroad, which was graciously granted' (1700: 104). No matter how strong the King's Men's connections with the court had become by the 1630s, they were still 'Common Players' to many observers.

The mid-1630s repertory thus points in two directions: the court and the playhouse. The King's Men's performance of plays by courtiers – Thomas Killigrew's *The Princess* (c. 1636) and *The Parson's Wedding* (c. 1640), Sir John Suckling's *Aglaura* (1638) and *The Goblins* (c. 1638), Sir William Barclay's *The Lost Lady* (1638), William Habington's *The Queen of Aragon* (1640), William Cavendish, Earl of Newcastle's *The Country Captain* and *The Variety* (c. 1641) and John Denham's *The Sophy* (1642) – all suggest a company that was looking away from a popular audience. Such a conjecture might be supported by the court-driven performance of *The Royal Slave* and, in 1637–8, another Oxford play, Jasper Mayne's comedy *The City Match*, was played by the King's Men at court and the Blackfriars. New or recent plays by established professional dramatists such as

Massinger and Shirley are also absent from what we know of the court repertoire of 1635–42, although these records are very incomplete.[8]

Yet, while the King's Men 'seem deliberately to have capitalized on court favour', as Martin Butler acknowledges, '[t]he vast bulk of the players' incomes came commercially' (1984: 101). Dramatists absent from the surviving court repertoire were still writing plays for them. Massinger's *The Bashful Lover* was licensed by Herbert for the company on 9 May 1636, followed by a series of plays that are now lost: *The King and the Subject*, licensed on 5 June 1638; *Alexius or the Chaste Lover*, licensed on 25 September 1639; and *The Fair Anchoress of Pausilippo* licensed on 26 January 1640 (Bawcutt 1996: 198, 203, 205, 206). Their most regular dramatist from 1639 to 1642 was James Shirley. Moreover, some court seasons did include the work of professional dramatists. Richard Brome's *The Northern Lass*, originally licensed for the company on 29 July 1629, was performed twice at court in 1638–9, alongside plays by Davenant and Carlell, and old favourites such as *The Merry Devil of Edmonton*, Jonson's *Volpone*, Shakespeare's *Julius Caesar* and *The Merry Wives of Windsor*, and Fletcher's *Chances*, *The Custom of the Country*, *The Spanish Curate* and *Beggars' Bush*. It is sometimes difficult, in fact, to separate courtly and popular tastes. A performance of the old-fashioned political drama *Alphonsus, King of Aragon* at the Blackfriars on 5 May 1636 was attended by the queen and the Palatine princes.[9] Similarly, Shirley appears to have been involved with bringing Cavendish's plays to the stage. Herbert describes *The Variety* having 'several reformations made by Shirley' and comments, 'My My Lo[d] Newcastle, as is said hath some hand in it' (Bawcutt 1996: 209).

The place of Shakespeare's plays in this repertory is intriguing. It is noticeable that he is represented in the 1636–7 court repertory by tragedies, even though there is evidence, outlined in Chapter 3, that *Pericles* was current on the stage around 1636. The place of plays such as *The Winter's Tale* and *Cymbeline* is instead taken by the tragicomedies of Carlell and Davenant. *Arviragus and Philicia* itself draws heavily on *Cymbeline*. The young Prince of Pictland in Carlell's play, Arviragus, draws his name from one of Innogen's lost brothers in *Cymbeline*, and his kinsman and later enemy, Guiderius, is named after Innogen's other brother. Moreover, Carlell builds on this borrowing by including in the first part of *Arviragus and Philicia* a scene that is clearly modelled on *Cymbeline*, in which Arviragus and Philicia – brought up together since infancy like Posthumus and Innogen – exchange a ring and a bracelet to confirm their vows to one another (1639: B9r). Yet, having influenced the work of the new generation of courtier dramatists, Shakespeare is presented at court through the plays that look least like theirs, suggesting that part of his value as a theatrical commodity to the King's Men lay in his generic and stylistic range.

5

Summer Days at the Globe: *Richard II*, *Henry VIII* and the Politics of Playing

This final chapter revisits some of the questions surrounding authority and service that are raised by the 1603 letters patent that authorized the company to perform as the King's Men. The newly arrived James I, we recall, stresses the role of the company in providing 'for the recreation of our loving Subjects as for our Solace and pleasure when wee shall thincke good to see them duringe our pleasure'.[1] But what happened when the 'recreation' of the monarch's subjects was achieved through topical and political drama, when the demands of court patronage might clash with the desire to make a profit?

This chapter explores a remarkable series of political plays that were staged at the Globe over a forty-year period, from the commissioned performance of a play about King Richard II in 1601 to the licensing of Henry Glapthorne's Thirty Years War drama, *The Tragedy of Albertus Wallenstein, Duke of Friedland*, in 1639. I argue that summer performances at the outdoor playhouse were a crucial focus for political debate, and that Shakespearean histories such as *Richard II* and *Henry VIII, or All is True* helped to fuel and structure a vibrant line of political drama. Viewed from this perspective, *Henry VIII* looks less like a late revival of the chronicle history play and more like one element of a persistent Jacobean and Caroline tradition. Moreover, examining this tradition of political drama further complicates the idea that the Globe was considered downmarket by the 1620s (see Parr 2014).

As a group, the political plays of the King's Men suggest the complexity of the ways in which the company engaged with royal authority. Some were passed for the stage only after extensive negotiation with the Master of the Revels, but others appear to have been not only condoned but also actively supported or encouraged. The delighted rumours that circulated in England in 1624 that Prince Charles, the Duke of Buckingham and even King James himself were only pretending to be displeased by the anti-Spanish satire of Middleton's *A Game at Chess* may have been mistaken, but Buckingham does appear to have sponsored a revival of Shakespeare and Fletcher's *Henry VIII* in 1628. In doing so, he took advantage of the dual position of the King's Men as royal 'servants' and as the object of attention from the paying audience. Yet this relatively privileged position did not protect the company from censorship and scrutiny, as their repeated interactions with the Master of the Revels and even, on occasion, King Charles himself suggest. In June 1638, Massinger wrote a play for the King's Men called *The King and the Subject*, now lost. During a prolonged controversy over its licensing, the play manuscript eventually reached the king, who is said by Sir Henry Herbert to have written '[t]his is too insolent, and to bee changed' against a speech in which a Spanish king proposes to wring money from his people through underhand taxation, declaring, 'Wee'le rayse supplies what ways we please' (Bawcutt 1996: 203–4).[2] It is not surprising that the king, who was trying to impose his own taxes in the 1630s, was sensitive to such material, but his comment also shows the extent to which 'insolence' was a valuable commodity in the political drama of the King's Men. It titillated audiences and brought them to the Globe, but it could not be taken too far.

This chapter begins with a survey of the history of political drama at the Globe, making a case for its commercial and cultural importance to the King's Men, and looking at the profit that these 'summer days' accrued. It then looks in detail at a group of plays, including *Richard II* and *Henry VIII*, that raise especially intriguing questions in relation to their staging of political power and agency, first in the responses of spectators to them, and second in the techniques that the company employed. Shakespeare and Fletcher's play crystallizes some of the means through which the King's Men animated political narratives, and the role of spectators in making meaning from political drama. Playgoers such as the astrologer and physician Simon Forman found lessons for their own lives in political plays, while plays also held political figures of the past and present-day up for scrutiny. When the Globe burned down during a performance of *Henry VIII* in June 1613, the diplomat Sir Henry Wotton famously commented that the play was 'set forth with many extraordinary circumstances of Pomp and Majesty […] sufficient in truth within a while to make greatness very familiar, if not ridiculous' (Smith 1907: 2.32–3). Wotton's comment suggests the ways in which politics was embodied through stage spectacle, and he was not wrong to identify this as a crucial technique in the plays of the King's Men. The interplay between verbal and visual effects, and the embodiment of historical and contemporary figures by individual actors, was crucial to the impact of political drama. Through these means, the company made matters of state 'familiar' and legible to spectators at the Globe, their broadest possible public.

Staging Politics at the Globe

The Globe was still relatively new in February 1601, when the Chamberlain's Men were paid by supporters of the Earl of Essex to revive an old play on the subject of the reign of King

Richard II – probably Shakespeare's *Richard II*, first performed in the mid-1590s.³ The performance took place just before the events that have become known as the 'Essex Rising', during which Essex and his followers planned an 'aristocratic intervention' in which they would petition the queen to arrest the Earl's political enemies, a scheme that ended in failure and the execution of Essex and some of his followers for treason (Hammer 2008: 3–18; Dickinson 2012: 43–64). One of the Chamberlain's Men, Augustine Phillips, was interviewed by the Privy Council, but this experience does not appear to have lessened the appetite of his colleagues for political drama.⁴ In December 1604, the King's Men performed a lost play, *The Tragedy of Gowrie*, which portrayed a conspiracy against King James during the earlier part of his Scottish reign (Wiggins 2011–18: 5.1451–2). In 1608, *Richard II* was reissued with a title-page advertising 'THE Tragedie of King Richard the Second: With new additions of the Parliament Sceane, and the deposing of King Richard. As it hath been lately acted by the Kinges Majesties seruantes, at the Globe', suggesting that the play had recently been current on the Globe stage. A different play on the same subject was seen there by Simon Forman on 30 April 1611.⁵

By 1611, the King's Men had access to two playhouses, the Blackfriars and Globe, but they continued to view the Globe as an important venue for new plays and, especially, political drama. *Henry VIII* was described as a new play that 'had beene acted not passing 2 or 3 times before' when it was performed at the Globe on 29 June 1613, a performance during which – notoriously – the playhouse caught fire and burned down.⁶ Fletcher and Massinger's *Sir John Van Olden Barnavelt*, which represented the recent political turmoil in the Netherlands, was staged at the Globe in mid-to-late August 1619 (Bentley 1941–68: 1.114, 3.415–17). Middleton's celebrated satire *A Game at Chess*, which examined religio-political tensions between England and Spain, was licensed for the King's Men on 12 June 1624 and performed for an outrageous run of nine days between 5 and 14 August

(Bawcutt 1996: 152). Robert Davenport's lost play 'The Historye of Henry the First', licensed for the King's Men on 10 April 1624, may also be part of the same tradition (Bawcutt 1996: 151).

The same pattern continued after the death of King James and the accession of his son, Charles I. *Henry VIII* was performed again at the Globe in August 1628, in a revival sponsored by George Villiers, Duke of Buckingham, who 'stayd till ye Duke of Buckingham was beheaded, & then departed'.[7] As described in Chapter 3, Massinger's *Believe as You List*, refused a license by the Master of the Revels, on 11 January 1631 'because itt did contain dangerous matter', was finally passed for performance on 6 May (Bawcutt 1996: 171–2). Another political play appeared later in that season. Herbert had come to an arrangement in which he took a cut of the profits of one play performed by the King's Men in the winter and one in the summer. He records that he received £5 6s. 6d. 'for the benefitt of their summer day' at a performance of 'Richard ye Seconde', the second of that season, at the Globe on 12 June 1631 (Bawcutt 1996: 173). As I will explore in detail later in this chapter, 'Richard ye Seconde' was probably Shakespeare's play, but may have been the one seen by Forman in 1611.

Three years later, in 1634, the King's Men commissioned Thomas Heywood and Richard Brome to write a play about a recent witchcraft case, *The Late Lancashire Witches*, which was staged at the Globe in August and acted 'by reason of ye great concourse of people 3 days togither'.[8] In June 1638, as noted above, the licensing of Massinger's *The King and the Subject* provoked a controversy that drew in not only the Master of the Revels but also the king himself. This experience did not deter the King's Men from their strategy of performing political drama at the Globe, since Henry Glapthorne's *The Tragedy of Albertus Wallenstein, Late Duke of Friedland*, which focuses on a Bohemian veteran of the Thirty Years War, who was assassinated in 1634, was licensed for that playhouse in 1639 (Bawcutt 1996: 205).

Gathered together, these performance records suggest that from at least the 1610s, and perhaps earlier, the King's Men used political and topical plays as a way of drawing audiences to the Globe during the quieter summer months when the law courts did not sit, the court dispersed and many of their more affluent spectators left London to escape the heat and the potential contagion of the plague. By the 1630s, the idea of the 'vacation play' had become embedded in theatrical culture. In *Madagascar with Other Poems* (1638), Davenant prints an epilogue originally written for *News from Plymouth*, licensed for the Globe on 1 August 1635, as 'Epilogue, To a Vacation Play at the Globe' (1638: F10v), while Glapthorne includes a prologue 'To a reviv'd Vacation Play' in his *Poems* (1639: E1v–E2r). Focusing such plays on political and topical subjects appears to have been an effective way to bring crowds to the Globe. John Chamberlain commented to Ralph Winwood on 18 December 1604 that the performance of *The Tragedy of Gowrie* was attended by 'exceding concourse of all sortes of people', Henry Bluett remarked in a letter dated 4 July 1613 that '[t]here came many people to see it [*Henry VIII*] insomuch that the house was very full', and Nathaniel Tomkyns noted not only the 'great concourse of people' watching *The Late Lancashire Witches* at the Globe in August 1634, but also observed that he 'found a greater appearance of fine folke gent^{men} and gent^{women} then I thought had bin in town in the vacation'.[9]

Staging such material brought with it, however, the risk of official censure. On 14 August 1619, Thomas Locke wrote to Sir Dudley Carleton, the English ambassador in the Hague, telling him, 'The Players heere were bringing of Barnavelt vpon the stage, & had bestowed a great deale of mony to prepare all things for the purpose, but at th'instant were prohibited by my Lo: of London.'[10] Locke refers to John King, Bishop of London, here extending his role as a censor of drama in print to the stage itself. The company found a way of getting the play licensed in the face of King's opposition, perhaps through a strategic alliance with the Master of the

Revels, and Locke wrote to Carleton on 27 August, 'Our players haue fownd the meanes to goe through with the play of Barnvelt, & it hath had many spectators and receaued applause.'[11] These comments suggest the level of the King's Men's investments in these summer plays, and the rewards that might come from them.

Even more evidence survives from the scandalous extended nine-day run of *A Game at Chess* in August 1624. On 10 August 1624, Don Carlos Coloma wrote to Gaspar de Guzmán, Conde-Duque de Olivares:

> there were more than 3000 persons there on the day that the audience was smallest. [...] All this has been so much applauded and enjoyed by the mob that here, where no play has been acted for more than one day [consecutively], this one has already been acted on four, and each day the crowd is greater. [...] [D]uring these last four days more than 12,000 persons have all heard the play of *A Game of Chess*, for so they call it, including all the nobility still in London.[12]

Rumours about the profits that the King's Men had accrued before *A Game at Chess* was finally suppressed were rife. John Woolley wrote to William Trumbull on 11 August, 'the Players looseth no tyme, nor forbeareth to make haye while the Sunn shyneth, acting it euery day without any intermition and it is thought they haue already gott neere a thousand pound by it'.[13] One reader recorded in his copy of the second quarto edition of the play, 'I have heard some of the acters say they tooke fiveteen hundred Pounde.'[14] On 14 August, Sir Francis Nethersole told Carleton that 'the players haue gotten 100li a day euer since'.[15] Amerigo Salvetti, the Florentine Ambassador, wrote to Sir John Scudamore on the same day, 'Gondemar is dailie upon the stage with great applause of the people, but greater of the plaiers, that get well nigh 200l. a day.'[16] *A Game at Chess* was exceptional, but even a small portion of the profits that the King's Men allegedly made from Middleton's play would have been substantial.

Spectatorship

The part-scandalized, part-amused response to the staging of *A Game at Chess* is just one part of the broader reception of political drama at the Globe. On 30 April 1611, Simon Forman went to the playhouse to see a play on the subject of the reign of King Richard II of England. He wrote some recollections of its events, and their potential lessons for contemporary spectators, in a manuscript labelled 'The Bocke of Plaies and notes therof p*er* formans for Common Pollicie'. His comments are worth quoting at length:

> Remember therin howe Iack strawe by his overmuch boldnes not beinge pollitick nor suspecting Anye thinge. was Soddenly at Smithfeld Bars stabbed by Walworth the major [i.e. mayor] of London & soe he and his wholle Army was overthrowen [...] Also remember howe the duke of gloster. The Erell of Arundell Oxford and others. crossing the kinge in his humor. about the duke of Erland and Bushy wer glad to fly and Raise an hoste of men. and beinge in his Castell. Howe the D of Erland cam by nighte to betray him w*ith* 300 men. but hauinge priuie warning ther of kept his gates faste And wold not suffer, the Enimie to Enter, w*hi*ch went back Again w*ith* a flie in his eare. and after was slainte by the Errell of Arundell in the battlell Remember also: when the duke and Arundell cam to London w*ith* their Army. kinge Richard came forth to them and met them and gaue them fair words. And promised them pardon and that all should be well yf they wold discharge their Army. Vpon. whose promises and faier Speaches they did yt and Afftter the king byd them all to A banket and soe betraid them And Cut of their head*es* &c because they had not his pardon vnder his hand & sealle be fore [i.e. before] but his worde/Remember thein Also howe the ducke of Lankaster pryuily contryued all Villany. to set them all together by the ears and to make the nobility to Envy the kinge and mislyke of him and his gouernmentes by which means. he made his own sonn king

which was henry Bullinbroke. Remember also howe the duke of Lankaster asked A wise man, wher him self should ever be kinge And he told him no, but his sonn should be a kinge. And when he had told him he hanged him vp for his labor. because he should not brute yt a brod [i.e. abroad] or speke ther of to others.

(fol. 201r–v)

Forman's attention is caught by moments in the play at which politics becomes personal, dealing with matters of miscalculation or betrayal: Jack Straw's lack of political acumen; the events that see Robert de Vere, Duke of Ireland, attempt to betray the Duke of Arundel, only to be betrayed in turn; King Richard's beheading of the rebellious nobles on a legalistic pretext; and John of Gaunt, Duke of Lancaster, stirring up trouble for the king and hanging the wise man in order to keep his prophecy secret. This last event prompts Forman's most extensive commentary: 'This was a pollicie in the common wealthes opinion But I sai yt was a Villains parte and a Iudas kisse to hange the man. for telling him the truth Beware by this Example of noble men/and of their fair wordes & sai lyttell to them, lest they doe the like by thee for thy good will' (fol. 201v). As a purveyor of astronomical assistance, predictions of future events and horoscopes himself, Forman clearly sees a disturbing precedent in the treatment of the 'wise man' at the hands of the Duke of Lancaster. In his injunction to himself not to trust powerful men, and to 'Beware [...] their fair wordes', he puts political drama to his own personal use.

Although his interaction with the play of Richard II is private, Forman's desire to connect its events with his own experience has much in common with the far more public spectatorship of George Villiers, Duke of Buckingham. In 1624, Buckingham was presented onstage in the figure of the White Duke in Middleton's *A Game at Chess*, and some commentators speculated that he, Prince Charles and even King James himself were not altogether displeased by the play.

John Woolley wrote to William Trumbull on 20 August 1624, shortly after *A Game at Chess* had been suppressed, reporting that it was thought that the Master of the Revels had licensed it 'not without leaue, from the higher powers I meane the P. and D. if not from the K. for they were all loth to haue it forbidden, and by report laught hartely at it'.[17] He wrote further to Trumbull on 28 August, 'Some say (how true it is I know not) that the Players are gone to the Courte to Act the game at Chesse before the Kinge. w*hi*ch doth much truble the Span*iss*ish Amb*assador*.'[18] Woolley's gossip network may have been feeding him false information, but the idea that *A Game at Chess* had official approval was clearly attractive to some politically aware individuals in the fervid atmosphere of summer 1624.

It is notable, therefore, that Buckingham was again thought to have provided official encouragement for a performance by the King's Men four years later, in August 1628. Robert Gell reported to Sir Martin Stuteville in a letter dated Wednesday 9 August, 'On teusday his Grace was present at ye acting of K. Hen. 8 at ye Globe, a play bespoken of purpose by himself', while another newsletter adds the information that Buckingham was accompanied by 'ye Savoian Ambassadour, y^e [...] Earle of Hollande & others'.[19] Thomas Cogswell and Peter Lake describe this performance of spectatorship as 'a full-blown exercise in propaganda', aimed not only at the audience within the Globe but also the 'wider political nation' through the circulation of newsletters like the ones I have just quoted (2009: 255). They suggest that the Globe was 'an unlikely venue in 1628 for a duke, an earl, and a foreign envoy' (254), but this is to overlook the tradition of summer performances that this chapter traces. The Globe was a regular venue for political performance and spectatorship, and an important node within the network of communications that they describe.

Buckingham abruptly left the Globe during the first scene of the second act, a scene that itself pivots on questions of spectatorship. The execution of his dramatic counterpart – referred to as 'the Duke' here to avoid confusion – is not presented onstage. Instead, Shakespeare and Fletcher dramatize the immediate aftermath of his trial, and make the sentence vividly clear through stage action as he enters '*Tipstaves before him, the axe with the edge towards him, Halberds on each side, accompanied with* Sir Thomas LOVELL, Sir Nicholas VAUX, Lord SANDYS, [*Attendants*] *and Common People*' (2.1.53SD). The middle section of the scene is dominated by the Duke, who has three speeches of 22, 12 and 35 lines each (55–78, 82–94, 100–35), interspersed by only six lines from Lovell and Vaux (79–81, 95–7). Appealing to both the '*Common People*' onstage and the offstage spectators in the playhouse – 'All good people, / You that thus far have come to pity me' (55–6) – he presents himself as willing to embrace a Christian 'good death' by forgiving his enemies. Yet faultlines appear in the Duke's attempt to reconcile himself to his sentence. He claims that he bears the law 'no malice for my death', but he is more equivocal in his treatment of his political opponents:

> But those that sought it I could wish more Christians.
> Be what they will, I heartily forgive 'em.
> Yet let 'em look they glory not in mischief
> Nor build their evils on the graves of great men
>
> (62, 64–7)

As Gordon McMullan notes, his resentment against his enemies is 'at best barely contained' (Shakespeare and Fletcher 2003: 271n.), as the Duke oscillates between forgiveness and resentment, repeatedly reversing his position across these four successive verse lines.

The Duke's remaining speeches similarly oscillate between quiescent acceptance and raw emotion. The hostility that bubbles under his second speech – 'I forgive all. / There cannot be those numberless offences / 'Gainst me that I cannot take peace with' (2.1.83–5) – rises to a head in his final speech, which culminates in a lesson for his on- and offstage audience:

> Where you are liberal of your loves and counsels,
> Be sure you be not loose; for those you make friends
> And give your hearts to, when they once perceive
> The least rub in your fortunes, fall away
> Like water from ye, never found again
> But where they mean to sink ye.
>
> (2.1.126–31)

It is easy to imagine spectators like Simon Forman noting this advice down in order to turn it to their future advantage, and these comments on the changeability of public opinion demonstrate why the play was useful to Buckingham in the 1620s.

Performance at the Globe, rather than the Blackfriars, made Buckingham's political performance more 'public' not only because it followed the political uses to which the outdoor playhouse was put in 1619 and, especially, 1624, but also because the Globe itself accommodated a broad spectrum of the 'people' to whom the Duke in *Henry VIII* appeals, creating a political cross-section within its sphere. Yet this very multiplicity made the meanings of the Duke's actions hard to control. The sequence dominated by the Duke is book-ended by two exchanges between the First and Second Gentlemen, figures who will comment similarly on the coronation of Anne Bullen in Act 4, Scene 1. The Gentlemen's exchanges provide a frame and filter for central events in the play; as Rory Loughnane comments, 'their position as observers at the court's periphery connects them to the viewing playhouse audience' (2013: 110). Moreover, their dialogue has a similar function to the letters in which people like John Woolley and Robert Gell circulated political gossip in their own historical moment.

The First Gentleman reports on the Duke's trial for the Second Gentlemen, providing the crucial context that the Duke 'pleaded still not guilty and alleged / Many sharp reasons to defeat the law' (2.1.13–14) and that his rhetoric was ineffective: 'Much / He spoke, and learnedly, for life, but all / Was either pitied in him or forgotten' (27–9). The First Gentleman also reports that the Duke was unable to fully control his emotions during his trial, telling the Second Gentlemen that when he was sentenced 'he was stirred / With such an agony he sweat extremely / And something spoke in choler, ill and hasty' (31–4). Through these speeches the Duke's dignity and his political skills are both undermined. The Gentlemen then gossip about the role of Wolsey in the Duke's downfall; the Second Gentleman also comments on the hatred of 'the commons' for Wolsey and their love for the man they call 'bounteous Buckingham / The mirror of all courtesy' (49, 51–2). The Duke enters precisely at this moment, meaning that the Second Gentleman's lines frame his appearance, but the dialogue between the two Gentlemen also helps to accentuate the emotional fault-lines – discussed above – within the Duke's own speeches. After the Duke's exit, the Gentlemen briefly pity him and speculate on the fate that might await his accusers, but they quickly move on to a new 'secret': 'Did you not of late days hear / A buzzing of a separation / Between the King and Katherine?' (146–8). The Duke's news value expires quickly, another potential scandal taking its place.

We do not know at what point precisely Buckingham and his companions left the 1628 performance. Gell comments that Buckingham 'stayd till ye Duke of Buckingham was beheaded, & then departed', while the other contemporary account states that 'ye Savoian Ambassadour, ye Duke, Earle of Hollande & others [...] stayed only ye disgracing not ye beheading of ye great Duke of Buck'.[20] These reports suggest that Buckingham made his exit at the same time as his stage counterpart; if he stayed until the end of the scene, he risked diminishing the parallel and allowing his story to become subsumed within the divorce narrative. As a whole, the scene suggests the problems with using political drama in this very public manner: the comments of the First and Second Gentlemen offer a deconstructive frame that not only presents the Duke's fall as news, and the subject of speculation as well as pity among the 'common people', but also draws attention to the other political parallels that exist between the narrative of *Henry VIII* and current events in 1628. Gell comments of Buckingham's staged spectatorship: 'Some say, he should rather have seen ye fall of Cardinall Wolsey, who was a more lively type of himself, having governed this kingdom 18 yeares, as he hath done 14.'[21] Where Buckingham sought to present himself as the innocent, noble victim of false accusation, others saw a political opportunist, a figure who had more in common with Wolsey, who owed his position of power to the favour of the monarch and is presented in *Henry VIII* as abusing that position to the detriment of the state.[22]

The scene's impact may have been heightened by the casting of the Duke in the 1628 performance. This is the fifth largest role in the play, with 199 lines, after King Henry (460 lines), played by John Lowin (Downes 1708: 24); Wolsey (429 lines), probably played by Joseph Taylor; Katherine (377 lines), probably played by John Honeyman or John Thompson; and Norfolk (209 lines), a role for which the casting is less clear. Moreover, the concentration of the Duke's lines into only two scenes means that this is an important role for a supporting player – the actor has fewer lines than those of the actor who plays Norfolk, but he makes a stronger impact. If we look at the cast-lists in two Massinger plays, *The Roman Actor* (1626) and *The Picture* (1629), roles of this size and prominence are taken by Elliard Swanston, Robert Benfield, Richard Robinson and Richard Sharpe. The casting of Benfield, who is often assigned the roles of kings and other authority figures in surviving actor-lists, would have given the Duke additional weight and gravitas onstage, while the casting of Swanston or Sharpe, both of whom appear to have been rising to star status in the late 1620s, would have reinforced the idea that this is a play without a clear lead, in which four characters – the Duke, Wolsey, Katherine and King Henry – tussle for prominence. In either case, Buckingham may have been happy to take such a performer as his theatrical avatar.

Summer performance at the Globe forms an important context for the ways in which plays such as *Barnavelt*, *A Game at Chess* and *Henry VIII* were received by spectators. Although the King's Men do not appear to have maintained separate repertories at their two playhouses until the 1630s, they seem quickly to have realized the potential that lay in staging political drama at the Globe during the summer months. Not only did the tendency of the king and court to withdraw from London at this time provide the company with opportunities to stage plays that courted political controversy, but such plays were also capable of drawing the large crowds – and, in particular, the high-status playgoers – that would make the outdoor playhouse more profitable. As I will explore in the next section, moreover, the Globe offered an environment in which spectacle and the details of performance combined, perhaps paradoxically, to offer spectators an especially intimate view of political process. A useful starting point for such a discussion can be found in *Henry VIII*, if we leave the late 1620s and look back to its first performances in 1613.

The Politics of Performance

The events of 1628, described above, were not the first time that *Henry VIII* had been the subject of scrutiny outside the playhouse. On 29 June 1613, when the play had been 'acted not passing 2 or 3 times before', the discharging of a small cannon in Act 1, Scene 4 set fire to the thatched roof of the playhouse.[23] Thomas Lorkins wrote to Sir Thomas Puckering on 30 June that the flames '<catch'd &> fastened vpon the thatch of ye house and <there> burned so furiously, as it consumed <the whole house &> all in lesse then two houres'.[24] This was a disaster for the King's Men, yet it also created some valuable commentary on the ways in which the company staged political material. The most detailed of the reports on the fire, in a letter written by Sir Henry Wotton to Sir Edmund Bacon on 2 July, is deeply interested in these techniques; the play, he writes, was 'set forth with many extraordinary circumstances of Pomp and Majesty, even to the matting of the stage; the

Knights of the Order, with their Georges and garters, the Guards with their embroidered coats, and the like: sufficient in truth within a while to make greatness very familiar, if not ridiculous' (Smith 1907: 2.32–3). In the context of this chapter, what interests me about Wotton's response to *Henry VIII* is the play's reported capacity to render historical figures and political events 'familiar' in the sense of being both well known and overly intimate. At the Globe, where spectators represented a wider social range and were, on average, of lower status than their counterparts at Blackfriars, a play's ability to render history and politics 'familiar' might itself become unsettling, as Wotton's comments suggest, potentially holding up important figures of the past to popular scrutiny and scorn. Political drama has the capacity to reveal the extent to which politics is itself theatrical, and representation can easily tip into satire.

Such anxieties appear to inform some of the comments that the Master of the Revels, Sir George Buc, made in the surviving playhouse manuscript of *Sir John Van Olden Barnavelt* (1619). 'I like not this: neith^r do I think y^t the pr[ince]. was thus disgracefully vsed. besides he is to much presented', he writes in the margin against the sequence in which the Prince of Orange is barred from the council chamber in Act 1, Scene 3 (Fletcher and Massinger 1980: margins of ll. 388–92). Orange and Barnavelt were probably played by two of the leading actors of the King's Men in August 1619, John Lowin and Joseph Taylor.[25] Barnavelt is by far the largest role in the play, with 793 lines, overshadowing the second largest, the Prince of Orange, who has only 384 lines. As we have seen in earlier chapters, it is not unusual for a King's Men play to have one outsize role. It is not unlikely, however, that the smaller size of the Prince's role also relates to the anxiety of Buc, himself a former diplomat who had direct experience of the Netherlands, about presenting prominent – and living – politicians onstage.[26]

A similar problem appears to have affected the performance of *The Tragedy of Gowrie* in 1604. John Chamberlain was struck by the theatrical translation of political history 'with all the action and actors', commenting, 'whether the matter or manner be not well handled, or that yt be thought unfit that princes should be played on the stage in theyre life time, I hear that some great counsailllors are much displeased with yt: and so is thought shalbe forbidden' (McClure 1939: 1.199). The precise subject of the play is unclear since two historical conspiracies against James centred on the Gowrie family. The first, in 1582, involved William Ruthven, first Earl of Gowrie; the second, in 1600, involved his second son, John Ruthven, the third Earl, and his brother Alexander. Scholars have generally argued that the second conspiracy, which includes the enticingly dramatic detail of the young earl dabbling in magic, is more likely to have been the source of the events represented in the play (Wiggins 2011–18: 5.1451–2; Turner 2006). However, there is an intriguing allusion to the Gowrie conspiracy in *Sir John Van Olden Barnavelt*: responding to Barnavelt's prolonged attempt to justify his actions in Act 5, Scene 3, the Second Lord exclaims,

> Examine all men
> branded wth such fowle syns as yo^u now dye for,
> and yo^u shall find their first stepp still, Religion:
> *Gowrie* in *Scotland*, 'twas his maine pretention:
> was not he honest too? his Cuntries Father?
>
> (ll. 2938–42)

Although the reference is probably to historical events rather than the earlier play, it is suggestive that the first Earl was the 'Gowrie' who lingered in the repertory of the King's Men, and the events of 1582 would also have made for good drama.

The 1582 conspiracy was motivated by tensions among the Scottish nobility during the minority of King James. Esmé Stewart, Sieur d'Aubigny and Duke of Lennox, and James Stewart of Ochiltree, Earl of Arran, wrested power from the regent, James Douglas, Earl of Morton, a move that was thought to threaten both the Protestant religious settlement and the lands and goods of other nobles. Making a decisive move to counter the new power of Lennox and Arran, the conspirators seized the king, who was only fifteen at the time, keeping him in captivity between 23 August 1582 and 20 May 1583, and Gowrie was placed at the head of the government (Reid 2016). It is easy to imagine Gowrie as a good role for an actor such as Richard Burbage, particularly as he was renowned for his performance as another usurper, Richard III. Some support for the idea that *The Tragedy of Gowrie* indeed staged this conspiracy rather than the later one might be found in its apparent representation of James I onstage. The King's Men may have felt that they could avoid censure for presenting the new king as a dramatic character if they did so in the figure of a teenage boy who was kept offstage, under various forms of house arrest, for much of the narrative before triumphantly regaining his freedom at its conclusion.

Plays such as *The Tragedy of Gowrie*, *Barnavelt* and *Henry VIII* see the King's Men repeatedly grappling with the question of how to make political figures and events 'familiar'. One of the ways in which they do so is through the very mechanics of theatre itself. Chamberlain reported that *Gowrie* was staged 'with all the action and actors', the term 'action' potentially referring not only to the representation of events but the histrionic techniques through which they were presented. Reflecting such practice, the surviving plays are suffused with self-conscious theatricality. In the final act of *Barnavelt*, for example, Barnavelt's servant remembers his master's former greatness in theatrical terms:

> the whole Court attending
> when he was pleasd to speake, and with such murmo^{rs}
> as glad Spectators in a Theater
> grace their best Acto^{rs} with, they ever heard him
> (ll. 2475–8)

Barnavelt himself declares towards the end of the same scene, in the face of a death sentence, 'I shall not play my last Act worst' (2694). By collapsing the politician into the familiar form of the actor, the play enables spectators to respond directly to their long-time favourite John Lowin, his powerful stage presence carrying Barnavelt with him.

The theatricality of *Henry VIII* is yet more intense. *Barnavelt* largely eschews spectacle, but Shakespeare and Fletcher's play was staged from the first with extravagant attention to detail, and it renders its protagonists 'familiar' not merely through costume, as Wotton suggests, but through stage action and gesture. At the start of the play, the political and personal relationship between king and advisor is long established, and the characters' intimacy is signalled in the way in which Henry first enters '*leaning on the* Cardinal's *shoulder*' in the play's second scene (1.2.0SD). Later in the play, however, that intimacy is dispelled and, following the Duke of Buckingham (and his real-life counterpart in 1628), Wolsey exits the play early, in Act 3, Scene 2. Like the Duke's final appearance, this scene makes use of an onstage audience, in a sequence that pivots on a series of self-consciously framed performances. When Wolsey enters with Cromwell, he is watched by a group of nobles who can see his movements but are unable to hear his words. The playhouse audience, in contrast, are able to hear not only Wolsey's fretful comments about the new prominence of Anne Bullen and Thomas Cranmer but also the words of the nobles. Norfolk's comments direct their attention towards gesture and expression: 'Observe, observe: he's moody' (3.2.75); 'He's discontented' (91); 'He is vexed at something' (104). Later in the scene, Norfolk describes Wolsey's expressions and gestures in detail to King Henry:

> Some strange commotion
> Is in his brain. He bites his lip, and starts,
> Stops on a sudden, looks upon the ground,
> Then lays his finger on his temple; straight
> Springs out into fast gait; then stops again,
> Strikes his breast hard, and anon he casts
> His eye against the moon. In most strange postures
> We have seen him set himself.
>
> (3.2.112–19)

Wolsey is still onstage, so the commentary cues spectators to 'read' the gestural language of the actor's performance and to continue to do so as the scene progresses. At the moment at which the king distances himself from his former adviser, Wolsey is subjected to a scrutiny that makes him 'familiar' to the Globe audience.

At the end of the scene, Henry presents Wolsey with two papers, saying 'Read o'er this, / And after this, and then to breakfast with / What appetite you have' (3.2.201–3). He then exits '*frowning upon the Cardinal; the nobles throng after him, smiling and whispering*' (203SD), and the disorientated Wolsey is left alone onstage, attempting to gauge the king's intentions from his body language and gesture, as the sequence's dramaturgy circles back on itself:

> What should this mean?
> What sudden anger's this? How have I reaped it?
> He parted frowning from me, as if ruin
> Leaped from his eyes.
>
> (3.2.203–7)

Wolsey lapses into soliloquy, but this is very different from the confiding tone that characters such as Iago adopt, closer to an interior monologue than direct address to the audience. The sequence presents politics as theatre. It deploys all of the means through which early modern drama creates intimacy between actors and spectators, such as soliloquy and aside, but its use of onstage spectatorship, and its self-conscious exploitation of the mechanics of performance, such as gesture and facial expression, mean that it renders its powerful political figures both 'familiar' and potentially 'ridiculous'.

The capacity of political theatre to work through forms of dramatic intimacy, and the lessons offered by Shakespeare and Fletcher, are clear in Middleton's *A Game at Chess*, which uses costume and the details of performance in a yet more self-consciously theatrical manner. In presenting contemporary English and Spanish political figures as white and black chess pieces respectively, and surrounding them with emblematic figures representing scheming Jesuits and naive English Protestants, the play makes the 'real' people sufficiently distant as to make staging them even possible, but it simultaneously creates an odd kind of intimacy through the allegorical framework itself, and the attention to detail that it required. The figure of the Black Knight was immediately recognizable to playgoers as the former Spanish ambassador to England, Don Diego Sarmiento de Acuña, Conde de Gondomar; indeed, the King's Men went to considerable efforts to make the parallels clear. Chamberlain reported to Carleton on 21 August 1624 that he had heard that the company had 'counterfeited his person to the life, with all his graces and faces, and had gotten (they say) a cast sute of his apparell for the purpose, with his Lytter'.[27] Gesture here aims not – as it does in *Henry VIII* – to render historical figures legible as politicians in the here and now, but to ensure that the targets of the play's satire were visible through its allegory.

As Gary Taylor suggests, playgoers did not see chess pieces. Instead, they saw 'a series of recognizable historical figures [...] and individuals who belonged to recognizable social categories' (2007: 1826). Also important here was the familiarity of the actors who played these roles. Taylor rightly observes that '[t]he protagonist of *A Game at Chess* is not a person but a party', but his statement that the play 'emphasizes ensemble; it is not built around a single dominant "star"' (1826) is more questionable given the balance of its roles. Although *A Game at Chess* demands strong casting throughout, the Machiavellian Black Knight is by far its largest role. Indeed, in the *Later Form* edited by Taylor in *Thomas Middleton: The Collected Works*, which aims to reconstruct 'the play as collaboratively produced and performed in August 1624', the Black Knight has over 700 lines where the next largest parts, the Virgin White Queen's Pawn and the Jesuit Black Bishop's Pawn, have around 380 and 330 apiece.[28] It is highly likely that the Black Knight was played by John Lowin; his casting would bring to the role the ability to simultaneously engage and repel audiences, an ability that characterizes Iago, manipulating the 'ghost' of the earlier performance. Similar qualities would also be evident in later Lowin roles, such as the Emperor Domitian in *The Roman Actor*, the insinuating Iacomo in *The Deserving Favourite* and the implacable Titus Flaminius in *Believe as You List*.

Similar questions should also be brought to bear on the play of 'Richard ye Seconde' performed at the Globe in 1631. If this was the play seen by Forman in 1611, some intriguing possibilities surround its revival and the casting of its leading roles. Forman's summary of the narrative features prominently some events that took place in Richard's youth and early manhood, such as the Peasants' Revolt (1381), which took place when the king was thirteen, and the Battle of Radcot Bridge (1387), which took place when he was twenty; its latest events appears to be the execution of Richard FitzAlan, Earl of Arundel, and the murder of Thomas of Woodstock, Earl of Gloucester, both of which took place in September 1397, when he was thirty. Who would have played such a role? It is easy to imagine an actor in his early twenties playing Richard at thirty, but it would have been difficult for an actor like Burbage, who was forty-two in 1611, to play the boy-king effectively. The role of Richard may instead have been written for a younger actor, perhaps William Ostler, whose prominence with the company in this period I have described earlier in this book.

Was the 'Richard ye Seconde' performed at the Globe in 1631 Shakespeare's play or this 1611 play? The possibility that it was the latter play is offered some slight support by Massinger's *The Emperor of the East*, licensed by Herbert on 11 March 1631 (Bawcutt 1996: 172). The protagonist of *The Emperor of the East*, like that of the 1611 Richard II play, is a young man barely out of boyhood who has to struggle to assert his political maturity. The play's epilogue suggests that this part was originally designed for a particular actor and that he was unavailable to perform it, meaning that another had to step in:

> *Wee haue reason to be doubtfull, whether hee*
> *On whom (forc'd to it by necessitie)*
> *The maker did conferre his Emperours part*
> *Hath giuen you satisfaction, in his art*
> *Of action and deliuerie; 'tis sure truth*
> *The burden was too heauie for his youth*
> *To vndergoe: but in his will wee know*
> *Hee was not wanting, and shall euer owe*
> *With his, our seruice, if your fauours daine*
> *To giue him strength, heereafter to sustaine*
> *A greater waight. It is your grace that can*
> *In your allowance of this write him man*
> *Before his time, which if you please to doe*
> *You make the Player, and the Poet too.*
>
> (Epilogue, 1–14)

As I have described earlier in this book, by the early 1630s Richard Sharpe was challenging Lowin and Taylor for leading roles. In another play of 1631, *The Swisser*, he takes the second-largest role, that of the King of the Lombards, but his name does not appear in the playhouse manuscript of Massinger's *Believe as You List*, licensed on 7 May 1631. This is probably because his role did not require specific props, as the leading actors are only listed in the manuscript if their roles require them to handle letters or other small objects. However, Sharpe's early death in January 1632 may have been preceded by a period of illness, and it is possible that he was unable to perform in *Believe as You List* or *The Emperor of the East*. The stand-in actor was possibly the eighteen-year-old John Honeyman, who had graduated very recently from playing female roles and is given small but eye-catching adult male roles in John Clavell's *The Soddered Citizen* (c. 1630) and *Believe as You List* (1631). Reviving the 1611 Richard II play in summer 1631 would thus provide a role appropriate either for the actor originally designed to play the Emperor in Massinger's play or his stand-in, if he were as successful as the prologue hopes.

Potential correspondences between the 1611 play and *The Emperor of the East* do not, of course, prove that the 'Richard ye Seconde' performed at the Globe in 1631 was not Shakespeare's play, and *Richard II* offers its own possibilities in an early 1630s context. Like *Believe as You List*, *Richard II* is structured around two leading roles. It pivots on the contest for the crown between King Richard – who has the largest role, with 618 lines – and Henry Bolingbroke, who has the second largest role, with 385 lines (King 1992: 178). Similarly, *Believe as You List* centres on the pursuit of the former king Antiochus by the Roman official Titus Flaminius. These roles are more evenly matched in terms of their size, Antiochus having 680 lines and Titus Flaminius 597 lines (King 1992: 111), and – as discussed in Chapter 3 – we know that they were played by Joseph Taylor and John Lowin respectively. We cannot be certain which actors would have played Richard and Bolingbroke in a 1631 revival of *Richard II*, but it is not unlikely that these roles were also taken by Taylor and Lowin.

As I have noted above, the casting of well-known actors such as Lowin and Taylor is one of the ways in which political narratives might be rendered 'familiar' to playgoers, and dramatists regularly exploited the connections between theatrical and political performance. Like *Henry VIII*, *Richard II* features multiple moments of political theatre: the abortive duel between Bolingbroke and Mowbray in Act 1, Scene 3, which culminates the moment when King Richard '*throws down his warder*' (1.3.117SD), asserting his authority over the scene and his argumentative subjects; the king's gesture of touching the ground when he returns to England; his later action of sitting 'upon the ground' to 'tell sad stories of the death of kings' (3.2.155–6); and his appearance '*on the walls*' in the following scene (3.3.61SD). Especially powerful is the emblematic business with the crown and mirror in Act 4, Scene 1, in a scene that is – as Bart Van Es notes – 'driven by a series of claims for dramatic and personal authority' (2013: 117). Richard both stage-manages the use of these props and seeks to control their meaning as political signs.

'Give me the crown', he tells an attendant, before turning to Bolingbroke with the words

> Here, cousin, seize the crown. Here, cousin.
> On this side my hand, on that side thine.
> Now is this golden crown like a deep well
> That owes two buckets, filling one another,
> The emptier ever dancing in the air,
> The other down, unseen and full of water.
> That bucket down and full of tears am I,
> Drinking my grief, whilst you mount up on high.
>
> (4.1.182–9)

The image of the two actors standing with their hands upon the crown is a powerful political symbol, but it also encapsulates something of the tension that often exists where there are two leading roles in a play, a tension that I have explored in detail in Chapter 2 in relation to *Othello* and *The Alchemist*. The business with the glass later in the scene also creates the impression that the actor who plays Richard, as much as the character, is eking out their part, unwilling to leave the stage. The political business is done, but Richard seeks to remain at the centre of attention, enjoying but unable to capitalize upon the intimacy with spectators that the casting of a familiar actor facilitated.

*

The plays on which this chapter has focused – *Richard II*, *Henry VIII*, *Sir John Van Olden Barnavelt* and *A Game at Chess* – provide potent examples of the ways in which the staging of political drama depended not only on narrative itself but also on the embodied performances of actors such as Burbage, Lowin or Taylor. They offered opportunities for leading performers at the Globe to capitalize on the showcase that the outdoor playhouse provided, as they stood at the centre of spectators' attention, and they dramatized the tensions between political 'actors' through forceful exchanges between players. The fact that Herbert chose to take a cut of the proceeds from the King's Men's performance of 'Richard ye Seconde' in 1631 also underlines the importance of political and topical plays to the company's summer repertory, and the powerful performances that successive King's Men casts were able to conjure from them. Like Forman and Buckingham, albeit in a more literal form, Herbert saw the profit in these plays.

Late in the 1630s, the king himself became part of this process of engaged spectatorship when he wrote '[t]his is too insolent, and to bee changed' against a speech by the tyrannical monarch in Massinger's *The King and the Subject*. The fact that Charles wrote 'too insolent' and not 'insolent' sums up the interaction between politics, profit and representation that structured the 'summer days' at the Globe. The King's Men are unlikely to have had a consistent political project, but they strategically exploited the gap between 'insolent' and 'too insolent', using politics as part of a broader commercial strategy.

The plays licensed for the Globe and revived there did not comprise the company's entire political repertory; moreover, until the 1630s the King's Men appear to have made little effort to develop separate indoor and outdoor repertories, meaning that the plays examined in this chapter could have moved between the company's two playhouses. Nonetheless, the material gathered in this chapter makes a case for the continued importance of the Globe across the decades, and for the continued life of Shakespeare's plays on its stage. As my concluding discussion of *Richard II* suggests, Shakespeare's histories set a pattern for the plays of the King's Men, in which political events and debates are staged through overtly theatrical means. This style perhaps reached its highest point in the allegorical spectacle of *A Game at Chess*, but its seeds were sown in works from *Richard II* to *Henry VIII*, and revivals of these plays and others – notably the *Henry IV* plays – ensured that the political theatre of the King's Men retained its links with its Shakespearean roots.

Epilogue: *Hamlet* without the Prince, 1642–60

The final court performance of the reign of Charles I, on 6 January 1642, involved the King's Men, but they did not present one of Shakespeare's plays. Sir Henry Herbert noted in his office-book: 'the prince had a play called The Scornful Lady [...], but the kinge and queene were not there; and it was the only play acted at courte in the whole Christmas' (Bawcutt 1996: 211). The image of the eleven-year-old Prince Charles watching Beaumont and Fletcher's comedy in his parents' absence is a powerful one, especially given what we now know about the events of the 1640s and 1650s. With the outbreak of the Civil War, the lives of both the court and the theatre industry were transformed. On 2 September 1642, a resolution was passed by both Houses of Parliament that ordered that plays be suppressed because 'publike Sports doe not well agree with publike Calamities, nor publike Stage-Playes with the Seasons of Humiliation, this being an Exercise of sad and pious Solemnity, and the other being Spectacles of Pleasure, too commonly expressing lacivious Mirth and levitie' (Anon 1642). Plays were out of step with the public mood, or at least the public mood as Parliament wanted to present it.

Histories of the King's Men often stop in 1642, but the events of the 1640s and 1650s offer important perspectives on the questions of authority, service, commodity and collaboration that have helped to organise this book.[1] When royal authority was threatened by Parliament, the structures that had articulated that authority within the theatre industry were also dislodged. What did it mean to be the King's Men when the monarch's ability to protect his 'servants' was compromised? In *Historia Histrionica*, James Wright claims the company swapped one form of service for another: '[m]ost of 'em, except *Lowin, Tayler* and *Pollard,* (who were superannuated) went into the King's Army, and like good Men and true, Serv'd their Old Master, tho' in a different, yet more honourable, Capacity' (1699: 7). A notable exception was Elliard Swanston, whose sympathies appear to have been with Parliament (Wright 1699: 8; Hotson 1928: 14–15), but even he collaborated with his old colleagues to sign the dedication to the folio edition of the plays of Fletcher and his collaborators (Beaumont and Fletcher 1647: A2v).

Parliament was unable to stamp out playing altogether, and surreptitious performances are known to have taken place in 1643–6. However, the ability of the actors to profit from their industry was limited and the 'traffic' in plays and players was curtailed. At two points in the later 1640s it looked as if the restrictions might be eased. A concerted attempt to revive the commercial theatre came in 1647, when the first and most intense phase of fighting had ceased (Hotson 1928: 16–20; Rollins 1921: 277–9). Many players appear to have thought that the ordinance of 1642 had lapsed; as Hyder E. Rollins comments, performances began at the Cockpit, Fortune, Salisbury Court and, probably, the Red Bull, 'with little or no concealment, on a fairly regular schedule' (1921: 279). Parliament's hostility towards playing continued, however, and it passed orders on 16 July and 16 October renewing the ban and increasing penalties against players who transgressed it (Hotson 1928: 25, 27). When the July 1647 order expired, the players began to perform openly again, only to be faced with another order, passed on 9 February 1648, which took a much stronger ideological line against playing. Its stance is clear in its opening statement that playing was 'condemned by ancient

Heathens, and much lesse to be tolerated among Professors of the Christian Religion' (Anon 1648: A2r). It declares that players 'are, and shall be taken to be Rogues' (A2v) and therefore punishable under Elizabethan and Jacobean statutes against vagabonds and vagrants, authorizes the Lord Mayor and sheriffs of London, Westminster, Middlesex and Surrey to 'pull down and demolish all Stage-Galleries, Seats and Boxes [...] erected and used for the acting, or playing, or seeing acted or plaid [...] Stage-Playes, Interludes, and Playes' (A2v), sets out punishments for players caught in the act of playing, orders that their takings should be handed over to the churchwardens of the parishes in which the performances took place and seeks to levy fines against anyone who attended a surreptitious performance.

The Blackfriars and Globe playhouses may have been casualties of these orders. A parliamentarian newsbook, *The Perfect Weekly Account*, noted on 10 October 1647, 'Plays begin to be set up apace neverthelesse not without disturbance yet they give out that it shall go forward at three houses, and blacke Fryars is repairing to the end that may be one' (Anon 1647b: P2v). However, although surreptitious performances continued at the Red Bull, Fortune, Cockpit and Salisbury Court, both the Globe and Blackfriars appear to have been silenced by the 1650s, if not before. In 1651, Richard Burbage's son, William, sold the Blackfriars property to George Best, merchant, for £700, and by 1655 'messuages or tenements' had been erected 'where the playhouse called the Globe stood and upon the ground thereunto belonging'.[2] It is also likely that the property of the King's Men was dispersed: Theophilus Bird was to claim that in 1642 his fellow actors had 'seized upon all the [...] apparel, hangings, books, and other goods [...] and sold and converted the same to their own uses'.[3]

Despite these losses, there is evidence that the King's Men attempted to retain some kind of corporate identity. In March 1646, 'the King's Players' petitioned Parliament to be paid money owed to them by the king (Anon

1767–1830: 8.234, 4.496). This may have been the same group as the ten former sharers – John Lowin, Joseph Taylor, Richard Robinson, Robert Benfield, Elliard Swanston, Thomas Pollard, Hugh Clarke, William Allen, Stephen Hammerton and Theophilus Bird – who signed the dedication of the Beaumont and Fletcher folio in 1647. A few months later, on 28 January 1648, the same group, minus Swanston and Allen, signed a bond to finance a new version of the King's Men.[4] But the difficulty of maintaining the structures of the Caroline stage can be seen in the fact that other former King's Men, such as Richard Baxter, Walter Clun, Charles Hart, William Hart and Nicholas Burt, were part of a different group that emerged in December 1648 and 'united togeather as a Company or Socyety of Actors for the actinge & performinge of Comedies Tragedyes and other interludes for the service of his late Majesty'.[5] Neither group appears to have gained much stability or to have lasted long, and it is perhaps unsurprising that members of both appear in an account given by Wright in *Historia Histrionica* of an interrupted performance of Fletcher and Massinger's *Rollo, Duke of Normandy, or The Bloody Brother* at the Cockpit, 'in which *Lowin* Acted Aubrey, *Tayler* Rollo, *Pollard* the Cook, *Burt* Latorch, and I think *Hart* Otto' (1699: 9).

The plays of the King's Men may have been similarly dispersed. Another news-book, *Perfect Occurrences*, reported on 6 October 1647:

> A Stage-play was to have been acted at Salisbury Court this day (and Bills stuck up about it) called *A King and No King*, formerly acted at the Black-Fryers, by his Majesties servants, about 8. yeares since, written by *Francis Beaumont*, and *Iohn Fletcher*.
>
> The Sheriffs of the City of *London* with their Officers went thither, and found a great number of people; some young Lords, and other eminent persons; and the men and women with the Boxes, [that took monies] [*sic*] fled. The Sheriffes brought away *Tim Reade* the Foole, and the people

cryed out for their monies, but slunke away like a company
of drowned Mice without it.

(Anon 1647a: 2Q4r)

Given the febrile political atmosphere in October 1647, with
King Charles in custody at Hampton Court, it must have been
as irresistible for the actors to perform the resonantly titled
A King and No King as it was for the news-books to report
on those performances. The author of *Perfect Occurrences*
pointedly refers to the earlier performance of the play 'at
the Black-Fryers, by his Majesties servants', but in 1647
its ownership must have been less clear. Timothy Reade, a
famous comic performer, had belonged to Queen Henrietta
Maria's Men at Salisbury Court before the outbreak of war,
so this performance of Beaumont and Fletcher's play evidently
combined the personnel and resources of different Caroline
companies.

There are no records of Shakespeare's plays receiving
performances of the kind described here, but it is not unlikely
that they took place, especially given the uses to which his
works are put in Civil War commentary and satire. Falstaff
is the most frequently invoked character, but there were also
frequent references to plays such as *Hamlet*.[6] For example,
a 1644 pamphlet, *The Great Eclipse of the Sun, or Charles
his Wain Overclouded*, imagines 'a thing call'd Conscience'
pursuing the king and his followers: 'it is worse then *Hamlets*
Ghost; for it will haunt him every where, and cry unto
him, O King expect revenge for the blood of thy subjects'
(Anon 1644: A3r). Shakespeare's plays are also prominent
in another form of playing that emerged during this period,
that of the droll. Drolls were short playlets, often cut down
from longer plays, which may have developed as a result of
the disruptions to performance conditions (Hotson 1928: 47;
see also Randall 1995: 150–6; Depledge 2018: 16–23). There
are some links specifically between the King's Men and the
performance and repertoire of the drolls. The most famous
performer of drolls was Robert Cox, who is named with

Baxter and the other former King's Men in the agreement of December 1648, and one of his drolls – an adaptation of *A Midsummer Night's Dream*, titled *Bottom the Weaver* – was printed by an enterprising publisher, Francis Kirkman, 'As it hath been often publikely Acted by some of his Majesties Comedians' (Cox 1661).

Sixteen of the drolls in a collection published by Kirkman in 1662 derive from King's Men plays: Shakespeare's *1 Henry IV* and *Hamlet*, Jonson's *The Alchemist*, Beaumont and Fletcher's *The Scornful Lady*, *Philaster*, *A King and No King* and *The Maid's Tragedy*, Fletcher and Massinger's *Beggars' Bush*, *The Spanish Curate*, *Rollo* and *The Custom of the Country*, Fletcher's *Rule a Wife and Have a Wife*, *The Humorous Lieutenant* and *The Chances*, Fletcher and Rowley's *The Maid in the Mill* and Cavendish and Shirley's *The Variety*. The similarity between this list and the plays commissioned for court performances, described above, is striking, suggesting some strong continuities of taste between courtly audiences of the 1630s and their popular counterparts in the 1640s and 1650s. Yet the impact of the drolls in performance would have been very different to those of the full-length plays from which they are drawn. As Emma Depledge notes, drolls 'centre on characters more than plots' (2018: 19), often gathering together several scenes to make a narrative that centres on a specific comic character or group of characters – *Bottom the Weaver* centres on the transformation of Bottom and the performance of the Pyramus and Thisbe play, while *The Bouncing Knight, or The Robbers Robbed* extracts material from *1 Henry IV* that centres on Falstaff in the tavern and the battlefield.

The third Shakespeare droll, *The Grave-makers*, extracts just one scene, the discussion between Hamlet and the Gravedigger in Act 5, Scene 1 of *Hamlet*. In doing so, it underlines the extent to which drolls also create detachable modules of action, a structural feature that also figures in *Bottom the Weaver* and *The Bouncing Knight*. *The Grave-makers* is headed with an argument, '*While he is making the*

Grave, for a Lady that drown'd her selfe, Hamlet *and his friend interrupt him with several Questions*', and its running title reads '*The Humors of / The Gravemakers*' (Kirkman 1662: F4v–F5r). When Hamlet and Horatio (who is not named anywhere in the droll) enter, the entry direction reads simply '*Enter two Gentlemen*'. While all of the Gravedigger and his companion's lines are retained, the droll cuts several lines from Horatio and, especially, Hamlet. In particular, it streamlines Hamlet's remarks on Yorick's skull (5.1.174–84), which instead read, 'Alas poor *Yorick*, I knew him friend, a fellow of infinite jest, of most excellent fancy, but where be your Gibes now, your Gamboles, your Songs of merryment? quite chop fal'n?' The effect is to refocus the sequence on the 'Grave-maker'. The Gravedigger in *Hamlet* has the potential to upstage the prince, but the droll gives the comic performer the upper hand over the tragedian; this effect may have been heighted if the popular Robert Cox was playing the Gravemaker, even if his antagonist was an actor as talented as Charles Hart. In performance, the sequence probably aroused memories of Joseph Taylor's performance in the full version of Shakespeare's play, but such memories are allowed only to flicker within the sequence's new comic framework.

Thus, while the activities of the former King's Men in the 1640s and 1650s, and the continued circulation of their plays, preserved aspects of the traditions that had emerged around the performance of Shakespeare's plays, the Civil War and Commonwealth periods nonetheless marked a break with those traditions. This process intensified with the Restoration, when the plays of the King's Men, Shakespeare's among them, were divided between Sir Thomas Killigrew, who managed a new King's Company, and Sir William Davenant, who managed their rivals, the Duke's Company. The most popular plays of the period before the Civil War were shared between them. Davenant was assigned a set of plays including *Hamlet*, *Henry VIII*, *Much Ado About Nothing* and *Twelfth Night*, plus two months' right in *Pericles* and a group of Fletcherian plays, while Killigrew's share included *Cymbeline*, the two parts of *Henry IV*, *Julius Caesar*, *A Midsummer Night's Dream*, *Othello*, *Richard II*, *Richard III*, *The Taming of the Shrew* and *The Winter's Tale* (see Appendix). Both of the documents in which these lists appear make the nostalgic, authenticating gesture of linking the plays with the King's Men, describing them as 'ancient Playes that were playd at Blackfriers' and 'His Majesties Servants Playes as they were formerly acted at the Blackfryers', but some fundamental aspects of their performance had changed. Within a few years of the resumption of playing in 1660, all-male performance had been suppressed and new playhouses had emerged. Shakespeare's plays would never again be the exclusive property of one company, and their stage traditions began to diverge: not only were they performed by different groups of actors, but Davenant also pursued a policy of aggressively adapting and updating the plays that he had been allotted. Shakespeare was again 'in the theatre', but the time of the King's Men had passed.

APPENDIX

Shakespearean Plays in the Repertory of the King's Men, 1603–42

(1) Records of Performance

1603–4

?*As You Like It*	Possibly performed at Wilton (Cornish 1897: 168).
Measure for Measure	Likely date of earliest performances.
A Midsummer Night's Dream	Dudley Carleton wrote to John Chamberlain on 15 January 1604, 'On New yeares night we had a play of Robin goode-fellow' (TNA, SP 14/6, fol. 53).
?*Hamlet*	Printed 1603, '*As it hath beene diuerse times acted by his Highnesse seruants in the cittie of London: as also in the two vniuersities of Cambridge and Oxford, and else-where*' (Shakespeare 1603).

1604–5

'The Moor of Venis' (*Othello*)	Performed at court 1 November 1604 (TNA, AO 3/908 no. 13, fol. 2a). May have had earliest performances in 1603–4 (Wiggins 2011–18, 5.129).
The Merry Wives of Windsor	Performed at court 4 November 1604 (TNA, AO 3/908/13, fol. 2a).

The Comedy of Errors	Performed at court 28 December 1604 (TNA, AO 3/908/13, fol. 2a).
Love's Labour's Lost	Performed at court 1–6 January 1605 (TNA, AO 3/908/13, fol. 2a).
Henry V	Performed at court 7 January 1605 (TNA, AO 3/908/13, fol. 2b).
The Merchant of Venice	Performed twice at court 10 and 12 February 1605. (TNA, AO3/908/13, fol. 2b).
All's Well That Ends Well	Likely date of earliest performances.

1605–6

King Lear	Likely date of earliest performances.
Macbeth	Likely date of earliest performances.

1606–7

King Lear	Performed at court 26 December 1606 (Q1608; TNA, E 351/543, fol. 177a).
Antony and Cleopatra	Likely date of earliest performances.

1607–8

Timon of Athens	Likely date of earliest performances.
Pericles	Likely date of earliest performances; one performance attended by the Venetian ambassador, *c.* 1607–8 (Brown 1908: 600).
?*Richard II*	Reissued 1608, 'As it hath been lately acted by the Kinges Majesties servantes, at the Globe' (Shakespeare 1608).

1608–9

?Romeo and Juliet	Reissued 1609, 'As it hath beene sundrie times publiquely acted, by the Kings Maiesties Seruants at the Globe' (Shakespeare 1609b).
?Troilus and Cressida	Published in 1609, 'As it was acted by the Kings Maiesties seruants at the Globe' (Shakespeare 1609a).

1609–10

Coriolanus	Likely date of earliest performances.
Cymbeline	Likely date of earliest performances.
Othello	Performance attended by Prince Lewis Frederick of Wurttemburg at the Globe on 30 April 1610 (Rye 1865: 61).
?King Lear	Revised version in Shakespeare 1623 may date to this period (Wiggins 2011–18: 6.253).

1610–11

Othello	Performance attended by Henry Jackson in Oxford in autumn 1610 (Elliott et al., 2004: 2.1037–8).
Macbeth	Performance attended by Simon Forman at the Globe on 20 April 1611 (Bodleian Library, MS Ashmole 208).
The Winter's Tale	Performance attended by Simon Forman at the Globe on 15 May 1611 (Bodleian Library, MS Ashmole 208).
Cymbeline	Performance attended by Simon Forman, probably at the Globe in April–May 1611 (Bodleian Library, MS Ashmole 208).

| ?*Titus Andronicus* | Reissued 1611, '*As it hath sundry times beene plaide by the Kings Maiesties Seruants*'. |

1611–12

The Tempest	Performed at court 1 November 1611 (TNA, AO 3/908/14, fol. 1b). May have had earliest performances in 1610–11.
The Winter's Tale	Performed at court 5 November 1611 (TNA, AO 3/908/14, fol. 1b).

1612–13

The Tempest	Performed at court Christmas 1612–13 (Bodleian Library, MS Rawl. A. 239, fol. 47b).
Cardenio	Performed at court Christmas 1612–13 and 8 June 1613 before the Savoyard Ambassador (Bodleian Library, MS Rawl. A. 239, fol. 47b).
'The Hotspurr' (*1 Henry IV*)	Performed at court Christmas 1612–13 (Bodleian Library, MS Rawl. A. 239, fol. 47b).
'Sir Iohn Falstafe' (*1 or 2 Henry IV*, or *The Merry Wives of Windsor*)	Performed at court Christmas 1612–13 (Bodleian Library, MS Rawl. A. 239, fol. 47b).
'Caesars Tragedye' (*Julius Caesar*)	Performed at court Christmas 1612–13 (Bodleian Library, MS Rawl. A. 239, fol. 47b).
Much Ado About Nothing / 'Benedicte and Betteris'	Performed twice at court Christmas 1612–13. (Bodleian MS Rawl. A. 239, fol. 47b).
The Winter's Tale	Performed at court Christmas 1612–13 (Bodleian Library, MS Rawl. A. 239, fol. 47b).

'The Moore of Venice' (*Othello*)	Performed at court Christmas 1612–13 (Bodleian Library, MS Rawl. A. 239, fol. 47b).
'All is True' / 'the play of Hen:8' (*Henry VIII*)	Performed at the Globe on 29 June 1613 (Smith 1907: 2.32–3; BL, Harley MS 7002, fol. 268).

1613–14

The Two Noble Kinsmen	Likely date of earliest performances.
?*Antony and Cleopatra*	Pompey's line 'In me 'tis villainy, / In thee't had been good service' (2.7.75–6) is quoted in Anon 1614, B3r (Wiggins 2011–18: 6.330).

1616–17

?*Macbeth*	Conjectural date of revision by Middleton.

1617–18

Twelfth Night	Performed at court 6 April 1618 (TNA, E 351/544, 90b).
The Winter's Tale	Performed at court 7 April 1618 (TNA, E 351/544, 90b).

1618–19

Pericles	Performed at court 20 May 1619 (SP 14/109, fols 100–1 (no. 46)).

1619–20

Hamlet	Probably considered for court performance Christmas 1619–20 (BL, Cotton MS Tiberius E.X, fol. 197v).
The Two Noble Kinsmen	Probably considered for court performance Christmas 1619–20 (BL, Cotton MS Tiberius E.X, fol. 197v).

'[Seco]nd part of Falstaff' (*2 Henry IV*)	Probably considered for court performance Christmas 1619–20 (BL, Cotton MS Tiberius E.X, fol. 197v).
The Winter's Tale	Probably considered for court performance Christmas 1619–20 (BL Cotton MS Tiberius E.X, fol. 197v).

1621–2

?*Measure for Measure*	Conjectural date of revision by Middleton.
?*Othello*	Published 1622, '*As it hath beene diuerse times acted at the Globe, and at the Black-Friers, by his Maiesties Seruants*'.

1622–3

'Malvolio' (*Twelfth Night*)	Performed at court 2 February 1623 (Bawcutt 1996: 140).
?*A Midsummer Night's Dream*	Shakespeare 1623 includes reference in stage directions to King's Men's musician William Tawyer (O2v).
?*Much Ado About Nothing*	Shakespeare 1623 includes reference in stage directions to apprentice and musician John Wilson (I6r).

1623–4

The Winter's Tale	Re-licensed by Master of the Revels 19 August 1623; performed at court 18 January 1624 (Bawcutt 1996: 142, 149).

1624–5

'The First Part of Sir John Falstaff' (*1 Henry IV*)	Performed at court 1 January 1625 (Bawcutt 1996: 159).

1626–7

?The Two Noble Kinsmen	Published in 1634 as '*presented at the Blackfriers by the Kings Maiesties servants, with great applause*'; the two men mentioned in stage directions, '*Curtis*' (I4v, L4v) and '*T. Tucke*' (L4v) are likely to be Curtis Greville, actor with the King's Men *c.* 1626–31, and Thomas Tuckfield, listed among the company's musicians and attendants in 1624.

1627–8

Henry VIII	Performance at the Globe attended by the Duke of Buckingham, *c.* 8 August 1628 (BL, Harley MS 383, fol. 65; Northamptonshire Record Office, MS IL 2671, fol. 1v).

1629–30

'The Moor of Venise' (Othello)	Performed at the Blackfriars 22 November 1629 (Bawcutt 1996: 169).

1630–1

A Midsummer Night's Dream	Performed at court 17 October 1630 (Folger Shakespeare Library, MS X.d.110).
'Olde Castle' (*1* or *2 Henry IV*?)	Performed at court 6 January 1631 (Folger Shakespeare Library, MS X.d.110).
Pericles	Performed at the Globe 10 June 1631 (Bawcutt 1996: 173).
'Richard ye Seconde' (?Richard II)	Performed at the Globe 21 June 1631 (Bawcutt 1996: 173).
?Love's Labours Lost	Published 1631, '*as it was acted by his Maiesties Seruants at the Blacke-Friers and the Globe*' (Shakespeare 1631b).

| ?*The Taming of the Shrew* | Published in 1631, 'As it was acted by his Maiesties Seruants at the Blacke Friers and the Globe' (Shakespeare 1631b). |

1633–4

Richard III	Performed at court 17 November 1633 (Bawcutt 1996: 184).
The Taming of the Shrew	Performed at court 26 November 1633 (Bawcutt 1996: 185).
Cymbeline	Performed at court 1 January 1634 (Bawcutt 1996: 185).
The Winter's Tale	Performed at court 16 January 1634 (Bawcutt 1996: 186).

1634–5

| 'ffalstaffe' (*1* or *2 Henry IV* or *The Merry Wives of Windsor*) | Performance attended by John Greene 9 April 1635 (Elliott 1993: 192). |
| 'the More of Venice' (*Othello*) | Performance at the Blackfriars attended by Sir Humphrey Mildmay 6 May 1635 (Bentley 1937: 67). |

1635–6

| *Pericles* | Performance alluded to in Anon 1636: fol. 9r–v. |

1636–7

'the Moore of Venice' (*Othello*)	Performed at court 6 December 1636 (TNA, AO 3/908/22).
Hamlet	Performed at court 24 January 1637 (TNA, AO 3/908/22).
Julius Caesar	Performed at court 31 January 1637 (TNA, AO 3/908/22; Bawcutt 1996: 200).

1637–8

| 'ould Castel' (*1* or *2* *Henry IV*?) | Performed at court 29 May 1638 (Wright 1887: 10). |

1638–9

| *Julius Caesar* | Performed at court 13 November 1638 (Wright 1887: 10). |
| *The Merry Wives of Windsor* | Performed at court 15 November 1638 (Wright 1887: 10). |

(2) Restoration Attributions of Plays to the Blackfriars

(a) Shakespearean plays in a list of 'some of the most ancient Playes that were playd at Blackfriers […] granted […] unto […] Sir William Davenant' (1660), TNA, LC 5/137, p. 343:

> the Tempest, measures, for measures, much adoe about nothinge, Rome and Juliet, Twelfe night, the Life of King Henry the Eyght […] King Lear, the Tragedy of Mackbeth, the Tragedy of Hamlet prince of Denmarke […]

The warrant concludes by granting Davenant two months' right in six further plays, including 'Persiles prince of Tyre', but it does not specify that these are Blackfriars plays.

(b) Shakespearean plays in 'A Catalogue of part of his Majesties Servants Playes as they were formerly acted at the Blackfryers & now allowed of to his Majesties Servants at ye New Theatre' (1669), TNA, LC 5/12, pp. 212–13.

The Winters Tale
King John
Richard the Second […]
The Gentlemen of Verona

The Merry Wives of Windsor
The Comedy of Errors
Loves Labour Lost
Midsomer Nights Dreame
The Merchant of Venice
As you like it
The Taming of ye Shrew
Alls well y^t Ends well
Henry ye fourth
The second part [...]
Richard ye third
Coriolanus
Andronicus
Julius Ceaser
The Moore of Venice
Anthony & Clopatra
Cymbelyne

(3) Other Plays Attributed to the King's Men and Shakespeare or 'W.S.'

The London Prodigall As it was Plaide by the Kings Maiesties Seruants. By William Shakespeare (1605).

A Yorkshire Tragedy Not so New as Lamentable and True. Acted by his Maiesties Players at the Globe. Written by W. Shakspeare (1608).

The True Chronicle Historie of the Whole Life and Death of Thomas Lord Cromwell As it Hath Beene Sundry Times Publikely Acted by the Kings Maiesties Seruants. Written by VV.S. (1613).

NOTES

Original documents marked with a dagger (†) are available on *Shakespeare Documented*.

Preface

1   †Enrolment of letters patent, 19 May 1603, TNA, C 66/1608, m. 4.

2   For an overview of the different kinds of players that made up a company, see Bentley 1984: 25–146.

3   †Warrant for payment for court performance, TNA, E 351/542, m. 207d; see Cook and Wilson 1961: 29.

4   †Account of Edmund Tilney, 1604–5, TNA, AO 3/908/13, fols 2a–b; †Account of Sir John Stanhope, Baron Stanhope of Harrington, Treasurer of the Chamber, 1612–13, Bodleian Library, MS Rawl. A. 239, fol. 47b. See Streitberger 1986: 8–9; Cook and Wilson 1961: 55–6.

5   For a recent reappraisal of Shakespeare's plays at court, see Dutton 2016; on court performance more broadly, see Astington 1999.

6   Beinecke Library, Yale University, Osborn MS b 7, fol. 18r; Roberts 2006: 88; Syme 2019a. I am grateful to Holger Schott Syme for drawing this document to my attention, and for sharing his work ahead of publication.

7   See, for instance, the pattern of revivals for *The Winter's Tale*. Simon Forman saw it at the Globe on 15 May 1611, and it was performed at court on 5 November; it was re-licensed by Herbert on 19 August 1623 because 'the allowed booke was missinge' and played at court on 18 January 1624. See †Account of Sir George Buc, Master of the Revels,

1611–12, TNA, AO 3/908/14, fol. 1b; †Bodleian Library, MS Ashmolean 208; Bawcutt 1996: 142, 149.

8   As Streitberger notes (1986: xxxi), a re-examination of the document by A. E. Stamp in the late 1920s has convinced most of its authenticity.

9   †Schedule of plays performed at court in 1636–7, TNA, AO 3/908/22. For a transcription of the warrant to which the schedule is attached, see Cunningham 1842: xxiv.

Prologue

1   †Account of Edmund Tilney, Master of the Revels, 1604–5, TNA, AO 3/908/13.

2   I discuss this play in greater detail in Chapter 5.

3   On Lowin's roles, see pp. 9–10, 16. In the folio text of *The Merry Wives of Windsor*, Falstaff has 424 lines (16%), Ford has 304 lines (12%) and Mistress Page has 279 lines (11%) (King 1992: 213–14). The quarto text is more dominated by Falstaff, who has 333 lines (22%) compared with Ford's 171 (11%) and Mistress Page's 124 (8%) (King 1992: 212). On Carlo Buffone, see Baldwin 1927: 439–40 and casting-chart between 434 and 435; Wiles 1987: 145–50; Shakespeare 2002: 78–9.

Chapter 1

1   For commentary on Lowin's roles, see Bowers 1987: 15–35; Kawai 1992: 17–34; Astington 2010: esp. 131–4, 163; Wooding 2013.

2   BL, Add. MS 22608; see Kirsch 1969.

3   The revival of *The Duchess of Malfi* must have taken place after 9 February 1620, when Robert Pallant Junior, who played Cariola, was apprenticed to John Heminges (Kathman 2005: 233–4), and before the death of Nicholas

Tooley, who played Forobosco and a madman, in early June 1623.

4   See Wiltshire and Swinton History Centre, MS 865/502/2 (*Soddered Citizen*); BL, Add. MS 36759 (*Swisser*); BL, Lansdowne MS 807b (*Second Maiden's Tragedy*); BL, Add. MS 18653 (*Barnavelt*); BL, Egerton MS 2828 (*Believe as You List*). For an overview of these materials, see King 1992: 34–40, 43–8, 58–60.

5   Dulwich College MS XIX; for a digital facsimile, see Ioppolo 2005. On its date, auspices and casting, see Kathman 2004b; 2011; Dutton 2018: 205–17.

6   Huntington Library, 499968, discussed in Riddell 1969. See Chapter 2, Figures 5 and 6.

7   Folger Art Inv. 271 no. 10e (2), discussed in George 1974: 9.

8   Beinecke Library, Yale University, Osborn MS b 7, fol. 18r; Syme 2019a: 233.

9   'Io: ffletcher', 'An Elegie on the Death of the Famous Acto^r Rich*ard* Burbage, who died 13° martij A° 1618', BL, Stowe MS 962, fols 62v–63v (62v). For a detailed commentary on this elegy see Döring 2005: 60–71.

10 The last actor-lists in which Condell appears are for *The Loyal Subject*, licensed on 16 November 1618, and *The Humorous Lieutenant*, first performed after Burbage's death in 1619.

11 For a complete list of Taylor's known and reputed roles, see Astington 2010: 219–20.

12 See p. 7 above; Syme 2019b.

13 Clarke played the female lead, Gratiana, in James Shirley's *The Wedding* (1626), and Bess Bridges in Heywood's *The Fair Maid of the West* (*c*. 1630). Around 1634 he played an adult male role, Hubert, in Robert Davenport's *King John and Matilda*. It is therefore likely that he was born around 1610.

14 Prologue to *Philaster*, BL, Harley MS 6918, fol. 99r.

15 †Enrolment of letters patent, 19 May 1603, TNA, C 66/1608, m. 4. For a range of approaches to early modern acting, see Bevington 1984; Roach 1985: 23–57; Astington 2010: 23–4, 44–7; Karim-Cooper 2016; Tribble 2017.

16 I have corrected the final line quoted here (which reads 'without iust weight, weight to ballast it wth all' in BL, Stowe MS 962) against the other manuscripts.

17 For an account and critique of such approaches, see Lopez 2011: 167–80.

18 Shank appears in the actor-lists for *The Prophetess* (licensed 14 May 1622) and *The Lover's Melancholy* (licensed 24 November 1628); he is assigned roles in *The Picture*, *The Soddered Citizen* and *The Wild Goose Chase*. Wright also states that he played Roger in *The Scornful Lady* (1699: 4), which the King's Men probably acquired in the mid- to late 1610s.

19 These assessments draw on King 1992 and Baldwin 1927, casting chart between pages 198 and 199. The second edition of *Philaster* features a joke that does not appear in the 1620 edition, in which the rebellious Captain and citizens mock Pharamond: '2. *Ci.* He had no Hornes sir had he? / *Cap.* No sir, hee's a Pollard' (Beaumont and Fletcher 1622, K3v). A 'pollard' is a male deer that has cast its antlers (*OED* pollard, *n.* 1), but the choice of this term may also be an in-joke referring to the actor playing the role.

20 For recent scholarship on boy actors, see McMillin 2004; Kathman 2004a; 2005; Tribble 2009; Astington 2010: 76–107; Barker 2015; Kathman 2015.

21 Holcombe gave his age as nineteen in a 1620 pedigree of the family of Holcombe of Hole, Devon. See Anon 1874: 300.

22 'The Waste Booke of Robert Glover Scrivener Anno D*omi*ni :1613: :1614: :1615:', TNA, WARD 9/351.

23 In chronological order: Christopher Beeston, Robert Gough, John Edmonds, Nicholas Tooley, Alexander Cooke, John Rice, Richard Robinson, Richard Sharpe, Thomas Holcombe, George Vernon, John Honeyman, John Thompson, William Trigg, Alexander Gough, Stephen Hammerton, Walter Clun and Charles Hart. This list is based on information in Bentley 1941–68: vol. 2; Kathman 2004a; 2005; 2015. We might also add to the total William Ecclestone (see Kathman 2015: 255–6), Michael Bedell, apprenticed to John Lowin for ten years on 24 January 1612, if he is the 'Mighell' who played small adult roles in *Sir John Van Olden Barnavelt*

(see Kathman 2004a: 34). and Thomas Bedford if he is the 'Thomas' who played Megra in *Philaster* and a Lady in *The Passionate Lovers* around 1638–9 (see p. 37).

24 Ruoff (1956) suggests that '*Thom.*' is John Thompson, but boy actors are more often referred to by their first names in playhouse documents.

25 Milhous and Hume 1991: 490, citing *John Hall v John Lacy et al.*, Court of Chancery, 1665, TNA, C 24/903.

26 LMA, P69/GIS/A/002/MS06419/003.

27 TNA, LC 5/133, p. 47; Nicoll and Boswell 1931: 369.

Interlude: Playing the Court, 1612–13

1 †Account of Sir John Stanhope, Baron Stanhope of Harrington, Treasurer of the Chamber, 1612–13, Bodleian Library, MS Rawl. A. 239.

2 †Account of George Buc, Master of the Revels, 1611–12, TNA, AO 3/308/14, fol. 2r; Arber 1875–7: 3.216v.

3 The song in *The Captain*, 'Orpheus with His Lute', also appears in Shakespeare and Fletcher's *Henry VIII* (3.1.31–40).

4 On Beaumont and Fletcher's uses of Cervantes, see essays by Alexander Samson and Trudi L. Darby in Ardila 2009; for a range of perspectives on *Cardenio*, see Carnegie and Taylor 2012.

5 See Baldwin 1927, casting-charts between 110 and 111, 198 and 199.

6 Both roles are overshadowed by Lowin's Bosola, who has 824 lines, and the Duchess, who has 556.

Chapter 2

1 'Io: ffletcher', 'An Elegie on the Death of the Famous Acto[r] Rich*ard* Burbage, who died 13° martij A° 1618', BL, Stowe MS 962, fols 62v–63v.

2 *The Alchemist* was performed alongside *Othello* at court in 1612–13. It was performed there again on 1 January 1623 (Bawcutt 1996: 139), revived at Blackfriars on 1 December 1631, when Herbert claimed £13 for his winter benefit (Bawcutt 1996: 174), revived again in January 1638 (letter of Madam Ann Merrick to Mistress Lydall, 21 January 1639, State Papers, Domestic, TNA, SP 16/409, fol. 327), and seen by Sir Humphrey Mildmay in the company of Mistress James and 'her goodman' on 18 May 1639 (Bentley 1937: 69).

3 Huntington Library, 49968; see Riddell 1969.

4 Iago has 1,032 lines in the quarto (31% of the total) and 1,098 in the folio (31%); Othello has 811 lines in the quarto (27%) and 891 in the folio (25%). The third largest role, Desdemona, has 342 lines (11%) in the quarto and 381 lines (11%) in the folio. See King 1992: 220–2. Face has 1,215 lines in *The Alchemist* and Subtle 1,066; the third largest role, Sir Epicure Mammon, has 509 lines, followed by Doll with 223 lines and Surly with 222. See Baldwin 1927, casting-chart between 434 and 435.

5 On Rice's early career with the King's Men, see p. 61. Ecclestone appears in the actor-list for *The Alchemist* and he is not recorded with another company in the previous years, meaning that he may have begun his career with the King's Men. See Kathman 2015.

6 Beinecke Library, Yale University, Osborn MS b 7, fol. 18r. On Fletcher's association with the King's Men, see Roberts 2006: 88; Syme 2019a: 241–3.

7 Baldwin 1927, casting-chart between 110 and 111.

8 Field was a member of Lady Elizabeth's Men until at least 1614; he had left by 20 March 1616, when its sharers signed new articles of agreement with Edward Alleyn and Joseph Meade (Greg 1907: 86–91) and he appears in the actor-list for *The Mad Lover*, performed by the King's Men in 1616 (Beaumont and Fletcher 1679: C4r, 2H1v).

9 The King's Men had come to an arrangement with Herbert whereby he took a cut of the proceeds of two performances of his choosing, one in the summer and one in the winter.

10 BL, Add. MS 22608, fol. 84v, quoted in Kirsch 1969: 257.

11 I have found that 'William Eaglestone' was buried at St Benet, Paul's Wharf, on 30 August 1623 (parish register, LMA, P69/BEN3/A/001/MS05716), a date that tallies with his disappearance from the company's personnel around this time. On the deaths of Tooley and Underwood, see Honigmann and Brock 1993: 124–8, 142–5.

12 Another important variation is between the folio and the second quarto of 1630: 'Her' in l. 389 is taken from Q2, where F has 'My'.

13 Taylor may also have played the title character in *Monsieur Thomas*, probably written by Fletcher for Lady Elizabeth's Men around 1615, who is described by Alice as having 'A hansom browne complexion', to which Mary replies, 'Reasonable / Inclining to a tawney' (1.3.30–1).

14 Dyer 2007: 102. On current efforts to improve the lighting of black skin on film, see Latif 2017.

15 Karim-Cooper 2006: 12, 174. The foundational study of 'fairness' in early modern English culture is Hall 1995: 62–122; see also Iyengar 2005.

Interlude: Playing the Court, 1619–20

1 BL, Cotton MS Tiberius E.X, fols 70v, 197v, 211v; reproduced in Marcham 1925. Other scraps feature plays that appear to have belonged to Prince Charles's Men (Nicol 2006).

2 Developing a suggestion of Chambers (1925: 484), Wiggins (2011–18: 7.293) suggests that *The Scholar Turned to School Again*, *The False Friend*, *The Spanish Tragedy* and *Albumazar*, which all appear in a scrap that contains numbers in the left-hand side, were in other repertories and that Buc was considering alternatives for certain performance slots. However, I am not convinced that this is correct because there is substantial evidence that the King's Men owned *The Spanish Tragedy* in the early seventeenth century (see Syme 2013).

3 Line-counts are from Baldwin 1927, casting-chart between pages 198 and 199.

4   'Io: ffletcher', 'An Elegie on the Death of the Famous Acto^r Rich*ar*d Burbage, who died 13° martij A° 1618', BL, Stowe MS 962, fols 62v–63v; Cavendish 1975: 4.4.596–8.

Chapter 3

1. TNA, LC 5/132, p. 334; Nicoll and Boswell 1931: 361.
2. TNA, SP 14/107, fol. 61.
3. Sackville Papers, Kent History and Library Centre, U269, quoted from C.W. Wallace Papers, Huntington Library, Box 7.
4. Letter of Sir Gerrard Herbert to Sir Dudley Carleton, 24 May 1619, TNA, SP 14/109, fols 100–1. For a transcription by W. D. Selby of this section of the letter see Munro 1909: 1.276–7.
5. BL, Egerton MS 2592, fols 81–2, quoted from Shakespeare 2010: 67.
6. Line counts are taken from Baldwin 1927, casting-chart between pages 198 and 199.
7. LMA, P71/OLA/009.
8. On 1619 and its place in the history of slavery, see Guasco 2014: 1–10.
9. Warrant for payment with a list of plays, Folger MS X.d.110 (available on LUNA: Folger Digital Image Collection, https://luna.folger.edu).
10. These are my own counts.
11. See 37–8.
12. For a summary of various perspectives, see Gossett 2004: 49–54.

Interlude: Playing the Court, 1633–4

1. An incomplete account of expenses incurred by Anna's household includes a payment to Heminges 'for one plaie acted before her ma*jes*tie at Queenes court' on 21 December 1615 (TNA, E 101/47/8; Cook and Wilson 1961: 144), and it is

likely that similar performances by the King's Men took place for which the records have not survived.
2. The play was published in 1647 as *The Lovers' Progress*.
3. TNA, C 115/106/8416, quoted from Montagu 1997: viii.
4. British Museum, MS Harl. 454, quoted from Bentley 1937: 64; Bawcutt 1996: 187.

Chapter 4

1. Bodleian Library, MS Rawl. A. 239, fol. 47b (1612–13); TNA, E 351/544, fol. 90b (1618); †TNA, AO 3/908/22 (1636–7); Wright 1887: frontispiece, 10–11 (1638–9).
2. On the recorded performances of *The Winter's Tale* and *The Tempest*, see Appendix. On performances of *The Prophetess*, see p. 129. It was in a list of plays of the King's Men that the Lord Chamberlain protected from printing on 7 August 1641 (Nicoll and Boswell 1931: 398–9).
3. The *Henry V* prologue may be closer in date to *The Merry Devil of Edmonton* than is usually assumed: Richard Dutton thinks it 'likely' that the folio text of *Henry V*, which preserves the prologue and choruses, 'belongs to 1602, after the decisive (Agincourt-like) Battle of Kinsale' (2016: 177).
4. †Account of George Buc, Master of the Revels, 1611–12, TNA AO 3/908/14.
5. Huntington Library, 499968; Riddell 1969.
6. For a range of approaches, see Diehl 2008; Delsigne 2014; Roberts 1999; Schalkwyk 1992.
7. For a critique of this tendency, see Dawson 1988.
8. Baldwin 1927, casting-chart between pages 198 and 199.
9. King assigns the role to a boy in *Casting*, 24, and it makes sense given the characterization of Ariel and the lack of female roles in *The Tempest*. See also Vitkus 2003.
10. Baldwin assigns Diocles to Lowin, as one of his 'soldier potentate' roles and Maximinian to Taylor because he is described as 'young' (1927: 201, 384), but it is possible that the casting was reversed.

Interlude: Playing the Court, 1636–7

1. †Schedule of plays performed at court, 1637, TNA, AO 3/908/22. See also Cunningham 1842: xxiv–v, who transcribes the warrant to which the schedule is attached. Notices of the plays performed between 26 December 1636 and 21 February 1637, with the exception of *Hamlet*, were also transcribed by Edmond Malone from Sir Henry Herbert's office book (Shakespeare 1821: 3.239; Bawcutt 1996: 199–201). By 1636, the King's Men were being paid for a calendar year, rather than a single court season, so the original list includes plays performed in the later part of the 1635–6 season – earlier performances of Carlell's *Arviragus and Philicia*, Jonson's *Epicoene* and *Alphonsus, Emperor of Germany* 'at the Blackfryers for the Queene and the prince Elector' – and lacks those performed at Easter and the summer months of 1637.

2. TNA, AO 3/908/22.

3. Northumberland Papers, quoted in Anon 1872: 118 (no. 132).

4. BL, Add. MS 10419. For discussion, see Wiggins 2011–18: 9.459; Randall 1995: 357–8.

5. Laud 1700: 104; Bodleian Library, MS Twyne 17, p. 193, quoted from Elliott et al. 2004: 1.542.

6. TNA, AO 3/908/22.

7. TNA, LC 5/134, p. 165; Nicoll and Boswell 1931: 382–3; Bawcutt 1996: 200.

8. Partial lists survive of the court repertories of 1635–9; for 1639–42 we know of only one play, *The Scornful Lady* (6 January 1642).

9. TNA, AO 3/908/22.

Chapter 5

1. Enrolment of letters patent authorizing the King's Men, 19 May 1603, TNA, C 66/1608, m. 4.

2   On the controversies over Charles's attempts to levy ship money, see Sharpe 1992: 714–30.
3   For debates on the identity of this play, see Barroll 1988; Worden 2003; Hammer 2008.
4   †Examination of Augustine Phillips, TNA, SP 12/278, fol. 139r. This document is transcribed along with other examinations that discuss the performance in Chambers 1930: 2.34–5.
5   †Forman, 'The Bocke of Plaies', Bodleian Library MS Ashmole 208, fol. 201r–v.
6   Henry Bluett, letter to Richard Weeks, 4 July 1613, Somerset Record Office, DD/SF 3066, quoted from Cole 1981. On this and other accounts, see Shakespeare and Fletcher 2003: 9, 57–63.
7   Robert Gell, letter to Sir Martyn Stuteville, 9 August 1628, BL, Harley MS 383, fol. 65, quoted from Shakespeare and Fletcher 2003: 16.
8   Nathaniel Tomkyns, letter to Sir Robert Phelips, 16 August 1634, Somerset Record Office, DD/PH/212/12, quoted from Berry 1984: 212.
9   McClure 1939: 1.199; Somerset Record Office, DD/SF 3066; Somerset Record Office, DD/PH/212/12.
10 TNA, SP 14/110, fol. 25.
11 TNA, SP 14/110, fol. 57.
12 Biblioteca Nacional, Madrid, MS 18203, quoted from Middleton 1993: 194, 195, 197.
13 Berkshire Record Office, Reading, Trumbull alphabetical correspondence, 48/135, quoted from Middleton 1993: 198.
14 Victoria and Albert Museum, Dyce Copy, 25.D.42, quoted from Middleton 1993: 211.
15 TNA, SP 14/171, quoted from Middleton 1993: 202.
16 TNA, C 115/N1/8488, quoted from Middleton 1993: 201.
17 Trumbull alphabetical correspondence, 48/136, quoted from Middleton 1993: 203.
18 Trumbull alphabetical correspondence, 48/137, quoted from Middleton 1993: 207.

19 BL, Harley MS 383, fol. 65, quoted from Shakespeare and Fletcher 2003: 16; Newsletter, 8 August 1628, Isham of Lamport Manuscript Collection, Northamptonshire Record Office, MS IL 2671, fol. 1v, quoted from Chambers 1930: 2.348.

20 BL, Harley MS 383, fol. 65; Northamptonshire Record Office, MS IL 2671, fol. 1v.

21 BL, Harley MS 383, fol. 65.

22 On this point, see Cogswell and Lake 2009: 256–7.

23 Somerset Record Office, DD/SF 3066.

24 † BL, Harley MS 7002, fol. 268.

25 See Baldwin 1927, casting-chart between pages 198 and 199. It is also possible that Nathan Field played Orange, depending on when he died.

26 On Buc's career see Howard-Hill 1988: 44–9. For a reassessment of the play's place in European politics, see Hackett 2014: 157–76.

27 TNA, SP 14/171, quoted from Middleton 1993: 205. For a detailed exploration of the uses of costume in the play, see Lublin 2011: 163–80.

28 These are my counts.

Epilogue

1 An important exception is Gurr 2004: 200–16, which offers a detailed account of 'The Afterlife'.

2 See Wickham, Berry and Ingram 2000: 529, 622, quoting TNA, C 54/3579, m. 39–40 and Francis Brend v. Sir Robert Smyth et al., Court of Chancery, 1675, TNA, C 5/448/137.

3 Hotson 1928: 32, quoting Theophilus Bird v. Thomas Morrison, Court of Chancery, 1655, TNA, C 5/434/21.

4 Hotson 1928: 32–3, quoting TNA C 5/434/21. See also Milhous and Hume 1991: 491–2.

5 Milhous and Hume 1991: 496, quoting Richard Baxter et al. v. Elizabeth Conway and William Ridges, Court of Chancery, 1661, TNA, C 10/62/8.

6 For a range of allusions, see Bentley 1945; Sirluck 1955.

REFERENCES

Anon (1609), *Pimlyco. Or, Runne Red-Cap*, London.
Anon (1614), *A Horrible, Cruel and Bloody Murder*, London.
Anon (1636), *The Booke of Bulls*, London.
Anon (1641), *The Brothers of the Blade*, London.
Anon (1642), *An Ordinance of Both Houses of Parliament for the Suppressing of Publike Stage-Playes*, London.
Anon (1644), *The Great Eclipse of the Sun, or Charles his Waine Over-clouded*, London.
Anon (1647a), *Perfect Occurrences of Every Dayes Journall in Parliament*, 1–8 October.
Anon (1647b), *The Perfect Weekely Account*, 6–13 October.
Anon (1648), *An Ordinance of the Lords and Commons Assembled in Parliament, for the Utter Suppression and Abolishing of all Stage-Playes and Interludes*, London.
Anon (1767–1830), *Journal of the House of Lords [1509–1793]*, 39 vols, London: HMSO.
Anon (1872), *Third Report of the Royal Commission on Historical Manuscripts*, Appendix, London: HMSO.
Anon (1874), *Miscellanea Genealogica et Heraldica*, n.s., 1.
Anon (1930), *The Two Noble Ladies*, ed. Rebecca G. Rhoads, Oxford: Malone Society.
Anon (2000), *The Merry Devil of Edmonton*, ed. Nicola Bennett, London: Nick Hern Books.
Arber, Edward, ed. (1875–7), *A Transcript of the Registers of the Company of Stations of London, 1554–1640*, 5 vols, London: Privately Printed.
Ardila, J.A.G., ed. (2009), *The Cervantean Heritage: Reception and Influence of Cervantes in Britain*, London: Legenda.
Astington, John H. (1999), *English Court Theatre 1558–1642*, Cambridge: Cambridge University Press.
Astington, John H. (2010), *Actors and Acting in Shakespeare's Time: The Art of Stage Playing*, Cambridge: Cambridge University Press.
Bailey, Amanda (2013), *On Bondage: Debt, Property and Personhood in Early Modern England*, Philadelphia: University of Pennsylvania Press.

Bailey, Rebecca (2009), *Staging the Old Faith: Queen Henrietta Maria and the Theatre of Caroline England, 1625–42*, Manchester: Manchester University Press.

Baldwin, Thomas Whitfield (1927), *The Organization and Personnel of the Shakespearean Company*, Princeton: Princeton University Press.

Bancroft, Thomas (1658), *Time's Out of Tune*, London.

Barker, Roberta (2015), 'The "Play-Boy", the Female Performer, and the Art of Portraying a Lady', *Shakespeare Bulletin*, 33: 83–97.

Barroll, Leeds (1988), 'A New History for Shakespeare and His Time', *Shakespeare Quarterly*, 39: 441–64.

Bate, Jonathan (1993), *Shakespeare and Ovid*, Oxford: Clarendon Press.

Bawcutt, N.W. (1996), *Control and Censorship of Caroline Drama: The Records of Sir Henry Herbert, Master of the Revels, 1623–73*, Oxford: Clarendon Press.

Beal, Peter (1980), 'Massinger at Bay: Unpublished Verses in a War of the Theatres', *The Yearbook of English Studies*, 10: 190–203.

Beaumont, Francis, and John Fletcher (1622), *Philaster*, London.

Beaumont, Francis, and John Fletcher (1679), *Fifty Comedies and Tragedies*, London.

Bentley, Gerald Eades (1937), 'The Diary of a Caroline Theatergoer', *Modern Philology*, 35: 61–72.

Bentley, Gerald Eades (1941–68), *The Jacobean and Caroline Stage*, 7 vols, Oxford: Clarendon Press.

Bentley, Gerald Eades (1945), *Shakespeare and Jonson: Their Reputations in the Seventeenth Century Compared*, 2 vols, Chicago: University of Chicago Press.

Bentley, Gerald Eades (1948), 'Shakespeare and the Blackfriars Theatre', *Shakespeare Survey*, 1: 38–50.

Bentley, Gerald Eades (1984), *The Profession of Player in Shakespeare's Time 1590–1642*, Princeton: Princeton University Press.

Berry, Herbert (1984), 'The Globe Bewitched and El Hombre Fiel', *Medieval and Renaissance Drama in England*, 1: 211–30.

Bevington, David (1984), *Action is Eloquence: Shakespeare's Language of Gesture*, Cambridge, MA: Harvard University Press.

Bowers, Rick (1987), 'John Lowin: Actor-Manager of the King's Company, 1630–42', *Theatre Survey*, 28: 15–35.

Braithwaite, Richard (1631), *Whimzies, or a New Cast of Characters*, London.

Bratton, Jacky (2003), *New Readings in Theatre History*, Cambridge: Cambridge University Press.
Brewer, Thomas (1631), *The Life and Death of the Merry Devill of Edmonton*, London.
Britland, Karen (2006), *Drama at the Courts of Queen Henrietta Maria*, Cambridge: Cambridge University Press.
Britton, Dennis Austin (2018), 'Contaminatio, Race, and Pity in *Othello*', in Dennis Austin Britton and Melissa Walter, eds, *Rethinking Shakespeare Source Study: Audiences, Authors, and Digital Technologies*, 46–64, New York: Routledge.
Brown, Rawdon, ed. (1908), *Calendar of State Papers Relating to English Affairs in the Archives of Venice, Vol. 14, 1615–17*, London: HMSO.
Butler, Martin (1984), *Theatre and Crisis, 1632–1642*, Cambridge: Cambridge University Press.
Callaghan, Dympna (2000), *Shakespeare Without Women: Representing Gender and Race on the Early Modern Stage*, London: Routledge.
Carlell, Lodowick (1629), *The Deserving Favourite*, London.
Carlell, Lodowick (1639), *Arviragus and Philicia […] The First and Second Part*, London.
Carlell, Lodowick (1655), *The Passionate Lovers, A Tragi-Comedy. The First and Second Parts*, London.
Carlson, Marvin (2001), *The Haunted Stage: The Theatre as Memory Machine*, Ann Arbor: University of Michigan Press.
Carnegie, David, and Gary Taylor, eds (2012), *The Quest for Cardenio: Shakespeare, Fletcher, Cervantes, and the Lost Play*, Oxford: Oxford University Press.
Cavendish, William, Earl of Newcastle (1975), *A Critical Edition of Wit's Triumvirate, or The Philosopher*, ed. Cathryn Anne Nelson, Salzburg: Institut für Englische Sprache und Literatur, Universität Salzburg.
Cawdry, Robert (1609), *A Table Alphabeticall Contayning and Teaching the True Writing and Understanding of Hard Usuall English Wordes*, London.
Cerasano, S.P. (1998), 'Edward Alleyn's "Retirement" 1597–1600', *Medieval and Renaissance Drama in England*, 10: 98–112.
Cervantes, Miguel de (1619), *The Travels of Persiles and Sigismunda: A Northern History*, London.
Chakravarty, Urvashi (2012), 'Livery, Liberty, and Legal Fictions', *English Literary Renaissance*, 42: 365–90.

Chambers, E.K. (1923), *The Elizabethan Stage*, 4 vols, Oxford: Clarendon Press.

Chambers, E.K. (1925), 'The King's Office of the Revels, 1610–1622', *Review of English Studies*, 1: 479–84.

Chambers, E.K. (1930), *William Shakespeare: A Study of Facts and Problems*, 2 vols, Oxford: Clarendon Press.

Chapman, George (1910), *The Plays and Poems of George Chapman*, ed. Thomas Marc Parrott, London: Routledge.

Chapman, George (1965), *Bussy D'Ambois*, ed. Maurice Evans, London: Ernest Benn.

Clare, Janet (2014), *Shakespeare's Stage Traffic: Imitation, Borrowing and Competition in Renaissance Theatre*, Cambridge: Cambridge University Press.

Clavell, John (1936), *The Soddered Citizen*, ed. J.H.P. Pafford, Oxford: Malone Society.

Clubb, Louise George (1989), *Italian Drama in Shakespeare's Time*, New Haven: Yale University Press.

Cogswell, Thomas, and Peter Lake (2009), 'Buckingham Does the Globe: *Henry VIII* and the Politics of Popularity in the 1620s', *Shakespeare Quarterly*, 60: 253–78.

Cole, Maija Jansson (1981), 'A New Account of the Burning of the Globe', *Shakespeare Quarterly*, 32: 352.

Collins, Eleanor (2013), 'Ghosts in the Archive: Edmond Malone, Craven Ord, and the Missing Texts of Henry Herbert's "Office-Book"', *Critical Quarterly*, 55: 30–41.

Cook, David, and F.P. Wilson, eds (1961), 'Dramatic Records in the Declared Accounts of the Treasurer of the Chamber 1558–1642', *Malone Society Collections*, 6.

Cornish, F.W., ed. (1897), *Letters and Journals of William Cory*, London: Printed for the Subscribers.

Cox, Robert (1661), *The Merry Conceited Humors of Bottom the Weaver*, London.

Cunningham, Peter (1842), *Extracts from the Accounts of the Revels at Court in the Reigns of Queen Elizabeth and King James I*, London: Shakespeare Society.

Cutts, John P. (1955), 'Robert Johnson: King's Musician in his Majesty's Public Entertainment', *Music and Letters*, 36: 110–25.

Cyprian (1984), *The Letters of St Cyprian of Carthage*, trans. G.W. Clarke, 2 vols, New York: Newman Press.

Dadabhoy, Ambereen (2014), 'Two-Faced: The Problem of Othello's Visage', in Lena Cowen Orlin, ed., *Othello: The State of Play*, 121–48, London: Bloomsbury.

Davenant, William (1636), *The Platonick Lovers. A Tragaecomedy*, London.

Davenant, William (1638), *Madagascar with Other Poems*, London.

Davenant, William (1673), *News from Plymouth*, in *The Works of Sr. William Davenant, Kt.*, London.

Davies, John ([?1611]), *The Scourge of Folly*, London.

Dawson, Anthony (1988), '*Tempest* in a Teapot: Critics, Evaluation, Ideology', in Maurice Charney, ed., *Bad Shakespeare: Revaluations of the Shakespeare Canon*, 61–73, Rutherford, NJ: Fairleigh-Dickinson University Press.

de la Serre, Jean Puget (1639), *The Mirror Which Flatters Not*, London.

Delsigne, Jill (2014), 'Hermetic Miracles in *The Winter's Tale*', in Lisa Hopkins and Helen Ostovich, eds, *Magical Transformations on the Early Modern English Stage*, 91–110, Farnham: Ashgate.

Depledge, Emma (2018), *Shakespeare's Rise to Cultural Prominence: Politics, Print and Alteration, 1642–1700*, Cambridge: Cambridge University Press.

Dickinson, Janet (2012), *Court Politics and the Earl of Essex, 1589–1601*, London: Routledge.

Diehl, Huston (2008), '"Does not the stone rebuke us?": The Pauline Rebuke and Paulina's Lawful Magic in *The Winter's Tale*', in Paul Yachnin and Patricia Badir, eds, *Shakespeare and the Cultures of Performance*, 69–82, Aldershot: Ashgate.

Döring, Tobias (2005), 'Writing Performance: How to Elegize Elizabethan Actors', *Shakespeare Survey*, 58: 60–71.

Downes, John (1708), *Roscius Anglicanus, or An Historical Review of the Stage*, London.

Dustagheer, Sarah (2017), *Shakespeare's Two Playhouses: Repertory and Theatre Space at the Globe and Blackfriars, 1599–1613*, Cambridge: Cambridge University Press.

Dutton, Richard (2016), *Shakespeare, Court Dramatist*, Oxford: Oxford University Press.

Dutton, Richard (2018), *Shakespeare's Theatre: A History*, Oxford: Wiley Blackwell.

Dyer, Richard (2007), *White: Essays on Race and Culture*, Abingdon: Routledge.

Edmond, Mary (1987), *Rare Sir William Davenant: Poet Laureate, Playwright, Civil War General, Restoration Theatre Manager*, Manchester: Manchester University Press.

Elliott, John R. (1993), 'Four Caroline Playgoers', *Medieval and Renaissance Drama in England*, 6: 179–93.

Elliott, John R., Alan H. Nelson, Alexandra F. Johnston and Diana Wyatt, eds (2004), *Records of Early English Drama: Oxford*, 2 vols, Toronto: University of Toronto Press.

Eyre, G.E. Briscoe (1913–14), *A Transcript of the Registers of the Worshipful Company of Stationers from 1640 to 1708 A.D.*, 3vols, London: Privately Printed.

Flecknoe, Richard (1664), *Love's Kingdom: A Pastoral Trage-comedy* [...] *With a Short Treatise of the English Stage*, London.

Flecknoe, Richard (1665), *Rich. Flecknoe's Aenigmatical Characters*, London.

Fletcher, John, and Philip Massinger (1980), *Sir John Van Olden Barnavelt*, ed. T.H. Howard-Hill, London: Malone Society.

Foakes, R.A. ed. (2002), *Henslowe's Diary*, second edition, Cambridge: Cambridge University Press.

Ford, John (1629), *The Lovers Melancholy*, London.

Fraunce, Abraham (1588), *The Arcadian Rhetorike*, London.

Freehafer, John (1969), '*Cardenio* by Shakespeare and Fletcher', *Publications of the Modern Language Association of America*, 84: 501–13.

Freeman, Arthur, and Janet Ing Freeman (2004), *John Payne Collier: Scholarship and Forgery in the Nineteenth Century*, New Haven: Yale University Press.

G[ainsford], T[homas] (1616), *The Rich Cabinet*, London.

Gayton, Edmund (1654), *Pleasant Notes Upon Don Quixot*, London.

George, David (1974), 'Early Cast Lists for Two Beaumont and Fletcher Plays', *Theatre Notebook*, 38: 9–11.

Gildon, Charles (1694), 'Some Reflections on Mr. *Rymer*'s *Short View of Tragedy*', in *Miscellaneous Letters and Essays on Several Subjects*, 64–118, London.

Glapthorne, Henry (1639), *Poems*, London.

Greg, W.W., ed. (1907), *Henslowe Papers*, London: A.H. Bullen.

Griffin, Eric J. (2009), *English Renaissance Drama and the Specter of Spain: Ethnopoetics and Empire*, Philadelphia: University of Pennsylvania Press.

Guasco, Michael (2014), *Slaves and Englishmen: Human Bondage in the Early Modern Atlantic World*, Philadelphia: University of Pennsylvania Press.

Gurr, Andrew (1989), '*The Tempest's* Tempest at Blackfriars', *Shakespeare Survey*, 41: 91–102.

Gurr, Andrew (1996), *The Shakespearian Playing Companies*, Oxford: Clarendon Press.

Gurr, Andrew (2004), *The Shakespeare Company, 1594–1642*, Cambridge: Cambridge University Press.

Gurr, Andrew (2006), '"The stage is hung with black": When Did Melpomene Lose Her Identity?', in Paul Nelson and June Schlueter, eds, *Acts of Criticism: Performance Matters in Shakespeare and his Contemporaries*, 58–73, Cranbury, NJ: Associated University Presses.

Gurr, Andrew, and Farah Karim-Cooper, eds (2014), *Moving Shakespeare Indoors: Performance and Repertoire in the Jacobean Playhouse*, Cambridge: Cambridge University Press.

Hackett, Kimberly J. (2014), 'The English Reception of Oldenbarnavelt's Fall', *Huntington Library Quarterly*, 77: 157–76.

Hall, Kim F. (1995), *Things of Darkness: Economies of Race and Gender in Early Modern England*, Ithaca: Cornell University Press.

Hall, Kim F., ed. (2007), *Othello: Texts and Contexts*, New York: Bedford.

Hammer, Paul E.J. (2008), 'Shakespeare's *Richard II*, the Play of 7 February 1601, and the Essex Rising', *Shakespeare Quarterly*, 59: 1–35.

Hand, Molly (2011), '"You Take No Labour": Women Workers of Magic in Early Modern England', in Michelle M. Dowd and Natasha Korda, eds, *Working Subjects in Early Modern English Drama*, 161–76, Farnham: Ashgate.

Hankey, Julie (2005), *Othello*, Shakespeare in Production, second edition, Cambridge: Cambridge University Press.

Harbage, Alfred (1936), *Cavalier Drama: An Historical and Critical Supplement to the Study of the Elizabethan and Restoration Stage*, London: Oxford University Press.

Harris, Jonathan Gil (2009), *Untimely Matter in the Time of Shakespeare*, Philadelphia: University of Pennsylvania Press.

Heywood, Thomas (1612), *An Apology for Actors*, London.

Heywood, Thomas (1613), *The Brazen Age*, London.

Highfill, Philip H., Kalman A. Burnim and Edward A. Langhans, eds (1973–93), *A Biographical Dictionary of Actors, Actresses, Musicians, Dancers, and Other Stage Personnel, 1660–1800*, 16vols, Carbondale: Southern Illinois University Press.

Honigmann, E.A.J., and Susan Brock, eds (1993), *Playhouse Wills, 1558–1642*, Manchester: Manchester University Press.

Hotson, Leslie (1928), *The Commonwealth and Restoration Stage*, Cambridge, MA: Harvard University Press.

Howard-Hill, T.H. (1988), 'Buc and the Censorship of *Sir John Van Olden Barnavelt* in 1619', *Review of English Studies*, 39: 39–63.

Howard, Skiles (1985), 'A Re-Examination of Baldwin's Theory of Acting Lines', *Theatre Survey*, 26: 1–20.

Ioppolo, Grace, dir. (2005), *Henslowe-Alleyn Digitization Project*, http://www.henslowe-alleyn.org.uk.

Iyengar, Sujata (2005), *Shades of Difference: Mythologies of Skin Color in Early Modern England*, Philadelphia: University of Pennsylvania Press.

Jonson, Ben (1616), *The Workes of Benjamin Jonson*, London.

Jonson, Ben (1631), *The New Inne, or The Light Heart*, London.

Karim-Cooper, Farah (2006), *Cosmetics in Shakespearean and Renaissance Drama*, Edinburgh: Edinburgh University Press.

Karim-Cooper, Farah (2016), *The Hand on the Shakespearean Stage: Gesture, Touch and the Spectacle of Dismemberment*, London: Bloomsbury Arden Shakespeare.

Kathman, David (2004a), 'Grocers, Goldsmiths, and Drapers: Freemen and Apprentices in the Elizabethan Theater', *Shakespeare Quarterly*, 55: 1–49.

Kathman, David (2004b), 'Reconsidering *The Seven Deadly Sins*', *Early Theatre*, 7: 13–44.

Kathman, David (2005), 'How Old Were Shakespeare's Boy Actors?', *Shakespeare Survey*, 58: 220–46.

Kathman, David (2011), '*The Seven Deadly Sins* and Theatrical Apprenticeship', *Early Theatre*, 14: 121–39.

Kathman, David (2015), 'John Rice and the Boys of the Jacobean King's Men', *Shakespeare Survey*, 68: 247–66.

Kawai, Shoichiro (1992), 'John Lowin as Iago', *Shakespeare Studies (Tokyo)*, 30: 17–34.

Killigrew, Thomas (1664), *The Princess, or Love at First Sight*, in *Comedies and Tragedies Written by Thomas Killigrew*, London.

King, T.J. (1992), *Casting Shakespeare's Plays: London Actors and Their Roles, 1590–1642*, Cambridge: Cambridge University Press.

Kirkman, Francis, comp. (1662), *The Wits, or, Sport upon Sport*, London.

Kirsch, Arthur C. (1969), 'A Caroline Commentary on the Drama', *Modern Philology*, 66: 256–61.

Kirwan, Peter (2015), *Shakespeare and the Idea of Apocrypha*, Cambridge: Cambridge University Press.

Knowler, William, ed. (1739), *The Earl of Strafford's Letters and Dispatches*, 2 vols, London.

Knutson, Roslyn L. (2006), 'What If There Wasn't a "Blackfriars Repertory"?', in Paul Menzer, ed., *Inside Shakespeare: Essays on the Blackfriars Stage*, 54–60, Selinsgrove: Susquehanna University Press.

Lamb, Charles (1811), 'On Garrick, and Acting, and the Plays of Shakspeare, Considered with Reference to their Fitness for Stage Representation', *The Reflector: A Quarterly Magazine*, 2: 298–313.

Latif, Nadia (2017), 'It's Lit! How Film Finally Learned to Light Black Skin', *Guardian*, 21 September.

Laud, William (1700), *The Second Volume of the Remains of the Most Reverend Father in God, and Blessed Martyr William Laud*, London.

Lopez, Jeremy (2011), 'Alleyn Resurrected', *Marlowe Studies*, 1: 167–80.

Loughnane, Rory (2013), 'Semi-Choric Devices and the Framework for Playgoer Response in *King Henry VIII*', in Andrew J. Power and Rory Loughnane, eds, *Late Shakespeare, 1608–1613*, 108–23, Cambridge: Cambridge University Press.

Lublin, Robert I. (2011), *Costuming the Shakespearean Stage: Visual Codes of Representation in Early Modern Theatre and Culture*, Farnham: Ashgate.

Lupić, Ivan (2012), 'Malone's *Double Falsehood*', in David Carnegie and Gary Taylor, eds, *The Quest for Cardenio: Shakespeare, Fletcher, Cervantes, and the Lost Play*, 95–114, Oxford: Oxford University Press.

Marcham, Frank (1925), *The King's Office of the Revels 1610–1622: Fragments of Documents in the Department of Manuscripts, British Museum*, London: Frank Marcham.

Massinger, Philip (1927), *Believe as You List*, ed. C.J. Sisson, Oxford: Malone Society.
McClure, Norman Egbert, ed. (1939), *The Letters of John Chamberlain*, Philadelphia: American Philosophical Society.
McManus, Clare (2015), '"Sing it like poor Barbary": *Othello* and Early Modern Women's Performance', *Shakespeare Bulletin*, 33: 99–120.
McMillin, Scott (2004), 'The Sharer and His Boy: Rehearsing Shakespeare's Women', in Peter Holland and Stephen Orgel, eds., *From Script to Stage in Early Modern England*, 231–45, London: Palgrave.
Menzer, Paul (2006), 'The Actor's Inhibition: Early Modern Acting and the Rhetoric of Restraint', *Renaissance Drama*, 35: 83–111.
Middleton, Thomas (1657), *No Wit, [No] Help Like a Womans*, London.
Middleton, Thomas (1909), *The Second Maiden's Tragedy*, ed. W.W. Greg, Oxford: Malone Society.
Middleton, Thomas (1993), *A Game at Chess*, ed. T.H. Howard-Hill, Manchester: Manchester University Press.
Milhous, Judith, and Robert D. Hume (1991), 'New Light on English Acting Companies in 1646, 1648 and 1660', *Review of English Studies*, n.s., 42: 487–509.
Montagu, Walter (1997), *The Shepherds' Paradise*, ed. Sarah Poynting, Oxford: Malone Society.
Munday, Anthony (1610), *Londons Love, to the Royal Prince Henrie*, London, 1610.
Munro, John, ed. (1909), *The Shakspere Allusion Book*, 2 vols, London: Chatto and Windus.
Munro, Lucy (2005), *Children of the Queen's Revels: A Jacobean Theatre Repertory*, Cambridge: Cambridge University Press.
Nicol, David (2006), 'The Repertory of Prince Charles's (I) Company, 1608–1625', *Early Theatre*, 9: 57–72.
Nicol, David (2012), *Middleton and Rowley: Forms of Collaboration in the Jacobean Playhouse*, Toronto: University of Toronto Press.
Nicoll, Allardyce, and Eleanore Boswell, eds (1931), 'Dramatic Records: The Lord Chamberlain's Office', *Malone Society Collections*, 2.3: 321–416.
Parr, Anthony (2014), 'The Caroline Globe', *Yearbook of English Studies*, 44: 12–28.

Potter, Lois (2002), *Othello*, Shakespeare in Performance, Manchester: Manchester University Press.

Potter, Lois (2012), *The Life of William Shakespeare: A Critical Biography*, Oxford: Blackwell.

Prager, Carolyn (1988), 'The Problem of Slavery in *The Custom of the Country*', *SEL: Studies in English Literature*, 28: 301–17.

Preiss, Richard (2014), *Clowning and Authorship in Early Modern Theatre*, Cambridge: Cambridge University Press.

Primrose, Gilbert (1625), *The Righteous Mans Evill, and the Lords Deliverances*, London.

Prynne, Willliam (1633), *Histrio-mastix*, London.

Randall, Dale B.J. (1995), *Winter Fruit: English Drama, 1642–1660*, Lexington: University of Kentucky Press.

Reid, Steven J. (2016), 'Of Bairns and Bearded Men: James VI and the Ruthven Raid', in Miles Kerr-Peterson and Steven J. Reid, eds, *James VI and Noble Power in Scotland, 1578–1603*, 32–56, London: Routledge.

Riddell, James A. (1969), 'Some Actors in Ben Jonson's Plays', *Shakespeare Studies*, 5: 284–98.

Roach, Joseph R. (1985), *The Player's Passion: Studies in the Science of Acting*, Newark: University of Delaware Press.

Roach, Joseph R. (1996), *Cities of the Dead: Circum-Atlantic Performance*, New York: Columbia University Press.

Roberts, Gareth (1999), '"An art as lawful as eating"?: Magic in *The Tempest* and *The Winter's Tale*', in Jennifer Richards and James Knowles, eds, *Shakespeare's Late Plays: New Readings*, 126–42, Edinburgh: Edinburgh University Press.

Roberts, Peter R. (2006), 'The Business of Playing and the Patronage of Players at the Jacobean Courts', in Ralph Houlbrooke, ed., *James VI and I: Ideas, Authority, and Government*, 81–106, Aldershot: Ashgate.

Rollins, Hyder E. (1921), 'A Contribution to the History of the English Commonwealth Drama', *Studies in Philology*, 18: 267–33.

Rous, Francis (1622), *The Diseases of the Time, Attended by Their Remedies*, London.

Ruoff, James E. (1956), 'The Dating of Carlell's *The Passionate Lovers*', *N&Q*, n.s., 3: 68–70.

Rye, W.B. (1865), *England as Seen by Foreigners*, London: John Russell Smith.

S., W. (1613), *The True Chronicle History of the Whole Life and Death of Thomas Lord Cromwell* [...] *Written by W.S.*, London.

Sanders, Julie (2004), 'Carlell [Carlile], Lodowick', *Oxford National Dictionary of Biography*, https://doi.org/10.1093/ref:odnb/4669.

Sawer, Patrick (2018), '"Traditional" Theatre Lighting Stage Design Discriminates against Black and Asian Actors, Warns Shakespeare's Globe', *Telegraph*, 12 August.

Schalkwyk, David (1992), '"A lady's 'verily' is as potent as a lord's": Women, Word, and Witchcraft in *The Winter's Tale*', *English Literary Renaissance*, 22: 242–72.

Schalkwyk, David (2008), *Shakespeare, Love and Service*, Cambridge: Cambridge University Press.

Shadwell, Thomas (1676), *The Virtuoso*, London.

Shakespeare, William (1599), *The Most Excellent and Lamentable Tragedy, of Romeo and Juliet*, London.

Shakespeare, William (1600), *Much Ado about Nothing*, London.

Shakespeare, William (1603), *The Tragicall Historie of Hamlet Prince of Denmarke*, London.

Shakespeare, William (1608), *The Tragedie of King Richard the Second*, London.

Shakespeare, William (1609a), *The Historie of Troylus and Cresseida*, London.

Shakespeare, William (1609b), *The Most Excellent and Lamentable Tragedie, of Romeo and Juliet*, London.

Shakespeare, William (1611), *The Most Lamentable Tragedie of Titus Andronicus*, London.

Shakespeare, William (1622), *The Tragœdy of Othello, the Moore of Venice*, London.

Shakespeare, William (1623), *Mr. William Shakespeares Comedies, Histories, & Tragedies*, London.

Shakespeare, William (1631a), *Loves Labours Lost: A Wittie and Pleasant Comedie*, London.

Shakespeare, William (1631b), *A Witte and Pleasant Comedie Called The Taming of the Shrew*, London.

Shaekspeare, William (1821), *The Plays and Poems of William Shakespeare*, ed. Edmond Malone and James Boswell, 21 vols, London.

Shakespeare, William (2001), *The First Quarto of Othello*, ed. Scott McMillin, Cambridge: Cambridge University Press.

Shakespeare, William (2002), *King Henry IV, Part 1*, ed. David Scott Kastan, London: Arden Shakespeare.

Shakespeare, William, and George Wilkins (2004), *Pericles*, ed. Suzanne Gossett, London: Arden Shakespeare.

Shakespeare, William (2010), *Shakespeare's Sonnets*, ed. Katherine Duncan Jones, revised edition, London: Arden Shakespeare.

Shakespeare, William, and John Fletcher (1634), *The Two Noble Kinsmen*, London.

Shakespeare, William, and John Fletcher (2003), *Henry VIII*, ed. Gordon McMullan, Arden Shakespeare Third Series, London: Thomson Learning.

Shakespeare, William, attr. (1605), *The London Prodigall […] By William Shakespeare*, London.

Shakespeare, William, attr. (1608), *A Yorkshire Tragedy […] Written by W. Shakespeare*, London.

Sharpe, Kevin (1992), *The Personal Rule of Charles I*, New Haven and London: Yale University Press.

Shirley, James (1640), *A Pastorall Called the Arcadia*, London.

Shirley, James (1653), *The Doubtful Heir. A Tragi-Comedie*, in *Six New Playes*, London.

Sirluck, Ernest (1955), 'Shakespeare and Jonson Among the Pamphleteers of the First Civil War: Some Unreported Seventeenth-Century Allusions', *Modern Philology*, 53: 88–99.

Smith, Ian (2013), 'Othello's Black Handkerchief', *Shakespeare Quarterly*, 64: 1–25.

Smith, Ian (2016), 'The Textile Black Body: Race and "Shadowed Livery" in *The Merchant of Venice*', in Valerie Traub, ed., *The Oxford Handbook of Shakespeare and Embodiment: Gender, Sexuality, and Race*, 170–85, Oxford: Oxford University Press.

Smith, Logan Pearsall (1907), *The Life and Letters of Sir Henry Wotton*, 2 vols, Oxford: Clarendon Press.

Stern, Tiffany (2011), '"The Forgery of Some Modern Author"?: Theobald's Shakespeare and Cardenio's *Double Falsehood*', *Shakespeare Quarterly*, 62: 555–93.

Stern, Tiffany (2016), 'Early Modern Tragedy and Performance', in Michael Neill and David Schalkwyk, eds, *The Oxford Handbook of Shakespearean Tragedy*, 489–504, Oxford: Oxford University Press.

Stevens, Andrea Ria (2013), *Inventions of the Skin: The Painted Body in Early English Drama, 1400–1642*, Edinburgh: Edinburgh University Press.

Streitberger, W.R., ed. (1986), 'Jacobean and Caroline Revels Accounts 1603–1642', *Malone Society Collections*, 13.

Syme, Holger Schott (2013), 'Shakespeare and *The Spanish Tragedy*: A Challenge for Theatre History', *Dispositio*, 31 August 2013, http://www.dispositio.net/archives/1667.

Syme, Holger Schott (2019a), 'The Jacobean King's Men: A Reconsideration', *Review of English Studies*, 70: 231–51.

Syme, Holger Schott (2019b), 'A Sharer's Repertory', in Tiffany Stern, ed., *Rethinking Theatrical Documents in Shakespeare's England* 33–51, London: Bloomsbury Arden Shakespeare.

Tailor, Robert (1614), *The Hogge Hath Lost His Pearle: A Comedy*, London.

Taylor, Gary (2007), Introduction to *A Game at Chess: A Later Form*, in Gary Taylor and John Lavagnino, eds, *Thomas Middleton: The Collected Works*, 1825–9, Oxford: Oxford University Press.

Taylor, Gary (2012), 'A History of *The History of Cardenio*', in David Carnegie and Gary Taylor, eds, *The Quest for Cardenio: Shakespeare, Fletcher, Cervantes, and the Lost Play*, 11–61, Oxford: Oxford University Press.

Taylor, Thomas (1618), *Christs Combate and Conquest*, London.

Theobald, Lewis (2010), *The Double Falsehood*, ed. Brean Hammond, London: Arden Shakespeare.

Thompson, Ayanna (2011), *Passing Strange: Shakespeare, Race, and Contemporary America*, Oxford: Oxford University Press.

Tosh, Will (2018), *Playing Indoors: Staging Early Modern Drama in the Sam Wanamaker Playhouse*, London: Arden Shakespeare.

Tribble, Evelyn (2009), 'Marlowe's Boy Actors', *Shakespeare Bulletin*, 27: 5–17.

Tribble, Evelyn (2017), *Early Modern Actors and Shakespeare's Theatre: Thinking with the Body*, London: Arden Shakespeare.

Turner, Gustavo Secchi (2006), 'The Matter of Fact: *The Tragedy of Gowrie* (1604) and Its Contexts', PhD diss., Harvard University.

Van Es, Bart (2013), *Shakespeare in Company*, Oxford: Oxford University Press.

Vaughan, Virginia Mason (2005), *Performing Blackness on English Stages, 1500–1800*, Cambridge: Cambridge University Press.

Vitkus, Daniel (2003), '"Meaner ministers": Mastery, Bondage and Theatrical Labour in *The Tempest*', in Richard Dutton and Jean E. Howard, eds, *A Companion to Shakespeare's Works:*

The Poems, Problem Comedies, Late Plays, 408–26, Oxford: Blackwell.
Webster, John (2007), *The Works of John Webster*, ed. David Gunby, David Carnegie and MacDonald P. Jackson, vol. 3, Cambridge: Cambridge University Press.
West, William N. (2013), 'Intertheatricality', in Henry S. Turner, ed., *Oxford Twenty-First Century Approaches to Literature: Early Modern Theatricality*, 151–72, Oxford: Oxford University Press.
Wickham, Glynne, Herbert Berry and William Ingram, eds (2000), *English Professional Theatre, 1530–1660*, Cambridge: Cambridge University Press.
Wiggins, Martin, in association with Catherine Richardson (2011–18), *British Drama 1533–1642: A Catalogue*, 9 vols, Oxford: Oxford University Press.
Wiles, David (1987), *Shakespeare's Clown: Actor and Text in the Elizabethan Playhouse*, Cambridge: Cambridge University Press.
Wilkins, George (1608), *The Painfull Adventures of Pericles, Prince of Tyre*, London.
Wilson, Arthur (1904), *The Swisser*, ed. Albert Feuillerat, Paris: Librarie Fischbacher.
Wooding, Barbara (2013), *John Lowin and the English Theatre, 1603–47: Acting and Cultural Politics on the Jacobean and Caroline Stage*, Farnham: Ashgate.
Worden, Blair (2003), 'Which Play Was Performed at the Globe Theatre on 7 February 1601?', *London Review of Books*, 25.13, 10 July, 22–4.
Wright, George R. (1887), *Archaeologic and Historic Fragments. A Facsimile of a Rare MS Page Dated 1638, Having Reference to Two of Shakespeare's Most Famous Plays*, London: Whiting & Co.
Wright, James (1699), *Historia Histrionica*, London.
Wroth, Lady Mary (1621), *The Countesse of Mountgomeries Urania*, London.

INDEX

The entries in bold are actors in the King's Men; basic biographical information (dates, pre-Restoration company membership and functions within the company) is provided in italics.

acting, commentaries on 19–20, 21–8, 39–41, 42, 51, 75, 131, 143
Acuña, Don Diego Sarmiento de, Conde de Gondomar 171
Admiral's Men (see also Prince Henry's Men) xiv
Allen, William *(fl. 1625–47; Queen Henrietta Maria's Men 1625-c. 1636; ?Dublin c. 1637; King's Men c. 1637–42; Groom of the Chamber 1641)* 10–11, 180
Alleyn, Edward 27, 50, 132, 200
Alphonsus, King of Aragon 148, 204
Anna of Denmark, Queen xiv, 95–6, 117, 128–9, 202
Ariosto, Ludovico 68
Aristotle 51, 68
Armin, Robert *(c. 1568–1615; Chandos's Men 1590s; Chamberlain's/King's Men c. 1599–1615: sharer by 1603)*
death 60
patentee xiii
playwright xv
roles 7, 29–30, 32, 43, 56, 57, 60
Astley, Sir John, Master of the Revels 129
audiences xv, xix, xxi–xxii, xxiv, 6, 7, 9–10, 11, 15, 16, 18, 19, 21, 22, 24, 25, 26, 27, 28, 34, 39, 41, 42, 51, 52, 53, 54, 64, 65, 67, 68, 70–1, 73, 75, 76, 77, 79–81, 82, 86, 87–8, 90, 91, 92, 94–5, 96, 99, 100, 102, 104–106, 112–13, 114–15, 120, 122, 124, 125, 126, 130, 131, 132, 134–5, 138–9, 147, 152, 153, 156–65, 166, 168–70, 171–2, 174, 175–6, 182. *See also* playgoers

Bacon, Sir Edmund 165
Bad Beginning Makes a Good Ending, A (lost play) 45–6, 49
Bailey, Amanda 98
Baldwin, Thomas Whitfield 16, 66

Bancroft, Thomas 26
Barclay, Sir William
  Lost Lady, The 147
Bate, Jonathan 129
Baxter, Richard *(c. 1593–c.1667; Queen Anna's Men c. 1606–24; King's Men c. 1628–42: hired man 1636; 'Company and Society of Actors', 1648)* 180, 182
Beaumont, Francis xvi, 46, 47–8, 50, 127
  Knight of the Burning Pestle, The 48
Beaumont, Francis, and John Fletcher
  Captain, The 17, 45–6, 47, 49, 50, 83, 199
  Coxcomb, The 48, 145
  King and No King, A 18, 19, 45–6, 48, 49, 139, 145, 180–1, 182
  Maid's Tragedy, The 9, 10, 18, 45–6, 47, 48, 49, 83, 84, 145, 182
  Philaster 14, 15, 16, 20–1, 24, 31, 37, 38, 45–6, 48, 49–50, 83, 84, 108, 145, 182, 198, 199
  Scornful Lady, The 10, 121, 177, 182, 198, 204
Bedell, Michael *(fl. 1612–19; King's Men c. 1612–19: apprenticed 1612 for ten years)* 198
Bedford, Thomas *(fl. 1621–65; ?King's Men c. 1638–40: apprentice)*, 37, 199
Beeston, Christopher 33, 198

Benfield, Robert *(?1583–1649; Lady Elizabeth's Men c. 1613–14; King's Men c. 1614–48: sharer by 1619)* 20–1, 57, 60, 96, 180
  roles 103, 164
Bennett, Nicola 133
Bentley, Gerald Eades 46–7, 127
Best, George 179
Betterton, Thomas 86
Bird, Theophilus (alias Bourne) *(1608–63; Queen Henrietta Maria's Men c. 1624–36; Beeston's Boys 1637–8; King's Men c. 1638–48: Groom of the Chamber 1641)* 10, 11, 108, 179, 180
Bird, William 132
Birche, George *(fl. 1610–25; King's Men 1610–25: apprenticed 1610 for eight years, hired man c. 1619, sharer by 1625)*
  apprenticeship 34, 57
  roles 34–5, 57, 60, 62, 138, 143
Birche, Richard *see* Birche, George
Blackfriars playhouse xvi, xxii–xxiv, 10, 11, 24, 37, 41, 46–7, 52, 62, 64, 75–81, 99, 107, 117, 118, 119, 121, 122, 124, 126–9, 131, 134, 137, 147, 148, 154, 162, 166, 179, 181, 184, 191, 192, 193–4, 200
Bluett, Henry 156

Book of Bulls, The 87–8, 90, 91, 107, 114
Bowyer, Michael *(c. 1595–1645; Queen Henrietta Maria's Men 1625-c. 1636; Dublin c. 1637; King's Men c. 1637–45: Groom of the Chamber 1641)* 10–11
Braithwaite, Richard
  Whimzies, or a New Cast of Characters 123–4
Brewer, Thomas
  Life and Death of the Merry Devil of Edmonton, The 124, 134
Britland, Karen 118
Britton, Dennis Austin 68
Brothers of the Blade, The 123
Brome, Richard xvi
  Northern Lass, The 148
  See also Heywood, Thomas, and Richard Brome
Buc, Sir George, Master of the Revels, xix, 16–17, 83–6, 166
Burbage, Cuthbert 60, 127
Burbage, Richard *(1568–1619; Chamberlain's/King's Men 1594–1619: sharer by 1603)* xvi–xvii
  apprentices of 34
  Blackfriars playhouse owner 127, 179
  death xxii, 16, 18, 50, 65, 77, 83–4, 85–86, 89, 95–6, 98, 197
  painter 23
  patentee xiii, xviii
  performance styles 23–8, 32, 67, 51, 72, 80
  physique 72
  roles xviii, 5, 7, 10, 15–18, 20, 24–5, 28, 43, 49–50, 51–2, 56–57, 61, 65, 66, 67, 68, 72, 73, 74, 77, 80, 82, 84, 85–6, 92, 124, 132, 136, 137, 143, 168, 172, 175
Burbage, William 179
Burt, Nicholas *(fl. 1630–60; King's Men early-mid 1630s: apprentice; Queen Henrietta Maria's Men/ Beeston's Boys early-mid 1630s–1642)* 180
Butler, Martin 148

Carew, Thomas 119
Carlell, Lodowick xvi, 65, 107, 119, 148, 149
  Arviragus and Philicia 145, 146, 149, 204
  Deserving Favourite, The 12, 19, 56, 62, 104, 119, 172
  Osmond the Great Turk 119
  Passionate Lovers, The 37, 199
  Spartan Ladies, The (lost play) 117, 119
Carleton, Dudley 95, 156–7, 171, 185
Carlson, Marvin xxi, 143
Cartwright, William 147
  Royal Slave, The 84, 120, 145, 146–7
Cavendish, William, Duke of Newcastle 26–7, 148

Country Captain, The 147
Variety, The 147, 148, 182
Wit's Triumvirate 26–7, 49–50, 85–6
Cawdry, Robert, 90
Cervantes, Miguel de
  Don Quixote 48
  Persiles y Sigismunda 96, 98
Chakravarty, Urvashi 89
Chamberlain, John 95, 156, 166–7, 168, 171, 185
Chamberlain's Men (see also King's Men) xiii–xiv, xvii, 12, 29, 33, 60, 85, 90, 153–4
Chapman, George
  Bussy D'Ambois 19–20, 50, 66, 67, 73, 108, 118
Charles I, King of England and Scotland 117, 119–20, 121, 145, 146–7, 152, 155, 159, 176, 177, 178, 179, 180, 181
Charles, Prince, later King Charles II 177
Charles Louis, Elector Palatine 146, 148, 204
Children of the Chapel xiv, 1, 17, 74, 90. *See also* Children of the Queen's Revels
Children of the Queen's Revels xiv, 1, 17, 20, 48, 120, 128. *See also* Children of the Chapel
Children of the Revels 108
Cinthio (Giovanni Battista Giraldi), 68
Civil War xxv, 177–83
Clare, Janet 90
Clarke, Hugh *(fl. 1626–53; Queen Henrietta Maria's Men c. 1626–36; King's Men c. 1636–48: Groom of the Chamber 1641)* 21, 107, 180
  performance style 21
  roles 21, 28, 65, 108, 197
Clavell, John, xvi
  Soddered Citizen, The xvi, 12, 18, 29, 30, 31, 35–6, 64, 108, 173, 198
Clubb, Louise George 90–1
Clun, Walter *(fl. 1635–64; King's Men early-mid 1630s–1642: apprentice early-mid 1630s–c. 1640: 'Company and Society of Actors' 1648)* 180, 198
  apprenticeship 11, 37–8
  roles 38, 108
Cockpit playhouse 10, 21, 178, 179
Cogswell, Thomas 160
Coloma, Don Carlos 157
Commonwealth xxv, 177–83
Condell, Henry *(1576–1627; Chamberlain's/King's Men 1590s–1627: sharer by 1603)* xvii
  patentee xiii
  retirement 18, 74, 85, 197
  roles 18, 56, 57, 197
Cooke, Alexander *(c. 1583–1614; Chamberlain's/King's Men 1597–1614: apprenticed 1597 for 8 years; sharer by 1607)* 56, 57, 60, 198
Cowley, Richard *(?1568–1619; Strange's Men 1593;*

INDEX

Chamberlain's/King's Men c. 1598–1619: sharer by 1603) xiii, 60
cosmetics 23, 52, 53, 72, 78–9, 80
Cox, Robert 181–2, 183
Crosse, Nicholas *(fl. 1614–23; apprenticed 1614 for 10 years)* 97
Cunningham, Peter xx, xxi
Cyprian, Saint 40

Dadabhoy, Ambereen 80
Davenant, William xvi, 86, 107, 119, 121, 148, 149, 183–4, 193
  Cruel Brother, The 119
  Just Italian, The 119
  Love and Honour 145, 146
  Madagascar and Other Poems 156
  News from Plymouth 77, 156
  Platonic Lovers, The 16
  Wits, The 118, 121
Davenport, Robert
  Henry I (lost play) 155
  King John and Matilda 197
Davies, John
  Scourge of Folly, The 50
Denham, John 147
Depledge, Emma 182
Devereux, Robert, Earl of Essex 153–4
d'Orléans, Gaston 118
Douglas, John, Earl of Morton 167
Downes, John 38, 72, 86
Dryden, John
  All for Love 38
Dustagheer, Sarah 47, 128

Dutton, Richard xviii, 203
Dyer, Richard 78

Ecclestone, William *(c. 1591–1623; King's Men c. 1610–11; Lady Elizabeth's Men 1611–13; King's Men 1614–23: apprentice c. 1604–10? sharer by 1619)*
  apprenticeship 56, 96, 198, 200
  death 65, 201
  roles 56–7, 65, 94, 96
Edmondes, John *(fl. 1604–19; King's Men c. 1603: apprentice; Queen Anna's Men 1618–19)* 198
Egyiawan, Kurt 78
Elizabeth I, Queen of England xiii, 154
Elizabeth Stuart, Princess, later Queen of Bohemia 45, 146
Evans, Henry 127

Fair Maid of Bristow, The 30
False Friend, The (lost play) 84, 201
Field, Nathan *(1587–c. 1619; Chapel/Queen's Revels 1600–13; Lady Elizabeth's Men 1613–c. 1615; King's Men c. 1615–19: sharer by 1619)*
  death 18, 20, 65, 66–7, 74
  performance style 20, 27
  playwright 84–5
  roles 17–18, 20, 27, 49–50, 57, 60, 65, 66–7, 74, 84–5, 200, 206

INDEX

Field, Nathan, John Fletcher
and Philip Massinger
Knight of Malta, The 83,
84–5, 97
Queen of Corinth, The 97
Fitch, Winifred Shank 38
Flecknoe, Richard 25, 26, 28
Fletcher, John xvi, xvii, xxii, 17,
18, 25, 30, 35, 46, 47–9,
65, 84, 124, 127, 129,
143, 178, 180
'An Elegie on ... Richard
Burbage' 17, 24–5, 27,
51, 67–8, 74, 85
Bonduca 17, 50
Chances, The 148, 182
Faithful Shepherdess, The
117–18, 119–20
False One, The 97
Humorous Lieutenant, The
31, 97, 182, 197
Island Princess, The 97
Little French Lawyer, The
97
Loyal Subject, The 16, 97,
117, 118, 121, 145, 197
Mad Lover, The 97, 200
Monsieur Thomas 201
Pilgrim, The 36, 72
*Rule a Wife and Have a
Wife* 31, 182
Valentinian 17, 50
Wife for a Month, A 31, 145
Wild Goose Chase, The 12,
16, 18, 28, 31, 36, 64,
72, 198
*Woman's Prize, or The
Tamer Tamed, The* 117,
118, 120–22
Women Pleased 97

See also Field, Nathan,
John Fletcher and Philip
Massinger; Fletcher, John,
and Philip Massinger;
Shakespeare, William,
and John Fletcher
Fletcher, John, and Philip
Massinger
Beggars' Bush 145, 148, 182
Cleander 117, 118–19 (*see
also Lovers' Progress;
Wandering Lovers, The*)
Custom of the Country, The
xxiii, 91, 95–100, 101,
102, 103, 107, 109, 148,
182
Elder Brother, The 145
Love's Pilgrimage 145
Lovers' Progress, The 97,
203 (*see also Cleander;
Wandering Lovers, The*)
Prophetess, The xxiii–xxiv,
97, 124–5, 129–31,
140–3, 144, 198, 203
*Rollo, Duke of Normandy,
or The Bloody Brother*
18, 145, 182
Sea Voyage, The 72, 129
*Sir John Van Olden
Barnavelt* xxiv, 12, 97,
154, 156–7, 164, 166,
167, 168–9, 175, 198
Spanish Curate, The 148, 182
Wandering Lovers, The
118 (*see also Cleander;
Lovers' Progress*)
Fletcher, John, and William
Rowley
Maid in the Mill, The 31,
182

Fletcher, Lawrence
    (fl. 1595–1608; Scotland
    c. 1595–1601; King's
    Men 1603–8: sharer by
    1603) xiii, xviii–xix, 56
Ford, John xvi
    Laws of Candy, The 97
    Lover's Melancholy, The 12,
    198
Forman, Simon 47, 127, 153,
    154, 158–9, 162, 172,
    176, 187, 195
Formido, Cornelius 146
Fortune playhouse 132, 178,
    179
Fraunce, Abraham 24
Frederick, Elector Palatine 45

Gainsford, Thomas 21–2
Garrard, George 119
Gayton, Edmund 19, 21, 23,
    24, 26, 73
Gell, Robert 160, 162, 163, 164
Gildon, Charles 73
Glapthorne, Henry 156
    *Tragedy of Albertus
    Wallenstein, The* 151,
    155
Globe playhouse xiii, xv–xvi,
    xxii–xxiv, 24, 41, 46–7,
    51, 52, 61, 68, 75–81, 92,
    100, 107, 124, 125–31,
    137, 143, 151–76, 179,
    186, 187, 189, 190, 191,
    192, 194, 195
Gough, Robert (fl. 1597–1624;
    King's Men c. 1597–
    1624: apprentice c.
    1597–1603; sharer by
    1619) 198

Gough, Alexander (fl. 1614–
    1655; King's Men
    c. 1626–48: apprentice
    c. 1626–35; hired man c.
    1636–48) 36, 64, 103, 198
Governor, The 145, 146
Greville, Curtis (1593–1655;
    Palsgrave's Men/Lady
    Elizabeth's Men 1622;
    King's Men 1626–31:
    hired man; Revels
    Company 1634; Queen
    Henrietta Maria's Men
    1635–40) 29
Gurr, Andrew, 127–9
Guzmán, Gaspar de, Conde-
    Duque de Olivares 157

Habington, William
    Queen of Aragon, The 147
Hall, Kim F. 78
Hammerton, Stephen (c. 1620–
    1653; Children of the
    Revels c. 1629–32; King's
    Men 1632–48: apprentice
    c. 1632–9; Groom of the
    Chamber 1641) 180
    apprenticeship 10, 11, 41,
        108, 198
    roles 9–10, 11, 108, 180
Hand, Molly 142
Harbage, Alfred 109
Hart, Charles (1625–83; King's
    Men c. 1638–42:
    apprentice; Europe
    1644–6: 'Company and
    Society of Actors' 1648)
    11, 37, 38, 180, 198
Hart, William (fl. 1636–1650;
    King's Men c. 1636–7:

hired man; 'Company and Society of Actors' *1648)* 37, 180
Heminges, John *(1566–1630; Strange's Men c. 1593; Chamberlain's/King's Men c. 1594–1630: sharer by 1603)* xvii, 45, 140, 202
  apprentices of 19, 32, 34, 41, 83, 97, 196
  patentee xiii
  retirement 60
  roles 5, 56, 57, 60–1, 74
Henrietta Maria, Queen of England and Scotland 117–20, 145, 146–7, 148, 177, 204
Henry Frederick, Prince of Wales 45, 61
Henslowe, Philip 57
Herbert, Sir Henry, Master of the Revels, xx, 62, 100, 101, 117–18, 120–21, 122, 140, 145, 146, 147, 148, 152, 155, 160, 172, 176, 177, 195, 200, 204
Herbert, Philip, Earl of Pembroke 96
Heywood, Thomas
  Ages plays 128–30, 136
  An Apology for Actors 90
  Brazen Age, The 136
  Fair Maid of the West, The 197
  Golden Age, The 128
  Silver Age, The 128–9
Heywood, Thomas, and Richard Brome
  Late Lancashire Witches, The 155, 156
Holcombe, Thomas *(c. 1601–25; King's Men 1618–25: apprenticed 1618 for eight years)*
  apprenticeship 33, 41, 83, 140, 198
  roles 96, 97, 140
Honeyman, John *(1613–36; King's Men 1626–36: apprentice c. 1626–32; Groom of the Chamber 1633)*
  apprenticeship 33, 64, 103, 173, 198
  roles 19, 30, 36, 41, 62–4, 103, 164, 173
Howard, Frances, Duchess of Richmond 119, 140

Jackson, Henry 52, 60, 79–80, 187
James VI and I, King of England and Scotland xiii–xiv, xviii–xix, xxiv, 1, 4, 5, 46, 61, 89, 95, 117, 140, 151, 152, 154, 155, 159–60, 167–8
James, Mistress 200
Jamestown, Virginia 98. *See also* slavery
Johnson, Robert 47
Jones, James 33
Jonson, Ben xvi, 1, 4, 5, 12, 15, 16, 46, 50, 84, 100, 127
  Alchemist, The xvi, xxii–xxiii, 9, 10, 15, 16, 17, 18, 28, 29, 34, 35, 38,

45–6, 47, 50, 51–82, 103,
138, 175, 182, 200
Catiline 60
Devil Is an Ass, The 123, 134
*Epicoene, or The Silent
  Woman* 9, 10, 28, 204
Every Man in His Humour
  1, 5, 6, 7
*Every Man out of His
  Humour* 1, 5, 6, 7
New Inn, The 100, 114
'Ode to Himself' 100
Poetaster, The 90
Sejanus 4, 5, 15–16, 56, 126
Staple of News, The 123,
  134–5
Volpone 9, 10, 15, 16, 17,
  18, 28, 34, 60, 62, 75, 83,
  84, 85, 138, 148

Karim-Cooper, Farah 78, 80
Kathman, David 33, 37, 41
Kawai, Shoichiro 16
Kemp, William xvii, 16, 29–30,
  31, 85
Killigrew, Thomas, xvi, 183–4
  Parson's Wedding, The 147
  Princess, The xxiii, 91,
    106–114, 147
King, John, Bishop of London
  156
King's Men (*see also*
  Chamberlain's Men)
  apprentices xv, xvii, xxi,
    xxiii–xxiv, 6, 7, 11, 19,
    32–42, 53, 56, 57, 61–4,
    79–80, 83, 88, 94–5,
    96–7, 99, 103, 108, 114,
    124, 135, 140–3, 190,
    196, 198–9

court performances xvii,
  xix–xxi, 1–7, 20, 43,
  45–50, 51, 66, 80, 83–6,
  95–6, 100, 117–22, 124,
  129, 137, 139, 140,
  145–9, 160, 177, 182,
  185–6, 188–93, 195, 200,
  202–3, 204
hired men xiv, 29, 34, 37,
  56, 89
playhouses
  see Blackfriars playhouse;
    Globe playhouse
repertory design xvi, xvii–
  xviii, xix–xxi, xxii–xxiv,
  xxv, 4–7, 42, 45–50, 52,
  66–7, 75–6, 82, 83–6, 91,
  99, 107, 110, 115, 117–22,
  123–4, 131, 135, 139,
  145–49, 153–7, 167, 176
roles xv, xviii, xxi–xxiv, 6–7,
  9–43, 49–50, 52, 53, 56–
  75, 77, 78, 79–82, 84–6,
  92–3, 94–5, 95–7, 102–4,
  107–8, 112–13, 124, 135,
  136–8, 140–3, 164, 166,
  168, 171–5, 183, 196,
  198–9, 200, 203
revivals xvii, xxii, 5, 9–10,
  12, 15, 19–20, 21, 31,
  34, 35, 36, 46, 51–2,
  56–67, 72–3, 74–5, 76,
  79–82, 83–4, 85–6, 91,
  95–6, 100–1, 103, 107,
  108, 118, 119–21, 122,
  123–4, 129, 132, 135,
  140, 144, 145, 148, 152,
  153–4, 155, 160–4, 172,
  173, 174, 176, 180–1,
  182–4, 185–94, 195,

196–7, 198, 200, 203, 204
  comedians and comic roles xxi, 7, 10, 15, 18, 19, 28–32, 37, 38, 56, 60, 62, 65, 73, 84, 88, 107–8, 115, 135, 181, 182–3, 198
  leading actors xv, xxi, xxiii, xxiv, 6–7, 9–11, 15–28, 32, 35, 38, 42, 49–50, 51, 52, 53, 54–5, 64–75, 79–82, 84–6, 88–9, 92–3, 95–6, 102–5, 107–8, 124, 131–2, 136–7, 142, 143, 164, 166, 169, 171–5, 183
  performances outside London xvi, 52, 60, 61, 79–80, 185, 187
Kirkman, Francis 182
Kirwan, Peter 137
Knot of Fools, The (lost play) 45–6
Knutson, Roslyn L. 131
Kyd, Thomas
  Spanish Tragedy, The 17, 27, 83, 84, 85–6, 201

Lady Elizabeth's Men 57, 61, 74, 84, 200, 201
Lake, Peter 160
Lamb, Charles 70–1, 74
Laud, William, Archbishop of Canterbury 120, 146–7
Lee, Nathaniel
  Rival Queens, The 38
Lehuc, Peter 147
letters patent xiii–xvii, xviii–xix, xxiv, 21, 56, 151

lighting 1, 47, 52, 75–81, 134
Lin, Erika 78
Locke, Thomas 156–7
London Prodigal, The 194
Lorkins, Thomas 165
Loughnane, Rory 162
Louis XIII, King of France 118
Lowin, John *(1576–1653; Worcester's Men c. 1602–3; King's Men 1603–48: sharer by 1607)* xv, 89, 121, 178, 180
  apprentices of 32, 198
  physique 10, 72, 120
  roles 7, 9–10, 15–16, 17, 18–19, 32, 35, 43, 56–57, 64–6, 71–2, 73, 85, 96, 102–4, 107, 108, 120, 121, 143, 164, 166, 169, 171–2, 173, 174, 175, 180, 199, 203
Lydall, Mistress 200

Mago, William *(1579–1632; Prince Charles's Men 1621; King's Men 1624–32: hired man)* 89
Malone, Edmond xx, 117, 204
Manners, Francis, Earl of Rutland 23
Marlowe, Christopher
  Doctor Faustus 125, 126, 132–4
Marston, John
  Malcontent, The 56
  Sophonisba 128
Massinger, Philip xvi, 18, 85, 106, 118–19, 148
  Alexius, or The Bashful Lover (lost play) 148

Bashful Lover, The (lost
   play) 148
Believe as You List xxiii,
   12, 18, 29, 31, 64, 65–6,
   91, 99, 101–6, 107, 108,
   110, 114, 155, 171, 173,
   174
Emperor of the East, The
   172–4
*Fair Anchoress of Pausilippo,
   The* (lost play) 148
Guardian, The 118–19
King and the Subject, The
   (lost play) 148, 152, 155,
   176
Picture, The 12, 16, 18, 19,
   30–2, 36–7, 62–3, 66, 67,
   164, 198
Roman Actor, The 12, 18,
   29, 62, 104, 164, 172
Unnatural Combat, The 31
See also Fletcher, John, and
   Philip Massinger
Mayne, Jasper
   City Match, The 147
McDougall, Ellen 78
McManus, Clare 63
McMillin, Scott 34–5
McMullan, Gordon 161
Meade, Joseph 200
Menzer, Paul, 22–3, 26
Merrick, Ann 200
*Merry Devil of Edmonton,
   The* xxiii–xxiv, 38, 45–6,
   49, 123–6, 129, 131–7,
   139–40, 142, 143–4, 148,
   203
Middleton, Thomas xvi, xvii,
   189, 190
   Black Book, The 123

Game at Chess, A xxiv,
   31, 152, 154–5, 157–8,
   159–60, 164, 170–2, 175,
   176
Mad World My Masters, A
   123
*Mayor of Quinborough or
   Hengist, King of Kent,
   The* 83, 84, 87–8, 90
*Second Maiden's Tragedy,
   The* 12, 34–5, 48, 49, 61
Yorkshire Tragedy, A 194
Mildmay, Sir Humphrey 76,
   121, 146, 192, 200
Montagu, Walter 120
   Shepherds' Paradise, The 120
Moseley, Humphrey 119, 146
Munday, Anthony 61–2

Nethersole, Sir Francis 157
'Niccolls' (playwright) 46
Nicol, David 31

Ostler, William *(c. 1588–1614;
   Chapel/Queen's Revels
   c. 1601–9; King's Men
   c. 1609–14: sharer by
   1611)*
   death 18, 60
   roles 17–18, 50, 57, 60, 74,
   172

Pallant, Robert *(fl. 1605–24;
   King's Men 1620–4:
   apprenticed 1620 for 8
   years)* 33, 196
Parliament xxv, 177–9
Pepys, Samuel xx
Perkins, Richard *(c. 1579–
   1650; Admiral's Men*

c. 1596–7; Pembroke's Men c. 1597; Admiral's Men ?1597–9; Worcester's/Queen Anna's/Revels ?1599–1622; King's Men 1623–25: sharer by 1625; Queen Henrietta Maria's 1626–41) 10
Pierre, Sebastian la 147
Phillips, Augustine *(fl. 1593–1605; Strange's Men 1593; Chamberlain's/King's Men c. 1597–1605: sharer by 1603)* xiii, xv, 5, 16, 56, 154
Pimlico, or Run Redcap 91–2
playgoers *see* audiences; Bancroft, Thomas; *Book of Bulls, The*; Cavendish, William; Flecknoe, Richard; Fletcher, John; Forman, Simon; Gayton, Edmund; James, Mistress; Henrietta Maria, Queen; Herbert, Philip, Earl of Pembroke; Mildmay, Sir Humphrey; Webster, John; Wright, James; Wright, Abraham; Wroth, Lady Mary
Pollard, Thomas *(1597–1653; King's Men c. 1617–48: sharer by 1624)* 178, 180
 apprenticeship 41
 performance style 31–2
 roles 10, 19, 29, 30, 31–2, 62, 65, 103, 108, 180, 198

Pope, Thomas *(fl. 1586–1603; Germany/Denmark 1586–7; Strange's Men 1593; Chamberlain's/King's Men 1597–1603)* xv, 7, 15, 16, 85
Porter, Endymion 121
Pory, John 120
Potter, Lois 4, 71, 73
Portman, George, 147
Prager, Carolyn 98
Preiss, Richard 30
Prince Charles's Men 201
Prince Henry's Men xiv
Protectorate xxv, 177–83
Prynne, William 28
Puckering, Sir Thomas 165
Puget de la Serre, Jean 123

Queen Anna's Men xiv, 1, 4, 33, 129. *See also* Worcester's Men
Queen Elizabeth's Men xiii
Queen Henrietta Maria's Men 10, 21, 100, 181

Rawlinson, Richard xx
Reade, Timothy 180–1
Red Bull playhouse 128, 130, 136, 178, 179
Rice, John *(c. 1590–1654; King's Men c. 1603–11: apprentice; Lady Elizabeth's Men 1611–c. 1614; King's Men c. 1614–25: sharer by 1621)*
 apprenticeship 56, 61, 198
 roles 61–2, 94
Rice, Dorcas 84

Rich, Henry, Earl of Holland 121, 160, 163
Richard the Second (lost play) 154, 155, 158–9, 172–4, 176
Roach, Joseph R. xxi, 143
Robins, William (alias Robinson) *(fl. 1616–45; Queen Anna's Men/Revels Company c. 1616–25; Queen Henrietta Maria's Men 1625–36; ?Dublin c. 1637; King's Men c. 1638–45: Groom of the Chamber 1641)* 10, 11, 29, 37
Robinson, Richard *(c. 1595–1648; King's Men, c. 1611–47: apprentice c. 1611–16; sharer by 1619)* 180
  apprentices of 37
  apprenticeship 34, 198
  roles 34–5, 61, 94, 164
Robinson, Winifred Burbage 34
Rollins, Hyder E. 178
Rowley, Samuel 132
Rowley, William *(?1585–1626; Prince Charles's Men c. 1609–23; King's Men 1623–6: sharer by 1625)* 29, 31, 182
Rous, Francis 40–1, 88, 90
Rupert of the Rhine, Prince 146, 148
Ruthven, William, Earl of Gowrie 167–8
Ruthven, John, Earl of Gowrie 167
Ruthven, Alexander 157

Salisbury Court playhouse 178, 179, 180, 181
Salvetti, Amerigo, Florentine ambassador 157
Sam Wanamaker Playhouse 78–9
Scaglia, Alessandro Cesare, Savoyard Ambassador 160, 163
Schalkwyk, David xv
Scholar Turned to School Again, The (lost play) 84, 201
Scudamore, John, Viscount 120, 157, 163
Seven Deadly Sins, The, Part 2 (lost play) 12, 17, 60
Shadwell, Thomas 19, 73
Shakespeare, William *(1564–1616; Chamberlain's/King's Men 1594–1616: sharer by 1603)*
  actor xiv, xvi–xvii, xix, 5, 12, 50, 56, 126, 143
  Blackfriars playhouse sharer 127
  collaborative writing xvi, xvii, xxii, xxiii, 17, 35, 48–9, 92, 103, 111
  See also Shakespeare, William, and George Wilkins; Shakespeare, William, and John Fletcher; Shakespeare, William, and Thomas Middleton
  company sharer xv, xvi, 5
  patentee xiii, xiv, xv
  plays
    All's Well That Ends Well 186, 194

INDEX

Antony and Cleopatra
   30, 186, 189, 194
As You Like It 29, 43,
   185, 194
Comedy of Errors, The
   xvii, 1, 5, 7, 186, 194
Coriolanus 92, 127, 187,
   194
Cymbeline 47, 49, 50, 56,
   117, 118, 127, 130,
   149, 183, 187, 192,
   194
Hamlet 10, 17, 18, 25,
   27, 30, 43, 83, 84,
   85–6, 104, 115, 145,
   177, 181–3, 185, 189,
   192, 193, 204
Henry IV, Part 1 xvii, 9,
   10, 16, 38, 43, 45–6,
   72, 176, 181, 182,
   184, 188, 190, 191,
   192, 193, 194
Henry IV, Part 2 xvii, 6, 9,
   10, 16, 38, 43, 45–6,
   72, 83, 84, 85, 176,
   181, 184, 188, 190,
   191, 192, 193, 194
Henry V xvii, 1, 5, 6, 7,
   125, 186, 203
Julius Caesar xvii, 45–6,
   49, 145, 148, 184,
   188, 192, 193, 194
King John 193
King Lear 17, 27, 29, 43,
   186, 187, 193
Love's Labour's Lost xvii,
   1, 5, 6, 7, 29, 186,
   191, 194
Macbeth 138, 186, 187,
   189, 193

Measure for Measure
   xvii, 1, 4, 6, 7, 30,
   185, 190, 193
Merchant of Venice, The
   xvii, xviii, 1, 5, 6, 29,
   186, 194
*Merry Wives of Windsor,
   The* xvii, 1, 5, 6, 7, 9,
   10, 16, 38, 43, 45–6,
   72, 148, 181, 185,
   188, 192, 193, 196
*Midsummer Night's
   Dream, A* 29, 182, 184,
   185, 190, 191, 194
*Much Ado About
   Nothing* xvii, 11, 29,
   45–6, 49, 183, 188,
   190, 193
*Othello, or The Moor of
   Venice* xvi, xvii, xviii,
   xxii–xxiii, 1, 4, 5–6,
   7, 10, 16, 17, 18, 27,
   30, 35, 43, 45–6, 49,
   51–82, 96, 104, 115,
   145, 175, 184, 185,
   187, 189, 190, 191,
   192, 194, 200
Richard II xxii, xxiv,
   151–2, 153, 154,
   174–6, 184, 186, 193
Richard III 17, 20, 43,
   66, 117, 118, 168,
   184, 192, 194
Romeo and Juliet 11, 29,
   90, 187, 193
Taming of the Shrew, The
   117, 118, 122, 184,
   192, 192, 194
Tempest, The xvii, xxii,
   xxiii–xxiv, 43, 45–6,

47, 49, 50, 124–5,
126–31, 133, 135–9,
142, 143, 144, 188,
193, 203
Titus Andronicus 188,
194
Troilus and Cressida
187
Twelfth Night 29, 43,
183, 189, 190, 193
*Two Gentlemen of
Verona, The* 49, 193
Winter's Tale, The xvii,
xxii, xxiii–xxiv, 45–6,
47, 49, 50, 83, 84,
118, 119, 124, 127,
137–43, 144, 148,
184, 187, 188, 189,
190, 192, 193, 195
playwright xiv, xvi, xvii, xix,
4, 6, 17, 127–8, 143–4
See also plays
retirement xvii, 43, 45, 139
writer of impresa 23
Shakespeare, William, and
George Wilkins
Pericles xvi, xxii, xxiii, 43,
87–115, 127, 148, 183,
186, 189, 191, 192, 193
Shakespeare, William, and John
Fletcher
Cardenio (lost play) xvii,
45–6, 47, 48–9, 50, 188
Henry VIII, or All is True
xxii, xxiv, 16, 35, 43, 72,
127, 151, 152, 153, 154,
155, 156, 160–6, 168,
169–70, 171, 174, 175,
176, 183, 189, 191, 193,
199

Two Noble Kinsmen, The
11–12, 35, 83, 84, 127,
189, 191
Shakespeare, William, and
Thomas Middleton
Timon of Athens 92, 186
Shakespeare's Globe 78–9
Shank, John *(fl. 1590s–1636;
Pembroke's Men 1590s;
Prince Henry's/Palsgrave's
Men c. 1610–15; King's
Men c. 1615–36: sharer
by 1619)* 29
apprentices of 32, 38, 41, 108
roles 10, 30–1, 32, 60, 135,
198
Sharpe, Richard *(1601–32;
King's Men 1616–31:
apprenticed 1616 for eight
years; sharer by 1624)*
apprenticeship 19, 33, 140,
198
death 19, 89, 173
performance style 35–6, 164
roles 19, 35–6, 96, 97, 140,
143, 164, 173
Shelton, Thomas 48
Shirley, James xvi, 107, 148
Arcadia, The 100–1
Cardinal, The 11, 37, 38, 197
Doubtful Heir, The 77
Sincler, John *(fl. 1592–1604;
?Germany 1596;
Chamberlain's/King's
Men c. 1597–1604: hired
man)* 56
slavery, enslaved people 91, 94,
98–9, 106, 107, 109–10,
113
Atlantic slave trade 88, 98

Sly, William *(?1573–1608; Admiral's Men c. 1594; Chamberlain's/King's Men c. 1597–1608: sharer by 1603)* xiii, 56
Smith, Ian xviii, 53
Stanhope, Sir John, Baron Stanhope of Harrington xx
Stewart, Esmé, Sieur d'Aubigny and Duke of Lennox 167
Stewart, James, of Ochiltree, Earl of Arran 167
Stuteville, Sir Martin 160
Swanston, Elliard *(fl. 1619–51; Lady Elizabeth's Men c. 1622; King's Men c. 1623–42: sharer by 1624)* 178, 180
  performance style 19–20, 26, 32, 73, 164
  physique 73
  roles 10, 19–21, 28, 32, 43, 62, 64, 65, 66, 67, 72–3, 108, 164
Suckling, Sir John
  Aglaura 147
  Goblins, The 147
Sumner, John 10
Syme, Holger Schott 7, 88–9

Tailor, Robert
  Hog Hath Lost His Pearl, The 92
Taylor, Joseph *(?1586–1652; Prince Charles's Men c. 1610; Lady Elizabeth's Men, 1611–16; Prince Charles's Men, 1616–19; King's Men 1619–48: sharer 1619)* 83, 89, 118, 120, 121, 180
  performance style 19, 21, 26, 28, 32, 86
  physique 72
  roles xxii–xxiii, 10, 18–19, 20–1, 26, 27, 28, 30, 36, 43, 52, 62, 64–7, 72, 73, 74–5, 77, 81, 84–6, 89, 95–6, 102–4, 107, 108, 110, 143, 164, 166, 173, 174, 175, 178, 183, 201, 203
  successor to Richard Burbage xxi–xxii, 18, 52, 77, 83, 85, 86, 89, 95
Taylor, Gary 171
Taylor, Thomas 39–40
Theobald, Lewis 48
  Double Falsehood, The 48
Thomas, Lord Cromwell 194
Thompson, Ayanna 78
Thompson, John *(fl. 1620–34; King's Men c. 1620–34; apprentice c. 1620–31; Groom of the Chamber 1633)*
  apprenticeship 41, 198
  performance style 35, 36, 63–4
  roles 19, 32, 36, 41, 62–4, 103, 164, 199
Tilney, Sir Edmund, Master of the Revels, xix, xx, 1–3, 7
Tomkins, Thomas
  Albumazar 84, 201
Tomkyns, Nathaniel 156
Tooley, Nicholas *(alias Wilkinson) (fl. 1597–1623; Chamberlain's/*

King's Men 1597–1623: apprentice c. 1597–1603; sharer by ?1605)
  apprenticeship 60, 198
  death 65, 196–7
  roles 57, 65, 96, 196–7
Tourneur, Cyril
  Nobleman, The (lost play) 45–6, 47
  Tragedy of Gowrie, The (lost play) 4–5, 154, 156, 166–8
  Tragedy of the Spanish Maze, The (lost play) 1, 4–6
Tribble, Evelyn 22, 35, 131–2
Trigg, William *(fl. 1612–52; King's 1626–36; Beeston's Boys c. 1637–9: apprenticed 1625 for 12 years; hired man 1636)*
  apprenticeship 33, 198
  roles 35, 36, 64, 103
Trumbull, William 157, 160
Twins' Tragedy, The (lost play) 45–6, 139
Two Noble Ladies, The 130

Underwood, John *(c. 1587–1624; Chapel/Queen's Revels 1600–c. 1608; King's c. 1610–24: sharer by 1619)* 57, 65, 96

Van Dyck, Antony 146
Van Es, Bart 174
Vaughan, Virginia Mason 79
Vernon, George *(c. 1603–30; King's Men 1617–30: apprenticed 1617 for 7 years; sharer by 1625)* 198
Villiers, George, Duke of Buckingham 152, 155, 159–60, 162–4, 169, 176, 191

Webster, John xvi, 23, 25
  'An Excellent Actor', 23–4, 25–6, 28, 42, 51, 75, 131, 143
  Duchess of Malfi, The 12, 13, 16, 17, 18, 19, 34, 35, 36, 50, 97, 140, 195–6, 199
Wentworth, Thomas, Earl of Strafford 119
'White' *(King's Men c. 1638–40: apprentice)* 37
Whitefriars playhouse 92
Wilkins, George xvi, xvii, xxii, 92
  Painful Adventures of Pericles, Prince of Tyre, The 92, 113–14
  See also Shakespeare, William, and George Wilkins
Wilson, Arthur
  Swisser, The 12, 29, 36, 64, 72
Wilson, John *(1595–1674; King's Men 1611–22: apprenticed 1611 for eight years; musician/composer)* 190
Winwood, Ralph 156
Woolley, John 157, 160, 162
Worcester's Men xiv, 15. *See also* Queen Anna's Men

Wotton, Sir Henry 153, 165–6, 169
Wright, Abraham 11, 64–5, 69
Wright, James 5, 9–11, 12, 32, 37, 52, 64, 65, 72, 85, 86, 178, 180

Wroth, Lady Mary 39
Wycherley, William
 Country Wife, The 38

www.ingramcontent.com/pod-product-compliance
Lightning Source LLC
Chambersburg PA
CBHW072136290426
44111CB00012B/1892